Faith and Resistance

The Politics of Love and War in Lebanon

Sarah Marusek

First published 2018 by Pluto Press
345 Archway Road, London N6 5AA

www.plutobooks.com

British Library Cataloguing in Publication Data
A catalogue record for this book is available from the British Library

ISBN   978 0 7453 9993 5   Hardback
ISBN   978 0 7453 9992 8   Paperback
ISBN   978 1 7868 0193 7   PDF eBook
ISBN   978 1 7868 0233 0   Kindle eBook
ISBN   978 1 7868 0232 3   EPUB eBook

Sarah Marusek is a Research Fellow at the University of Leeds and a Research
Associate Fellow at the University of Johannesburg. She is the co-author of
a series of Spinwatch reports on the overlapping funders of the transatlantic
Islamophobia network, neoconservative movement and Israeli settlements.

This book is printed on paper suitable for recycling and made from fully
managed and sustained forest sources. Logging, pulping and manufacturing
processes are expected to conform to the environmental standards of the
country of origin.

Typeset by Stanford DTP Services, Northampton, England

Simultaneously printed in the United Kingdom and United States of America

Contents

List of Illustrations

Preface

In the novel *Invisible Cities* by the Italian writer Italo Calvino, a fictional explorer named Marco Polo describes 55 cities to an ageing emperor, Kublai Khan, to convince the latter of his dying empire's vastness. 'I speak and speak,' Marco says, 'but the listener retains only the words he is expecting ... It is not the voice that commands the story: it is the ear' (Calvino 2010: 123). This quotation beautifully captures the predicament of Western scholarship when it comes to understanding Islam and the Middle East: ever since the Age of Enlightenment, what has been accepted as knowledge is deeply biased because the ear commanding the story has been a white, bourgeois, Western Christian male. In the contemporary era, this ear wants to hear that the Islamic resistance movement in Lebanon represents hatred and terrorism, not a legitimate challenge to the dominant coloniser/colonised relation that is foundational to Western secular modernity. As somebody who sees too much violence and oppression in today's status quo, I aim to present an alternative view – that the Islamic resistance movement has comparable goals to other post-colonial movements inspired by theologies of liberation. Furthermore, it is articulating its own way forward on its own terms.

By openly embracing the enchanted aspects of modernity and challenging the hegemony of Western secular liberalism, I argue that the Islamic resistance movement is resisting the continued hierarchy of European above non-European, what Quijano (2000) calls the coloniality of power. This is because Western colonialism was not only a political and economic system to extract wealth from the Global South, but also a wider cultural and intellectual project based on the idea that Europeans have the right to colonise non-Europeans. The Western colonial mission thus required two distinct phases of colonisation: the first physical, where Europeans occupied the Global South, subjugated non-European populations and built infrastructure; and the second structural, where the ideas and practices undergirding this colonial infrastructure – be they economic, political, religious, cultural or intellectual – reproduce the coloniality of power through institutionalising a conceptual system of hierarchical binaries: West/East (the Rest), rationality/faith, reason/

religion, modern/traditional, developed/backwards, etc. In this way, Europeans have crafted a particularly misleading conception of 'self' and 'Other' to justify the enslavement of non-Europeans, a binary now enshrined under Western secular liberalism. As a result, even though the physical structures of colonialism were dismantled in the last century, the coloniality of power remains intact. And as Nandy (2009: xi) points out, while the second colonisation was instituted to legitimise the first, 'Now, it is independent of its roots.'

This means that the coloniality of power continues to be reproduced on multiple levels that go beyond the scope of world systems theory, an economic explanation for the existing core, periphery and external nations reproduced under capitalism (Wallerstein 1974). While capitalism undoubtedly continues to reproduce colonial inequalities, and often dominates debates about decolonisation, the coloniality of power extends to politics, culture, religion and knowledge production more generally.[1] Ultimately, this means that decoloniality requires more than just challenging neoliberal capitalism. As Grosfoguel points out, 'Given its entanglement with other power relations, destroying the capitalist aspects of the world-system would not be enough to destroy the present world-system' (2007: 219). He further adds that, 'The idea here is to decolonise political-economy paradigms as well as world-system analysis and to propose an alternative decolonial conceptualisation of the world-system' (Grosfoguel 2007: 212). This does not mean rejecting modern politics and the economy, but reimagining their conceptual horizons from a different social and cultural geography.

Building on almost two-and-a-half years of ethnographic fieldwork in Lebanon, spread out between 2009 and 2017, I present an alternative view of the Islamic resistance movement by asking readers to re-examine their ideas not only about Islam and resistance,[2] but also about themselves, something I myself was forced to do throughout the course of this research. During my first few trips to Lebanon, my aim was to understand how the Islamic resistance movement deliberately integrates faith and rationality into their ideas and practices. However, some of these ideas and practices, while looking familiar to me, were impossible to properly articulate without first breaking free from the constraints of my own knowledge paradigm, one that was deeply shaped by the project of Western secular modernity. What I saw was not a rejection of secular liberalism, but an active negotiation with this conceptual framework based on faith and religious rationality, while firmly centred around resisting Western domination – what I call a resistance subjectivity, which I also discuss in a recent article (Marusek 2018); this is a faith and commitment to the cause of revolutionary Islamic activism. Therefore, I first had to dislocate my own world-view before being able to fully recognise the decolonial character of the Islamic resistance movement, liberating me from the limitations of what Sayyid (2003 and 2014) calls Westernese – locating the Western experience at the centre of all knowledge.

Boaventura De Sousa Santos (2007) refers to the dominant Western framework as a form of abyssal thinking, saying that: 'Beyond it, there is only nonexistence, invisibility, non-dialectical absence.' But these unfathomable geographies are rendered invisible precisely because they are sites of resistance to the coloniality of power. Therefore, I had to ask myself – acknowledging my own position as a white American scholar – if it was even possible for me to travel there. The concept of the hermeneutic circle partially helped me to arrive at an answer. The hermeneutic circle describes the process revealing that the position of any reader influences her interpretation of the text; therefore, knowing the cultural, historical and literary context of the text in question is necessary for any sound interpretation. As Heidegger explains: 'The entities of *which* one is talking must be taken out of their hiddenness; one must let them be something unhidden (*alethes*); that is, they must be *discovered*' (quoted in Packer and Addison 1989: 278). Although Heidegger's discourse of discovery is problematic,[3] when placed in the hands of liberation theologians, the hermeneutic circle becomes transformational, allowing readers to liberate texts and contexts from their colonial present and past. Esack explains that according to Juan Luis Segundo, a Christian liberation theologian from Uruguay, there are two preconditions for creating a hermeneutic circle: 'First, profound and enriching questions and suspicion about one's real situation. Second, a new interpretation of scripture that is equally profound and enriching' (Esack 2002: 11).

From the start, I approached the text/context with 'profound and enriching questions and suspicion' about our human situation, which ebbed and flowed throughout the course of my research. However, as an American scholar researching the Islamic resistance movement, there was more that I needed to do to before trying to apply a hermeneutic circle. After all, this is a population particularly demonised by my own government, which has designated many of its affiliated charities and spiritual leaders as terrorist.[4] Accordingly, I found that it was necessary to integrate love into my research process. Drawing inspiration from the work of Islamic and other theologies of liberation, including 'second-wave' black feminism, I sought to adopt what Jacobs (2001) calls a hermeneutics of love in my attempt to understand others. Jacobs (2001: 12) argues that understanding the 'love of God and neighbour' is required before we can read any text with 'the law of love' in our thinking and doing. Embracing the potential that love brings to how knowledge is produced is itself a revolutionary act; as I explain in more detail in Chapter 1, the Western project of secular modernity has privatised love and faith, thus marginalising them both as ways of knowing and being by reducing them to the barest of intimate relations (Bellah 1999).

The Islamic and Christian theologies of liberation that I outline in Chapter 2 critique the Western secular sciences for privatising these essential aspects of our shared humanity. For example, the Peruvian Christian liberation theologian Gustavo Gutiérrez (1995a and 1995b) argues that it is necessary to first struggle with the poor before finding a new language that can answer the question of how God loves the poor when they are suffering so unjustly in a world not of their own making. Gutiérrez believes that answering this question only in social scientific terms, with love and faith outside of this framework, is not enough. As he explains:

> Prophetic language is to take the language of the poor, to link God and the poor and to denounce injustice. And to name the reasons of poverty is the prophetic language. Justice is a central point. But Job is employing another language, a mystical language. God loves us gratuitously. To believe in God is to believe in gratuitous love. Human love must be gratuitous also. We need to employ both languages. Liberation theology is an effort to employ the two languages. The mystical language can be too abstract. And the language of justice can sometimes be nonhuman, where people who speak about justice believe they know better than the poor. In the mystical language it becomes human again. The poor need friendship also. Friendship is gratuitous love.
>
> (Gutiérrez 1995b)

Goizueta adds that, for Gutiérrez, the new paradigm of speaking and understanding will be 'revealed precisely at the point where the prophetic language of justice meets the silence of contemplative worship, at the point where the revolutionary and the mystic become one' (2004: 295). This notion of gratuitous love – especially in the face of the injustices that Lebanese Shi'is have suffered and continue to suffer – frames my understanding of the Islamic resistance movement. However, gratuitous love is not uncritical; it is human solidarity stripped to its barest meaning. The questions and suspicion will always remain, continually ebbing and flowing. Accordingly, this is a decentring not only of politics and geographies, but also of human conceptions of faith, love and knowledge.

In Chapter 3, I discuss how I try to apply love to social scientific research, proposing what I call a critical ethics of love, or the love for and of the stranger, as a decolonial method. I am particularly interested in building on the work of Alfred Schütz (1944) and Zygmunt Bauman (1991), who both developed profiles of the stranger that are critically engaging with the universal claims of Western security modernity and its objectification of 'the Other'. Schütz and Bauman argued that all systems of knowledge are incoherent and inconsistent, including Western secular modernity, and that culture and ideology shape all knowledges to give them the appearance of coherence and consistency. The stranger, however, has a different culture and ideology as a starting point for making sense of incoherence and inconsistency. As a result, Shütz (1944: 504) argues that the stranger must actively de-centre herself to understand another culture, in other words, learn a new way of making sense of incoherence and inconsistency, ultimately allowing her to realise what Bauman (1991: 236) calls solidarity – a joint destiny. By acknowledging that: (1) there is a lack clarity in all knowledge systems; and (2) there is a need to de-centre before understanding another knowledge paradigm, this allows the loving stranger to have a more honest engagement with others, one that seeks to understand without judgement and only then critically assess the acts of 'making sense' from within. That said, this is not an embrace of moral relativism; only a recognition that what is universal about our humanity is contested.

My analysis of the Islamic resistance movement builds on Esack's (2002) research on Islamic liberation theology in the context of apartheid South Africa, where the struggle against an oppressive political system brought together a diverse religious population. It also draws upon Grosfoguel's (2007) insights into decoloniality and Islam, contributing to a decentred understanding of modernity. And finally, it takes inspiration from Sayyid's (2003 and 2014) pioneering work that is laying the foundations of the newly emerging field of Critical Muslim Studies, which seeks to locate scholarship on the Islamicate, or the regions where Muslims are culturally dominant, away from the Orientalising gaze (ReOrient 2015: 5). My own aim is to apply a decolonial lens to understanding the Islamic resistance movement, demonstrating that what is supposedly hidden, or in the abyss, is very much visible and alive. The challenge is to search for decolonial praxis (Singh 2016), using decolonial theory to make sense of an empirical study of a movement that is forging its own way forward.

Considering my own positionality, my effort will be limited; however, the commitment remains. Although I am neither Muslim nor Lebanese, the field of Critical Muslim Studies overcomes the limitations of entrenched identity politics by shifting 'from the ontic towards a more ontological inclined understanding of matters Islamicate' (ReOrient 2015: 6). Furthermore, my own experiences of living in the Global South inform me of the desperate need for a politics of love in everyday lives, but one refracted through the dominant world system that currently privileges some over others. As Christian liberation theologians argue, there must be a preferential option for the poor; therefore, the duty to love the oppressed is non-negotiable. It is not for me to agree or disagree with the Islamic resistance movement, but to humanise its supporters and analyse its politics in a critical and loving way.

In this book, I present the result of these efforts, which I confess were lonely and difficult. I try to illustrate how the Islamic resistance movement is decolonising knowledge paradigms and proposing an alternative decolonial conceptualisation of the world-system by first locating itself as an Islamic resistance movement in Lebanon, centring its project in faith, religious rationality and a resistance subjectivity, and only then engaging with the dominant paradigm of secular liberalism, choosing its own way forward according to its own unique context. As such, the movement is not rejecting modernity, but only the idea that Western secular liberalism is universal. It does this by adopting certain ideas and practices that can be defined as secular and liberal, but sub-stantively repackaging them as something new, thus contributing to what (Mignolo 2011: 23) calls a pluriversal epistemology of the future.

Before offering some context on contemporary Lebanese politics to further prepare the reader for what is to come, I want to briefly address my own (mis)use of language. The 1979 revolution in Iran that inspired the Islamic resistance movement in Lebanon (in Arabic *al-muqawama al-islamiyya*) is known as the Islamic Revolution (in Persian *inqalab islam-e*). These social forces are both known, and self-define, as Islamic movements. And yet, at times I refer to them as Shi'i movements and describe Sunni Muslims according to their sectarian affiliation, rather than simply as Muslims. This is a contradictory and perhaps even unhelpful approach, reifying the recent sectarian cleavages in the Islamic world that have emerged in the wake of the US-led invasions and occupations of Afghanistan and Iraq (for more on this, see Chapter 6). Because the English language of Islam has Orientalist baggage, as discussed in Chapter 1, a decentred understanding should use the word Islamic or even Islamicate to open up the Western imagination to new understandings of Muslim societies (Hodgson 2009: 3). By sometimes using the term Shi'i to discuss the Islamic resistance movement and its supporters, I merely want to stress that it is not representative of all Lebanese Muslims and to acknowledge the politics of religious difference in Lebanon.

Because the reality is that Lebanon is a sectarian state; the French developed a confessional system during their mandate for Syria and Lebanon that privileged Christians above Muslims, while also creating internal sectarian hierarchies. This divisive system of colonial rule was entrenched with the Lebanese National Pact of 1943 and only slightly modified at the end of the civil–international war in 1989, even though the Lebanese population is diverse in beautiful ways. As is discussed in more detail in Chapter 2, altogether there are 18 recognised sects in Lebanon, but under the French mandate, the two most politically powerful identities were Maronite Christians and Sunni Muslims. However, more recently, Shi'i Muslims have also become economically and politically powerful (although less so socially – see Chapter 3), while the Druze often wield power as kingmaker. The distribution of power holds because the post-colonial Lebanese state continues to be politically, culturally and economically organised along sectarian lines. Although sectarianism is by no means a primordial identity, but rather something fluid, in the case of modern Lebanon, it must be taken seriously. As Salloukh, Barakat, al-Habbal, Khattab and Mikaelian explain:

> The disciplinary tentacles of the sectarian system reach deep into Lebanese society, and operate to reproduce sectarian identities, loyalties and forms of subjectification. They collectively manufacture disciplined sectarian subjects who embrace what is otherwise a very modern and historically constructed 'culture of sectarianism' as their primary and primordial identity. These tentacles stretch across the different public and private spheres of Lebanese life.
>
> (Salloukh et al. 2015: 4)

Lebanon's civil–international war between 1975 and 1989 largely pitted Christian militias against Muslim militias (the latter both Lebanese and Palestinian), but allegiances shifted throughout the war, especially when exacerbated by international actors. For example, Syrian forces initially intervened to assist Christian Lebanese (against the Palestinians), and yet during their subsequent occupation of the country, Lebanese Christians and Sunnis alike largely came to oppose them. Furthermore, battles were waged between Lebanese Shi'is and Palestinian Sunnis. The latter entered the country as refugees when Zionist military forces expelled them from their home in Palestine in 1948 and again in 1967. Other intra-sectarian conflicts also took place during Lebanon's civil–international war.

During the final days of the Syrian occupation of Lebanon (1976–2005), the most powerful cleavage to emerge was between Lebanese Shi'is and Sunnis, strengthened when the Sunni Prime Minister Rafik Hariri was assassinated in March 2005, a tragic crime blamed on Syria and/or Hizbullah. Since then, the Lebanese have generally been split into two factions: those who support the pro-Hariri Sunni–Christian 14 March alliance that is aligned with Saudi Arabia, France and the United States; and those who support the Shi'i–Christian-Druze 8 March alliance aligned with Iran and Syria. However, the recent civil–international war in Syria (2011–present) has disturbed even these alliances, leaving Lebanon internally fractured in precarious ways. According to the United Nations (2016), 1,011,366 Syrian refugees were registered in Lebanon as of 31 December 2016; but a UN worker told me that the number could be as high as 2 million (Lebanon's total population in 2010 was 4.25 million).[5]

Even before the civil–international war that engulfed Syria, the Sunni-Shi'i cleavage in Lebanon was building, escalating in May 2008 when the 14 March-led government moved to sack the general at the head of airport security, who was aligned with the 8 March coalition, while at the same time trying to disable Hizbullah's communication network. These provocative moves ended in large-scale street clashes between armed supporters of 8 March and 14 March, the latter reportedly supported by Saudi Arabia and perhaps even the United States.[6] The 8 March alliance quickly established control over Beirut, but this was controversial because Hizbullah deployed its military forces internally. The group is the only non-state army legally authorised to exist in Lebanon to defend the country from Israel; however, it is not meant to attack fellow Lebanese. The stand-off ended when the 14 March-led government reversed the two decisions that sparked the conflict. More political power was devolved to Shiʻis, raising their profile, and a unity government was formed. But it fell in 2011, leading to another series of political crises. While Saad Hariri, the son of Rafik and on-again-off-again prime minister of Lebanon, further cemented political alliances by retreating to Riyadh for several years, Saudi Arabia was unsuccessful in its efforts in late 2017 to use him to overturn the current pro-8 March unity government (Wedeman 2017).

And yet despite all these difficulties, the Lebanese people have persisted. The country has remained one of deep beauty, sophistication, culture and love, albeit one that continues to bare many painful scars. Despite the shifting political allegiances after Hariri's assassination, leading to the cross-sectarian alliances of 14 and 8 March, Lebanon continues to suffer from sectarian disagreements that are exacerbated by external actors. Indeed, the internationalisation of Lebanon's struggles has perhaps been the most destabilising force of all. Even today, the country is a major site of a proxy war between international powers that are struggling to maintain Western hegemony, and those that are willing to confront it. This means that the precariousness of Lebanese political alliances cannot be stressed enough. There are multiple identities and allegiances that intersectionally pull people in various directions beyond tribe, sect and nation. In this book, I attempt to analyse the Islamic resistance movement from the inside with the recognition that I will always be a loving stranger struggling to understand, contextualising why decisions are made before critiquing them.

My inclusion of the Imam al-Sadr Foundation in my analysis of the Islamic resistance movement today is another issue to acknowledge. When speaking of the resistance charities, the Lebanese usually refer only to Hizbullah and al-Mabarrat Association. The Imam al-Sadr Foundation is decidedly more liberal and depends on the international aid community for assistance. However, Imam al-Sadr played an essential role in laying the foundations of the resistance movement in southern Lebanon, as detailed in Chapter 2. I dedicate the entirety of Chapter 5 to the Imam al-Sadr Foundation, partly due to the amazing access that the foundation granted me, which was not the case with Hizbullah and al-Mabarrat Association (for understandable reasons that I explain in Chapter 3). More importantly, however, I include a comprehensive analysis of the Imam al-Sadr Foundation because I believe that it is necessary to stress the pluralities of Shiʻi activisms in

Lebanon – a population that is often homogenised into a deeply flawed caricature of Hizbullah as a terrorist militia. These misunderstandings say little about the many Shi'is I engaged with during my research and a lot about the people who seek to generate a vision of the world that is violent, unequal and centred in the geographies of Western power, reproducing coloniality.

In sum, in this book, I take seriously both the Islamic resistance movement as a counter-hegemonic force to the coloniality of power, and the wider aspirations for decoloniality in a complex, contradictory and interconnected world. Being a critical scholar researching a movement that has been named a terrorist group by my own government, thus limiting my own access to knowing, has only fuelled my desire to lovingly know even more. I have done my best to decentre this knowing, offering critique without judgement. And while there is much to critique, there is also much to admire. Sayyid argues that: 'People become without history not because they lack a past but because, paradoxically, they cannot narrate themselves into the future' (2014a: 2). My goal is to convey how the Islamic resistance movement is narrating its own future, inscribing decoloniality into the present by decentring human understandings of secular liberalism to present a counter-hegemonic force to Western secular modernity, reminding us all of the possibilities of faith, love and resistance.

Acknowledgements

I first want to express my deepest gratitude to everybody in Lebanon who helped me with my research, including those who took the time to speak with me, those who arranged for me to speak with others and those who could not assist me directly but who still supported me emotionally and politically. Your generosity and compassion truly moved me. I particularly want to thank Mohammad Bassam, Dr Yayah Ghaddar, Zeinab al-Saffar, Ali Rizk and Nabil Hallak, along with countless other Lebanese comrades whom I cannot mention by name. This research is dedicated to every one of you, and I hope that it contributes to new understandings of your past and present struggles to live dignified lives on your own terms.

I also need to thank the brilliant academics who pushed me to write a better book. I especially want to acknowledge Prof. Don Mitchell for inspiring me to keep going throughout my fieldwork, all the while providing exceptional critical insight into my work. In addition, I want to thank Prof. S. Sayyid for giving me hope and helping me to travel to decolonial horizons; Prof. Farid Esack for reminding me of the importance of always standing by the oppressed and providing me with the space that I needed to write this difficult book; and Prof. Maria Frahm-Arp for her amazing intellectual, spiritual and emotional guidance. And not least, I want to thank Prof. Mark Rupert, Prof. Mehrzad Boroujerdi, Prof. Miriam Elman, Prof. Osamah Khalil, Prof. Najib Hourani, Prof. Carol Fadda-Conwey and Dr Shirin Saeidi for being such amazing humans, scholars and friends.

Furthermore, I want to give a big shout out to my fabulous publishers at Pluto Press and particularly my editor David Castle. I am also grateful for the important institutional support provided by the Department of Religion Studies at the University of Johannesburg, the Middle Eastern Studies and Social Science programmes at Syracuse University, and the Center for Arab and Middle Eastern Studies at the American University of Beirut.

This research has benefitted from the thoughtful feedback I have received at numerous international workshops and conferences. I want to thank the organisers at the Free University of Brussels, University of Johannesburg, the International Institute for Islamic Thought, Oxford University, York University and the American University of Beirut.

And finally, this research would not have been possible without the generous financial and administrative support from the Mellon Foundation, the Institute of International Education and Fulbright-Hays. Additionally, I relied upon funding from Syracuse University (the Roscoe Martin Fund Dissertation Grant, Yabroudi Summer Research Grant and Goekjian Summer Research Grant) and earlier on in my research the Kosciuszko Foundation.

In so many ways, thank you. And especially, the biggest thank you of all to my mum.

This book is dedicated to Hussein.

1

Introduction

The rise of revolutionary religious activism

The Islamic resistance movement and other theologies of liberation challenge Western secular modernity, which aims to marginalise the role of faith in contemporary political struggles. The common assumption among many in the West is that religion is a conservative force, and thus religious movements are viewed as either reactionary or fundamentalist. However, this view fails to recognise the revolutionary potential of religious activism – think of Malcolm X and the Reverend Martin Luther King Jr during the American civil rights movement, or the Christian church in South Africa, which played an essential role in ending apartheid by releasing the Kairos Document.[1] In 2009, Palestinian Christians revived this strategy by declaring that: 'the military occupation of Palestinian land constitutes a sin against God and humanity.'[2] Since the imperialist project is one of the foundations of Western secular modernity, this kind of radical religious activism is a form of resistance.

Nevertheless, some continue to distrust religion because Western conceptions of faith and rationality were transformed during the Age of Enlightenment, as I describe below, and then forcefully exported to the Global South through colonial systems like the bureaucratic state and capitalist free market, both of which privilege a very particular form of instrumental rationality, often at the expense of what it means to be human. Within the dominant Western secular framework, rationality is now narrowly defined and is almost always linked to science, economics and politics, while faith is relegated to superstation, emotion and the private realm.[3] According to this framework, religious belief is inherently outside of reason, while secular myths about ourselves and the world are incorrectly reified as neutral and universal truths. As a result, many of today's religious activist movements are framed as irrational, when what they are really reminding us about is the radical potential of faith and religious rationality as ways of knowing, relinking knowledge to our humanness.

Viewed accordingly, the persistence of religious activist movements across the Global South, in particular, should not come as a total surprise. As Kassab (2012) points out, when societies have been defined by the colonial other, this produces a certain kind of reaction. Although this reaction may look somewhat different according to which society is in question, the reaction is nevertheless still recognisable. The rise of the Islamic resistance movement and other religious activisms that deliberately incorporate faith into their ideas and practices is one of the many expressions of this post-colonial reaction. While religion has always framed social struggles in mythical terms, doing so today allows for the indigenisation of not only religion, but also of ideas and practices embraced by Marxism. As Lancaster (1988: xvii) observes, historicising religion and myth is a way to link the religious past to the present, so that historically oppressed peoples can achieve redemption in the present day. This process also uproots religious geographies, challenging secular conceptions of space and time.

Lancaster is writing about the experiences of Christian liberation theology in Nicaragua, which, like Islamic activism in the Middle East, is a counter-hegemonic force in dynamic negotiation with secular modernity. Marx argued that with the introduction of capitalism, 'Christianity as a developed religion had completed theoretically the estrangement of man from himself and from nature' (1844). Christian liberation theologians and Islamic activists are seeking to reconnect humans to the self and to nature, including the many structures of oppression in their daily lives. Faith, according to this understanding, is a commitment to God and all of God's creation. A similar perspective can be found in critical Marxists like Terry Eagleton, who describes faith as a set of commitments:

> What moves people to have faith in, say, the possibility of a nonracist society is a set of commitments, not in the first place a set of preposisions. They must already have some allegiance to an idea of justice, and to the possibility of its realisation, if they are to be stirred to action by the knowledge that men and women are being refused employment because of their skin colour. The knowledge in itself is not enough to do it.
>
> (Eagleton 2009: 119–120)

As Peruvian Christian liberation theologian Gustavo Gutiérrez also explains, 'theology is not a matter of my faith – it is a reflection of my

faith. Theology is an answer to the questions of those living their faith.'
Gutiérrez calls this approach, quite simply, 'doing theology' (1995a).

Liberation theologians in Latin America and Islamic activists in the
Middle East seek freedom and social redemption for their communities
by re-imagining the dominant ideas and practices of Western secular
liberalism through a religious or mythical lens. As a result, expressions
of faith are more deliberate and frequently framed vis-à-vis oppression.
Or as Christian liberation theologians put it, there must be 'a preferential
option for the poor'. In this way, these activists have actually transformed
the liberal framework by incorporating religion. While Löwy (1988)
demonstrates that neither Marx nor Engels were as anti-religion as is
often assumed, he singles out the Italian Marxist Antonio Gramsci as
being the leading thinker of the Communist movement who is most
engaged with religious issues. While Gramsci was quite critical of Cathol-
icism, he still recognised the utopian social elements of religious ideas
(Löwy 1988: 7). For example, Gramsci suggested that: 'religion is the
most gigantic utopia, that is the most gigantic "metaphysics" that history
has ever known, since it is the most grandiose attempt to reconcile in
mythical form, the real contradictions of historical life' (2005: 405).

My point here is that when activists refuse to reconcile religion with
the unjust conditions of life, and instead use it to transform today's
world, religion can become a revolutionary force. For example, Enayat
(2011: 24) explains how Twelver Shi'is, citing several Qur'anic verses,
believe that the return of the Twelfth Imam, also known as the Hidden
Imam or Mahdi, will realise the ultimate victory over the 'forces of
injustice'. Throughout the greater part of Islamic history, this potential
was not seen as something that could happen in this world, only in the
next, sanctifying 'the submissive acceptance of the status quo', because
the realisation of this victory was 'beyond the reach of ordinary human
beings' (Enayat 2011: 25). However, when historicised by Islamic activists
in the twentieth century, 'this link between the return [of the Mahdi] and
the ultimate, global sovereignty of the righteous and the oppressed' in
the here and now becomes a potential tool of radical activism (Enayat
2011: 25).

Nevertheless, contemporary revolutionary projects also face contradictions. Beyond the difficulties inherent within all utopian thinking,
including socialism, of becoming authoritarian and exclusionary
in practice (Bauman 1976), another problem for religious activist
movements today is that they must also contend with the hegemony

of neoliberal capitalism – a world where Western secular modernity pervades both the dominant systems of knowledge and the entrenched structures of economic and political oppression, rendering a theology of liberation practically impossible. Compromises will be made. And thus, as scholars, we must honestly assess their implications. Accordingly, what can we expect then from doing a theology of liberation in today's corrupted and corrupting world?

Scholars have increasingly turned their attention to how contemporary religious movements are interacting with local and global economies (Bompani and Frahm-Arp 2010; Deeb and Harb 2013; Daher 2016; Dreher and Smith 2016), showing how deliberately incorporating faith into everyday social practices is a complex and contradictory political project that can be expressed in multiple ways. My concern with some of these studies is that Western-based scholars are not always being honest about their own positionality – where a researcher stands in relation to the people she is researching (Rose 1997; Mullings 1999; and Haney 2002). Critical engagement with religious movements is often located from a position that is decidedly centred, where the contradictions of living in cosmopolitan Western capitals and railing against neoliberal capitalism, all the while enjoying its material benefits, is not properly acknowledged when criticising religious movements for doing the same. Furthermore, post-colonial activists today are struggling against many layers of oppression; this is especially true for Shi'is in the Middle East. As Augustus Norton points out:

> In order to understand the Arab Shi'i it is necessary to come to grips with the social, political and, often, economic marginality which reflects contemporary patterns of discrimination and alienation, and then to see how such realities resonate within the mystical and symbolic richness of Shi'ism.
>
> (Norton 2005: 185)

Referring to the ideas of Frantz Fanon, Hudis adds that: 'Exploitation involves being robbed of the fruit of our labour, whereas alienation involves being robbed of our very being' (2015: Kindle edn). Accordingly, adopting a lens that accounts for the intersectional forces of oppression provides a more realistic framework.[4]

Perhaps my concern is also emblematic of a wider dilemma: those opposing neoliberal capitalism are strong on critique, but weak on offering any practical alternatives to it, all the while continuing to participate in this hegemonic system. The issue that we must all confront is this: if we are living in a historical moment where neoliberal capitalism is hegemonic, what form of engagement with this world system is acceptable for those committed to both a revolutionary politics and social justice? Especially when Albert Memni observed in his critical reflections on the effects of colonisation on the colonised that:

> The most serious blow suffered by the colonised is being removed from history and from the community. Colonisation usurps any free role in either war or peace, every decision contributing to his destiny and that of the world, and all cultural and social responsibility. The colonised … feels neither responsible nor guilty nor sceptical, for he is out of the game. He is in no way a subject of history any more. Of course, he carries its burden, often more cruelly than others, but always as an object.
>
> (Memni 1992: 91–92)

Commenting on Memni's work, Paolo Freire adds that: 'So often do [the oppressed] hear that they are good for nothing, know nothing and are incapable of learning anything – that they are sick, lazy, and unproductive – that in the end they become convinced of their own unfitness' (2005: 63). Taking these words to heart, I do not believe it is fair to judge those who were formerly colonised merely for participating in 'the game' when it means that they are able to contribute to their own destinies. For me a more fruitful, and human, approach is to ask if there are any radical possibilities within such an engagement, and if so, what are the parameters for assessing these? Because this predicament exists across the Global South; during a meeting on decolonising knowledge at the University of Johannesburg in 2016, one audience member questioned the possibility of ever realising decolonial ways of knowing and being when we are all complicit in one way or another in the global neoliberal capitalist system.[5] This question is precisely what I hope to further interrogate in this book by examining the ideas and practices of the Islamic resistance movement in Lebanon.

Re-Orienting 'the Orient'

Drawing upon the writings of Antonio Gramsci, Edward Said was the first to develop a sophisticated framework of Orientalism to analyse and critique Western representations of Islam and the Middle East. Said applied Gramsci's notions of 'common sense', or the unstable repertoire of ideas in popular culture, and 'hegemony', or the rule of consent without brute force, to explain how certain ways of seeing 'the Orient' have come to dominate the Western academy, arts, culture, media and politics. In his book *Orientalism*, Said (1979) described the European post-Enlightenment project to transform the peoples of the Middle East into an object of study, using a scientific methodology to claim objectivity while distorting their social realities. Said explained that when Europeans were confronted with the Orient, the experience was always framed by comparisons vis-à-vis the West, as if (so-called) Orientals did not exist before this encounter in their own right, with their own histories and their own ways of knowing and being. Instead, colonial representations of Orientals speak on their behalf, revealing more about the West than the East: within this framework, the Orient becomes a mirror reflection of all that is contemptible about Western society.

As Gregory (2004: 42) points out, representations are constructive, not merely mimetic; thus, through the eyes of the Western 'explorer' constructing knowledge of the Orient, 'the native, the peasant is *part* of the landscape.' Indeed, by the end of the nineteenth century, Said argued that Orientalism had established a certain coherence that was mostly unchallenged, where 'the word *Oriental* was a reference for the reader sufficient to identify a specific body of information about the Orient. This information seemed to be morally neutral and objectively valid' (1979: 205). Not only does this assumed neutrality position the Westerner outside of the Orient, but as Gregory (2004: 26) points out, it also spatialises difference. Over there – Islam and the Middle East – is imagined as outside of the Western universal. And yet as Said repeatedly noted, social knowledge is neither universal nor neutral: 'the general consensus that "true" knowledge is non-political (and conversely that overtly political knowledge is not "true" knowledge) obscures the highly if obscurely organised political circumstances obtaining when knowledge is produced' (1979: 10).

During the twentieth century, these scientifically 'neutral' experiences of the Orientalist paradigm began to dominate the Western episteme. Subjectivity became associated with emotion, passion, religion and 'the Other', whereas objectivity was linked with the 'real' sciences and the Western secular liberal project. Note that this framework is also decidedly gendered against women. Calling this positionality in the West that of the Default Man, the British artist Grayson Perry observes that:

> Women and 'exotic' minorities are framed as 'passionate' or 'emotional' as if they, the Default Men, had this unique ability to somehow look round the side of that most interior lens, the lens that is always distorted by our feelings. Default Man somehow had a dispassionate, empirical, objective vision of the world as a birthright, and everyone else was at the mercy of turbulent, uncontrolled feelings.
>
> (Grayson Perry 2014)

When Westerners scientifically evaluate themselves and others according to the position of the Default Man, it reinforces a notion of the West as technologically and culturally superior, in turn reproducing Orientalist industries of so-called expert knowledges of 'the Other'. Nevertheless, the West's process of understanding the Orient remains far removed from its own self-understanding. In his follow up book, *Culture and Imperialism*, Said adds that while,

> we assume that the better part of history in colonial territories was a function of the imperial intervention … there is an equally obstinate assumption that colonial undertakings were marginal and perhaps even eccentric to the central activities of the great metropolitan cultures.
>
> (Said 1994: 34)

This misunderstanding has long disfigured both Western self-awareness and its representations of 'the Other', with Said later arguing that: 'covering Islam [in the Western media] is a one-sided activity that obscures what "we" do, and highlights instead what Muslims and Arabs by their very flawed nature are' (1997: xxii).

And yet, as Asad (2003b) describes, Orientalism is only one of a series of interlinked projects that undergird Western modernity, the others being imperialism, secularism and liberalism. Together they forged a framework to help the powerful institutionalise principles based on Western Enlightenment and colonial experiences that create new formations of space and time. Indeed, it is only in the modern era that the division of West and East/the Rest began to conceptualise space, with the juxtaposition of modern/advanced (time) first justifying colonialism and then authoritatively describing the stages of economic progress or 'development' under neoliberal capitalism.[6] Ultimately, this paradigm determines how many of us think about everything ranging from democracy and freedom to cruelty and health. Those societies that do not embody the project of Western secular modernity are subjected to Orientalist characterisations via new technologies that are imagined to measure the Western Enlightenment principles objectively (Gouldner 1970; Habermas 1970; and Lyotard 1984). For example, Asad (2003a and 2003b) points out how questions of effectiveness and efficiency are now seen to be normative standards when determining the benefit of certain behaviours, often superseding essential ethical and moral concerns.[7]

Asad argues that, over time, many of us have socially internalised these principles, ultimately coming to believe that our modern experiences 'constitute "disenchantment" – implying a direct access to reality, a stripping away of myth, magic and the sacred;' this 'is a salient feature of the modern epoch' (2003a: 13). As Koshul (2005: 2) further explains, disenchantment signifies the rupture between religious rationalism and scientific rationalism. Up until the modern era, as is discussed below, there were intimate relations between faith and science. But under the projects interlinked with Western secular modernity, mythology and the sacred became conceptually isolated and assigned to inferiority or otherness, while faith developed into a way of knowing the supernatural only in parallel to knowledge about 'the *real* world' (Asad 2003a: 39). As Chakrabarty describes, secular history's time is godless, continuous, empty and homogenous. In other words, 'Gods, spirits and other "supernatural" forces can claim no agency in our narratives' (Chakrabarty, quoted in Deeb 2009: 244). However, as Whimster and Lash (2006: 6) correctly point out, 'science is singularly ill-suited to explaining the ultimate questions,' especially what it means to be human.

Within this conceptual framework, the hegemonic Western social forces are construed to appear as objective truths, not culturally contingent constructions.[8] And one of the most dangerous myths is that Western secular ideals are universal. Asad argues that when we ideologically disenchant liberalism by claiming that it is natural or neutral, it results in a translucent violence that is difficult for liberals to see, explaining that in order 'to make an enlightened space, the liberal must continually attack the darkness of the outside world that threatens to overwhelm that space' (2003a: 59). In other words, the Western liberal must always conquer the illiberal, even justifying violence as a means-ends calculation. As Asad also puts it,

> liberal politics is based on cultural consensus and aims at human progress. It is the product of rational discourse as well as its precondition. It must dominate the unredeemed world – if not by reason then, alas, by force – in order to survive.
>
> (Asad 2003a: 61)

At the same time, the staunch belief in the neutrality of Western liberal principles and technologies eclipses this violence and the resulting pain that is inflicted in the liberalising mission.

Needless to say, as Freire pointed out, the imperialist project is intrinsically violent simply by establishing 'a relationship of oppression' (2005: 55). And because imperialism is foundational to Western secular modernity, this oppressive relation (the coloniality of power) continues. Deconstructing the phenomenon of violence today, Žižek argues that it falls into two distinct categories: subjective or objective. The latter type of violence is the systemic violence that is inherent in the normal everyday state of affairs:

> Objective violence is invisible since it sustains the very zero-level standard against which we perceive something as subjectively violent. Systemic violence is thus something like the notorious 'dark matter' of physics, the counterpart to an all-too-visible subjective violence. It may be invisible, but it has to be taken into account if one is to make sense of what otherwise seem to be 'irrational' explosions of subjective violence.
>
> (Žižek 2008: 2)

Žižek's point is that by focusing only on the subjective violence of individuals and groups, we are ignoring the everyday violence created by the system (the rules and knowledges created by the Western coloniser, imperialist, capitalist and secular liberal). As a result, we fail to appreciate how the subjective violence of certain individuals and groups – many of whom the West designates as 'terrorist', including Hizbullah – is a response to already existing violence, or a form of resistance. By failing to recognise it as such, we propagate the very system that is producing and reproducing the objective violence.

Furthermore, when Western secular liberalism claims universality, it renders subjects with different frameworks based on other cultures and histories as darkness (Said 1994). According to Western Enlightenment principles, only particular understandings of religion are compatible with this project. Sayyid (2014b: 43) argues that secularism 'generates Muslims as permanently transgressive subjects, whose religious essence is constantly being undermined by the temptations of the political'. Here, the political is anything that challenges Western secular liberalism. As Brown adds, 'today the secular derives much of its meaning from an imagined opposite in Islam, and, as such, veils the religious shape and content of Western public life and its imperial designs' (2009: 10). Asad further explains that:

> when it is proposed that religion can play a positive political role in modern society, it is not intended that this apply to *any* religion whatever, but only those religions that are able and willing to enter the public sphere for the purpose of rational debate with opponents who are to be persuaded rather than coerced.
>
> (Asad 2003b: 183)

In order to be able to be persuasive, however, one's argument must be seen as rational according to a very particular understanding of rationality that is now dominant in the West today. Of course, this conception is also widely contested. The next section explains how Western ideas of rationality are historically determined and have a direct relationship with their accompanying conceptions of faith.

The transformation of faith and rationality

Looking back to origins of Christian thought in Europe, faith is defined as that which God requires of humans in their relationship with God. According to Wolterstorff, the root meaning of the word faith in classical and Hellenistic Greek, or *pistis*, is 'trust, reliance, belief in, or confidence', and in certain nuances faith even means 'to obey' (1983: 11). In the Old and New Testaments, faithfulness means 'fidelity, endurance and hope', both in the hearts and on the lips of the faithful (Wolterstorff 1983: 12). But as Wolterstorff also clarifies, faith is not just belief, because belief also requires faith in the one who is trusted (Wolterstorff 1983: 13). Plantinga elaborates on this point by explaining that: 'belief in God means trusting

God, accepting God, accepting his purposes, committing one's life to him and living in his presence' (1983: 18). Therefore, according to this understanding, the person who trusts in God also believes, and in the New Testament this acceptance is seen as a form of knowledge (Wolterstorff 198: 14). Accordingly, knowledge requires faith and the two are deeply intertwined.

However, as Said demonstrated, the Western Enlightenment and colonial projects transformed the dominant understandings of religion, faith and knowledge. Asad further points out how 'the constitution of the modern state required the forcible redefinition of religion as belief, and of religious belief, sentiment, and identity as personal matters that belong to the newly emerging space of private (as opposed to public) life' (2003b: 205). As a result, religious belief in the West became something that is privatised, personal and unconnected to the social world, whereas the 'objective' sciences started to dominate society and politics. Asad describes how the privatisation of religion in Europe accompanied the universalisation of Western conceptions of what religious belief entails, presenting 'belief as an alternative ideology from the consciousness of reality' (2003b: 46). Belief was no longer a social, relational experience, but rather something that is either accepted or rejected by the individual. Indeed, new ideas of religious conviction presupposed a certain belief system and were no longer seen as the product of lived experiences (Asad 2003b: 46). Thus, belief becomes something that is internally constructed, or private, where it is regarded not 'as the conclusion to a knowledge process, but as its precondition' (Asad 2003b: 47). Not only are faith and rationality separate according to this perspective, but faith is also a lower kind of knowing that precludes rationality.

Wolterstorff (1983) explains how the Western Enlightenment also transformed philosophical thinking, which became dominated by classical foundationalism, a theory of rationality developed by English philosopher John Locke that supposes there are two kinds of belief: what can be considered basic belief, and what is based on other beliefs. In other words, there are immediate starting points, or foundations, for all mediated beliefs. Classical foundationalism contends that basic beliefs must be either self-evident or incorrigible, the latter relating to a state of consciousness.[9] But according to Locke, religion is neither self-evident nor incorrigible; therefore, unless religious views are supported by evidence, they are not rational. Subsequently, most Western philosophers have examined how people arrive at their belief in God's existence according to Locke's framework of classical foundationalism.[10] As a result, religion and faith are conceptually separated from scientific and rational knowledges, and relegated to the private sphere.

Critical modernists and postmodernists, however, reject classical foundationalism's claim to Absolute Knowledge (Westphal 1992). Alvin Plantinga (1993), a well-known philosopher of religion and Christian apologetics, also challenges this framework by arguing that belief in God's existence is both basic *and* can be subject to rational argument. At the same time, Eagleton adds that 'a belief, for example, can be rational but not true,' while 'claims about the world can also be true but not in a sense rational' (2009: 112–113). Furthermore, he argues that this relationship is mutually conditioned:

> Knowledge is gleaned through active engagement, and active engagement implies faith. Belief motivates action, to be sure; but there is also a sense in which you define your beliefs through what you do. Moreover, because we have come to see knowledge primarily on the model of knowing things rather than persons, we fail to notice another way in which faith and knowledge are interwoven. It is only by having faith in someone that we can take the risk of disclosing ourselves to him or her fully, thus making true knowledge of ourselves possible.
>
> (Eagleton 2009: 121)

Eagleton is suggesting that science and religion, as well as rationality and faith, are deeply intertwined. Western philosophy has simply constructed a certain type of scientific knowledge that separates them, which is known as secular reason. Although the dominant conception of secular reason has delivered Western societies from many oppressive superstitions and religious practices, it also inherits a problematic colonial history that supports a narrow definition of rationality and a rejection of faith as a way of knowing. Furthermore, as Westphal argues, secular reason's critique of religion spurred it to make false claims of being a higher form of knowledge: 'the failure of the Enlightenment lies not in its critical goals but in an uncritical, arrogant view of reason that leaves it with pretensions to clarity and certainty that it cannot support' (1992: x).

The dominant form of secular reason is centred in the Western experience, while Muslims and Middle Eastern cultures are forced into the peripheries. This understanding of rationality is linked to scientific and mathematical theories and methods that also dominate the social sciences. And yet even for Max Weber, the influential German social theorist, the term rationality had a variety of meanings in his contemporary society.[11] Indeed, Weber believed there were a 'multiplicity of rationalisation processes that variously conflict and coalesce with one another at all societal and civilisational levels' (Kalberg 1980: 1147). Koch (1993: 133) nicely separates Weber's different conceptions of rationality into four general categories. He believes *conceptual rationality* means 'an increasing mastery of reality by means of increasingly precise and abstract concepts'. There is also *instrumental rationality*, or the 'attainment of a definitely given and practical end by means of an increasingly precise calculation of adequate means'.[12] *Formal rationality* means 'a systematic arrangement' of particular structures and practices, or as Kalberg explains, 'a structure of domination that acquired specific and delineated boundaries only with industrialisation' (1980: 1158). And finally, there is *substantive rationality*, which is value-based and 'may be applied to that process which distinguishes between valid norms and that which is empirically given'.[13]

Weber himself valued these four forms of rationality differently, believing they all worked together in concert. However, he was extremely critical of modern bureaucracies and capitalist societies, because he found that they are governed mainly by instrumental and formal rationality.[14] While these two systems were initially based upon Christian religious ethics, once they were formalised and reproduced, Weber feared that they started to undermine the very values that originally legitimated them. He was thus very pessimistic about the fate of societies ruled predominantly by formal and instrumental rationality, arguing that by the twentieth century the organising systems in the West had become 'bound to the technical and economic conditions of machine production,' constructing an 'iron cage' around humanity (Weber 2003: 117). Subsequent Western thinkers (Habermas 1970; Gouldner 1970; Lyotard 1984; and Hartmann and Honneth 2005) have similarly argued that the formalisation of secular modernity has mechanised humans, perceiving their value by capitalist and bureaucratic standards alone. And yet despite these criticisms, Western secular modernity continues to be perceived by its supporters as 'the unfolding of history itself', a necessary condition for non-Western societies to embrace in the contemporary world (Sayyid 2014a: 34). Perhaps this is why bringing faith back into fold of reason and rationality is one of the key goals of religious activists today.

In their volume on ethnographies of value, Bender and Taves (2012: 2) aim to illustrate how people around the world are complicating 'a simple "secular–religious" frame' in their everyday practices. Challenging this hegemonic framing, the editors argue that 'thinking about "spirituality" and "spirits" both breaks up the limitations of the binary and puts renewed emphasis on the ways that these terms work dynamically as part of processes of valuation' (Bender and Taves 2012: 3). The authors in the volume each show how spirituality transcends what are ordinarily considered to be secular and religious contexts. The political ramifications here are immense; as Sayyid (2014b: 74–75) reminds us, lived conceptions of the political are multidimensional; they include a decision, socialising that decision and bringing something new into the world, creating subjectivities and distinguishing between friend and enemy – or 'us' and 'them'. This creative aspect of the political is of the utmost importance for any effort to decolonise knowledge, as demonstrated by those who are negotiating with the secular liberal framework on their own terms by blurring established binaries.

Charity past and present

Scholars who research the charities affiliated with the Islamic resistance movement often overlook their radical potential by reproducing Western conceptions of charity. While the concept of charity is as old as religion, the historical experiences of Christian Europe, including industrialisation and secular modernity, transformed Western ideas and practices of charity. In the modern era, Western philanthropy (elite charity) plays an important role in reproducing the capitalist class hierarchies that it depends on (Ostrower 1995), including the American imperialist project (Roelofs 2007; Arnove and Pinede 2007). Writing about the United States, David Callahan argues that the 'big philanthropists', who are unaccountable, are now 'occupying a bigger seat at the table of power than at any time in the past century' (Cottle 2017). Gutiérrez, the Christian liberation theologian, also argues that: 'Charity is today a "political charity" … it means the transformation of a society structured to benefit a few who appropriate to themselves the value of the work of others' (2003: 116).

However, in the early years of Christianity, charity was not an elite project but an ordinary way of being in society defined by love. Indeed, charity was conceived as a moral requirement of the faithful. The Latin root of the word charity, *caritas*, can be understood as love for humanity; it is a theological virtue. Williams explains that back then, charity was 'Christian love, between man and God, and between men and their neighbours' (1985: 54). Jackson also points out that: 'Thomas Aquinas, for instance, considered almsgiving "a matter of precept"' (2009: 12). As Daly further explains:

> A consistent objective of the ancient covenant was to insure basic sustenance for all God's people and to prevent accumulations of land and power that would lead to deprivation and servitude among the people. Thus the laws of the covenant combined tithings earmarked for social welfare (Deut. 14:28–29) with redistributive policies such as Jubilee. Sustenance meant more than subsistence. In Hannah's prayer, God not only helps the poor, but reverses their fortunes: 'He raises the poor from the dust and lifts the needy from the ash heap; in order to give them a place with nobles, and have them inherit a throne of honour' (1 Sam. 2:8).
>
> (Daly 2009: xlii)

Importantly, this kind of religious charity included not only gifts to the poor and to the community, but also acts of human forgiveness. Jackson (2009: 12) notes that:

> When construed as a trait of character … such charity is the disposition to be patient and long-suffering. A charitable person is habitually compassionate, showing others leniency and understanding, giving them the benefit of the doubt, being slow to anger and quick to reconcile, and so on.
>
> (Jackson 2009: 12)

With the onset of European industrialisation and the formation of modern nation states, however, the meaning of charity in the West was soon constricted from 'Christian love' to 'benevolence towards the poor' (Jacobs 2001: 130). In this way, charity became an instrument for the elite to maintain the unequal status quo. Furthermore, the Marxist theorist Raymond Williams observed that when charity is something that the rich give to the poor, it becomes stigmatised; charity suddenly becomes one directional, voluntary and ultimately only given to 'the *deserving poor*', not out of 'neighbourly love' but as a 'reward for approved social conduct and the calculation in bourgeois political economy' (1985: 55). As Jackson further notes, since the more politically neutral terms 'welfare' and 'aid' have now replaced 'charity' in many Christian dominated countries, this means that:

> when aid to the unfortunate (private or public) is construed as morally optional, this represents a significant narrowing of the biblical and medieval meanings traditionally assigned to the term 'charity'. However much biblical and medieval contexts may have differed, both held that giving assistance to the poor and afflicted was an obligatory expression of love of neighbour, at least for Christians.
>
> (Jackson 2009: 12)

While the modern European welfare state has rendered this new 'secularised' version of charity into a liberal right, Offe (1984) argues that the bureaucratic state paternalistically determines needs, delivering only those services that are supposed to help the individual become a productive member of a capitalist society. Here, both charity and welfare are no longer ethical imperatives, but a means of social control (see Haney 2002). One result of these developments is that Christian charity today often has toxic effects upon the worldwide poor (Lupton 2011).

Nevertheless, it is still possible that charity can be imagined and practised differently. Gutiérrez advocates that the transformative capacity of charity 'ought to be directed toward a radical change in the foundation of society, that is, the private ownership of the means of production' (2003: 116). In the age of neoliberal capitalism, formalised practices of charity may always unintentionally reproduce some of the hierarchies within this system; however, as Hankela (2017: 51) suggests, we can still reformulate charity to become an aspect of social justice praxis, as potentially demonstrated by Shi'i charities in Lebanon. Since Islam is both orthopraxic and orthodoxic, the correct interpretation of rituals and myths are essential. As a result, charity has always been obligatory for Muslims; the Qur'an repeatedly urges believers to give alms to the poor and to pay the poor-rate on profits or luxuries. Giving a percentage of one's income, traditionally 2.5 per cent, is known as *zakat* and comprises one of the Five Pillars of Islam. According to Aslan, *zakat* literally means purification; it is 'not an act of charity but of religious devotion: benevolence and care for the poor were the first and foremost enduring virtues preached by [the Prophet] Muhammed in Mecca' (2005: 60).

Kochuyt (2009: 104) describes *zakat* as religiously inspired solidarity; however, he points out that its recipients do not extend beyond potential Muslim converts, perhaps reflective of the needs of the small Muslim community when Islam was revealed, although this is not true of voluntary acts of charity known as *sadaqah*. Otherwise, the recipients of *zakat* are extensive: the poor and needy, elderly and sick, public service workers, converts, slaves and captives, debtors, travellers (also refugees) and those who defend the 'cause of Allah' (Kochuyt 2009: 103). But while *zakat* is obligatory, Islamic scholars stress that paying it is an act of devotion, and so the *niyya* (the donor's intention) must be good (Kochuyt 2009: 11). Kochuyt further argues that the dualistic social science models of reciprocity are inadequate to adequately explain Islamic charity, because a believer's objective is to serve God. In addition to *zakat*, Shi'ism also established the practice of *khums*, which literally means one-fifth, or 20 per cent, and is often a tax paid on certain goods. For Shi'is, both *zakat* and *khums* are based on the mechanism of *taqlid*, or the emulation of another in manners of the law, in the sense that it is a duty of the believer to pay the religious tax to a *mujtahid*, or jurist.

Another important charitable institution in Muslim societies is the *waqf*, translated as an 'Islamic trust' or 'pious endowment', which emerged about one century after the birth of Islam (Kuran 2001: 842). The Islamic justification for *awqaf* is primarily found in the *hadith*, or the recollections and words of the Prophet Muhammad. For hundreds of years, the *waqf* was the only source of regular funding in Muslim societies for the *madrasa*, a school or provider of religious education (Shatzmiller 2001: 47). The institution also financed a wide variety of public services including the building of monuments, mosques, hospitals, universities, bathhouses, soup kitchens, hospices and lodging (Layish 1995: 146). The growth of endowments in Muslim societies suggests that they acquired great economic significance as the years progressed. Kuran (2001: 849) cites a study that showed around 'one-eighth of all cultivable soil in Egypt and one-seventh of that in Iran stood immobilized as *waqf* property' by the early twentieth century, although the secularising governments of both countries would soon challenge the sanctity of the institution of *waqf*.

It is important to remember that motivations for founding a *waqf* can be religious, but they can also be philanthropic or self-serving, unlike, at least theoretically, the practice of *zakat*. One objective for founding a *waqf* is to provide public services; however, pious acts also cultivate a favourable reputation, and in the past, endowments were generally not subject to government taxation. Furthermore, endowments also circumscribe the strict inheritance laws detailed in the Qur'an to prevent the gross accumulation of wealth; these laws explicitly outline how men and women are only allowed a 'stated portion' of what their parents and relatives leave to them (Surah IV 2005: 48–49). Thus, the potential for charity to become corrupting also exists in Islam (including Shi'i charities, although this is well beyond the scope of this book). Still, this concept of *obligatory love*, not only for one's neighbour, but also for and of the stranger, is key to my methodological approach for understanding the Islamic resistance movement in Lebanon, something I discuss in more detail in Chapter 3.

Islamic history and myth

Before going any further, I want to provide a brief history of Islam, which has two main sects: Sunnism and Shi'ism. About 90 per cent of contemporary Muslims are thought to be Sunnis, who comprise the majority in countries such as Algeria, Egypt, Indonesia, Kazakhstan, Saudi Arabia and the United Arab Emirates. This means that approximately 10 per cent of Muslims are thought to be Shi'is, who represent sizeable minorities in countries including Lebanon, Pakistan, Saudi Arabia, Syria, Turkey and Yemen, and majorities in Bahrain, Iran and Iraq. Shi'is in Lebanon are now thought to be the largest sect in the country; however, they do not comprise a majority of the overall population. There are also internal divisions within both Sunnism and Shi'ism, resulting in the creation of various internal subsects over time. And finally, there are Sufis, who follow Islam's mystical traditions as either Sunnis or Shi'is, sometimes even combining the two doctrines together.

The Sunni–Shi'i split emerged not long after the death of the Prophet Muhammad in 11 AH/632 CE when the Muslim community became divided over the issue of succession, with Sunnis preferring a consensus candidate chosen by the learned community, and Shi'is favouring those descended from the Prophet, known as *ahl al-bayt* – literally 'the people of the house' of the Prophet Muhammad (Moussawi 2011: 19). The first three of Muhammad's successors were chosen by the learned community and were not descendants of the Prophet; however, the fourth was both chosen and a descendent – Ali ibn Abi Talib, who was not only the Prophet's cousin, but also the husband of Fatimah, the Prophet's daughter. After Ali was assassinated, the disagreement over succession pulled the two factions even further apart. The Shiʻis, which in its original Arabic form *shiʻtu ʻali* means the followers of Ali, looked to his sons Hassan and Hussein for leadership, while the Sunnis looked to the Umayyad Caliphate in Damascus under Yazid ibn Muawiya. Although Hassan attempted to mediate the disagreement by signing a treaty with Yazid, he was poisoned.

In an act of resistance, his brother Hussein and 72 of his Shiʻi followers were killed in the Battle of Karbala in the year 61 AH/680 CE, reportedly by tens of thousands of Sunni Umayyad soldiers. As the story goes, for six days Imam Hussein and his small army resisted Yazid's forces. However, when the Umayyad soldiers blocked off their water supply, the Shiʻis slowly started to perish. Nevertheless, rather than die in retreat, on the tenth day of the battle, Imam Hussein and his remaining forces charged the attacking army and died.[15] The remaining women and children, under the leadership of Hussein's sister Sayyeda Zeinab, were taken captive and held as prisoners in Damascus before finally being released. This story of the Prophet's grandson, who bravely committed to battle against all the odds, has become essential to contemporary Shiʻi narratives. As a minority community in most Muslim countries, demonised by both orthodox Islam and Western powers, Shiʻis often look to the martyrdom of Imam Hussein for inspiration. The relevance of this history for Shiʻis today is revisited as well as critiqued in the chapters that follow.

The most popular subsect in Shiʻism is Twelver Shiʻism, which is the dominant religion in Iran and Iraq, and the largest minority in Lebanon. Twelver Shiʻis continued to follow the rule of the Prophet's descendants until Muhammad ibn al-Hassan al-Mahdi, the Twelfth Imam. As already mentioned, he is referred to as the Mahdi, or the Hidden Imam, because Twelver Shiʻis believe that he never died, but instead was hidden by God until the end of time. When the Mahdi reappears, Twelver Shiʻis believe that he will be the saviour for all humankind. In the modern era, Twelver Shiʻis have been religiously organised by a quasi-hierarchy with a *marjaʼ al-taqlid*, or source of emulation, at the top of the hierarchy, who is recognised by the title of Ayatollah. Intensive religious training and recognition by one's students and peers is required to reach this position. Today, there are very few Ayatollahs still living; since the death of Ayatollah Fadlallah in 2010, Lebanese Shiʻis have been left without a spiritual guardian living within their national borders.

Underneath or aside of the *marja'* are jurists who employ *ijtihad*, or interpretation, to craft Islamic laws based on the application of human reason and rationality (Rahnema 2005: 8). The jurist is called a *mujtahid* (from the root *jihad*, or struggle), because of his or her efforts in making religious rulings – although unusual, women in Iran and Iraq are sometimes educated at home to earn the right to be a *mujtahida* (Wiley 2001: 152). Often misunderstood, the word *jihad* means 'struggle', both inwardly and outwardly. As El-Hussein further explains, resistance is a form of *jihad*, but can be expressed in multiple ways: in the context of Lebanon, key Lebanese clerics supported both the military resistance against Israel's occupation of the country from 1982–2000, as well as *sumud*, or steadfastness, which is a more 'passive resistance manifest in a refusal to leave the land' (2008: 402–403).

Thus, despite its hierarchical structure, Shi'ism embraces a certain legal dynamism, whereas Sunni scholars have largely prohibited the application of *ijtihad* for many centuries (Rahnema 2005: 8). Nevertheless, numerous Sunni activist scholars have had similar radical visions to historicise Islam in the modern era, challenging the traditional *ulama*, or clerics, on questions of *ijtihad* and other key issues. Muhammad Abduh (1849–1905), an Egyptian jurist, set out to prove that Islam is a rational religion that can serve as the basis of life in the modern world (Haddad 2005: 44). The Indian philosopher, poet and politician Mohammad Iqbal (1877–1938),

> defined history as 'a continuous movement in time' that was always creative and never pre-determined. In the same vein, revelation was also a continuously evolving and creative project that despite having originated in an ancient past was spiritually invested in the conditions of the present.
>
> (Tareen 2013: 11)

Abul A'la Mawdudi (1903–1979), a Pakistani philosopher, rearticulated Islam to respond to urgent questions of nationalism, identity and the economy during the demise of British colonial rule – his political views were formed in debate with, rather than in conformity to, Western sources (Nasr 1996: 33). And Syrian politician and thinker Mustafa al-Siba'i (1915–1964) focused on reconciling socialism and Islam by exploring the different conceptions of property rights in the Qur'an (Enayat 2011: 144–150). According to Rahnema, these expressions of

'Islamic revivalism ultimately [aim] at the overthrow or radical transformation of a social system which it believes engenders decadence,
corruption, deprivation, social injustice, repression and impiety' (2005:
5). While in this book I focus exclusively on Shiʻi activism, this wider
post-colonial context to Islamic revivalism is important to keep in mind.

Decolonial horizons

In order to counter the hegemonic representation of the Islamic resistance
movement, I seek to intertwine different theologies of liberation to
introduce the possibility of a broader post-secular Marxist framework,
where love and knowledge are interconnected and our faith in God
and/or humans commits us to action. Here, it is the duty of the faithful to
resist against structures of oppression, whether conceptual, emotional or
material. Through a commitment to God and/or all humans, especially
the poor and those marginalised by capitalist, imperialist and sectarian
structures of oppression not of their own making, humans have the
potential to attain salvation not only by doing their own theology, but also
through creating new social formations, a framework that transforms
both the world we live in as well as ourselves. As previously noted, the
Italian Marxist Antonio Gramsci offers a conceptual framework that
resonates with this project because he takes culture seriously. Although
it may be somewhat paradoxical to look to a Western scholar in any
attempt to decentre knowledge, Gramsci sought to shape a new politics
dedicated to overcoming marginalisation by abolishing the distinction
between 'centres of prestige and peripheries of inferiority' (Germino
1990: 14).

Writing within the context of early twentieth century Europe, Gramsci
adopted a dual approach to politics, where 'ideas are not born of other
ideas, philosophies of other philosophies; [instead] they are a continually
renewed expression of historical development' (2005: 201). Elaborating
on the Marxist conception of materialism, Gramsci incorporated culture
to formulate a sophisticated theory of civil society and the struggle for
hegemony. He believed the power of ideas subtly elicits the tacit consent
to a social order, reasoning that members of a society willingly participate in structures of domination that keep them in subordinate roles.
Individuals engage in exploitative practices because the dominant ideas
about life either convince them that this is the desirable outcome, or
disable their critical faculties so that no other alternative appears feasible.

In Gramsci's formulation, civil society comprises both 'the political and cultural hegemony ... a social group exercises over the whole of society as the ethical content of the state' (Bobbio 1988: 10). This notion of civil society includes not only social institutions like schools, religious bodies, media and art, but also what ideas are refracted through them and how they are likely to be interpreted.

Hegemony is thus secured through civil society, offering a subtle but coercive means for the state and/or dominant class formation to preserve its social, cultural and political legitimacy (Gramsci 2005: 57). At the same time, however, Gramsci argued that civil society also provides the space for ideological struggle, where competing blocs may contest popular 'common sense' and create a new hegemony with a different history, eventually contributing to the formation of a new power (Bobbio 1988: 88). Here 'common sense' is the repertoire of popular culture. According to Gramsci, the ideologies comprising 'common sense' can be conservative or progressive and are open to multiple interpretations. These ideas are fragmentary, fluid, heterogeneous and contradictory. They are the historical accretion or sedimentation of multiple and various beliefs from religion, folklore, science, art, language and philosophy. A bloc secures hegemony by articulating the ideas and beliefs of 'common sense' in ways that resonate with the populace but mobilises them in new directions.

In this way, hegemony is never a fixed or unified position, but instead an unstable product. Legitimacy is continuously being contested in civil society by other reconstructions of popular 'common sense' with different kinds of political and social implications. This is a sophisticated way of explaining how a hegemonic group can institutionalise its power with the willing participation of the people, because Gramsci argued that hegemony is established by standardising particular ways of thinking and doing that appear to emanate from the self (Morton 2007: 93). It also illuminates how counter-hegemonic challenges can be made from within. Once a dominant group successfully wins the war of ideas, any necessary structural adjustments to secure its power are viewed as legitimate by the populace. Therefore, a new hegemony transforms not only the economic, cultural and political systems, but also the ways that people within the system perceive the world. Gramsci's synthesis of materialism and ideology is an important contribution to relational theories of power: he illustrated how ideology is integral to the political process because hegemony is a relation of consent through ideological leadership and not brute force. Here, religious ideas can either support or challenge the ruling bloc. Later Marxists, including Ernst Bloch and Lucien Goldman, also recognised both the revolutionary and oppressive potentials of religion (Löwy 8: 1988). Gramsci's conceptual framework provides for social and political possibilities that are decentred, empowering the margins, resonating with the goals of decolonial thinkers.

As discussed in the Preface, decolonial studies seek to challenge Europeanness – including its predetermined binaries of faith and rationality, religion and knowledge – 'as [the] master referent, in relation to which all things are measured and understood' (ReOrient 2015). The goal here is to decentre both knowledge production and knowledge itself. Or as Nelson Maldonado-Torres (2016) explains, decoloniality seeks to challenge the creation of identities that lock certain people into inferiority.[16] Sabelo Ndlovu-Gatsheni (2013) points out that the epistemological disobedience of decoloniality is 'premised on three domains of power, knowledge, and being'. In other words, questions regarding what are the appropriate constellations of social relations, ideas and practices are all up for grabs, to be determined by the non-European as she wishes and from her own location. To illustrate this point, Sayyid notes that, 'It is not that Islamists use ideas that are themselves Western, but the description of the ideas as Western retroactively constructs them as such' (2014a: 57).

The point of decoloniality is to decentre the West as the master referent (Sayyid 2003 and 2014a and 2014b). I argue that the Islamic resistance movement is doing this by constructing its own articulations of what it means to be human in today's world, on its own Islamic terms. This requires muddying established binaries, however unsettling – after all, destabilising Hall's (1992) conception of 'the West and the Rest' is the whole point. Breaking down boundaries also forces us to recognise the interconnectedness of knowledge and love. Barthes lamented that in Western societies:

> the lover's discourse is today of *an extreme solitude*. This discourse is spoken, perhaps, by thousands of subjects (who knows?), but warranted by no one; it is completely forsaken by the surrounding languages: ignored, disparaged, or derided by them, severed not only from authority but also from the mechanisms of authority (sciences, techniques, arts).
>
> (Barthes 1978: 2)

As detailed above, the dominant framework of Western secular modernity marginalises faith; however, it equally marginalises love. In response, a diverse array of radical scholars has articulated a conceptual framework to incorporate love into politics. Freire spoke of the post-colonial liberation struggle as constituting 'an act of love opposing the lovelessness which lies at the heart of the oppressors' violence' (2005: 45). Building on Freire's work to develop what she calls a methodology for the oppressed, Chela Sandoval defines love as a technology for social transformation, 'as a body of knowledges, arts, practices, and procedures for re-forming the self and the world' (2000: 4). Analysing the work of 'second-wave' black feminism, Jennifer Nash talks of love as not only 'a strategy for remaking the self', but also a means 'for moving beyond the limitations of selfhood' (2011: 3). Here, love 'forms the basis of political communities' and is 'rooted in a radical ethic of care' (Nash 2011: 14).

Throughout history, there have been a number of prominent Muslim scholars who also argued that love and knowledge are interconnected. According to William Chittick, the Persian theologian, jurist, philosopher and mystic, Al-Ghazali, 'stresse[d] that no one can love anything without knowing it first' (2011: 188). Ibn al-Dabbagh, the author of an influential classical treatise on love in Arabic, wrote that loving is an endless journey towards knowing:

> The many attributes witnessed from the Beloved are beyond count, and they cannot enter in upon the lover all at once. Rather, they follow one another in keeping with the increase in perception. Each attribute demands a trace in the soul, so the lover is always striving to seek increase. When a beautiful form of his Beloved appears to him, he yearns to perceive it so as to enjoy it. When he perceives it, he seeks to perceive what is higher, for the Beloved's self-disclosures have no end, and yearning drives the lover to embrace them all. In yearning to achieve them all, he suffers pain, and in gazing upon the beauty of what he witnesses from his Beloved, he lives in joy.
>
> (Quoted in Chittick 2011: 190–191).

Proponents of contemporary theologies of liberation use similar languages of love to respond to social injustice, as is discussed in greater detail in Chapter 2. For example, the Peruvian Christian liberation theologian Gustavo Gutiérrez argues that faith is expressed by a commitment to God and a love for the poor (Lewis 2005), and that 'poverty is one expression of the refusal to love' (Gutiérrez 1995b). As noted in the Preface, the question for Gutiérrez is: 'How to say to the poor, God loves you?' To answer this question, he believes it is necessary to struggle with the poor, because 'how to speak about God taking into account the sufferings of the poor is not easy. This question is larger than our possibilities to answer. We need to struggle with them against injustice in order to answer the question' (Gutiérrez 1995a). The Islamic theologian and activist Ayatollah Fadlallah (2011: 40) similarly believed that a political system must be based on the three principles of love, justice and mercy. Thus, one's love of God is what saves humans from feeling weak in the face of tyranny (Ayatollah Fadlallah 2011: 29), as well as what inspires them to necessary action when others are oppressed (Ayatollah Fadlallah 2011: 53).

This framework moves beyond the imperialist dynamic of Western liberal practices of toleration (Bauman 1991; Brown 2006), because as Gutiérrez explains, 'love exists only among equals' (2003: 17). Here, love is the ultimate equaliser, while at the same time potentially making us more aware of the structures of oppression that determine our inequality in the social world that currently exists (but which can be remade). While Jackson (2009: 15) notes that, 'love appreciates the plenitude and ambiguity of the world,' our current social world does not. For Hardt, this conception of political love means a love for and of the stranger, 'a love that functions through the play of differences, rather than the insistence on the same' (quoted in Schwartz 2009: 813). I expand upon this notion of a critical ethics of love as a decolonial method in Chapter 3. But first, I want to turn to the rise of Islamic activism and other theologies of liberation in the struggle to challenge power from the vantage of the oppressed.

2

The Rise of Religious Activism
in Lebanon and Beyond

Take responsibility and act.

— Ayatollah Fadlallah

To choose life is to be in solidarity with the poor, to fight poverty and strive for social justice, and for liberation. All this is life. Liberation is life.

— Gustavo Gutiérrez

The Islamic Renaissance

As discussed in Chapter 1, the twentieth century saw the rise of Islamic revivalism, especially in Muslim societies directly confronting colonialism. In this chapter, I focus on developments within Shi'ism in comparison to other theologies of liberation. Living as a minority sect within and among Sunni majority countries, Shi'is across the Middle East have often been marginalised.[1] Some conservative Sunni leaders in the Arab Gulf States consider Shi'is to be infidels and even sanction state violence against them (ICG 2005 and Farrell 2007). However, today's Sunni–Shi'i tensions must be contextualised by the reality that Muslims, together with many other religious sects, have largely coexisted in the region for many centuries without identity politics and conflict, which means that geopolitics likely play a more important role in understanding the sectarian divisions today.

According to the International Crisis Group, the US-led 2003 invasion and occupation of Iraq destabilised the sectarian political balance in the region (ICG 2005). This foreign intervention replaced the Sunni minority regime under Saddam Hussein with a Shi'i majority government aligned with the Islamic Republic of Iran, a country despised by many Arab Gulf States. Indeed, Zabad (2017: 137) argues that Sunnis have become threatened by the successes of political Shi'ism. Accordingly, while Sunni fighters from abroad initially crossed the borders into Iraq to challenge the US-led occupation, they later entered the country to confront Iran's influence over Iraq's autocratic government, aligning with the forces of imperialism. Many of these fighters went on to join the so-called Islamic State in Iraq and Syria (ISIS).

Of course, Shi'is are not always the victims of oppression and have also been the oppressors.[2] Nevertheless, the many narratives of Shi'i suffering are extremely powerful and have deeply shaped Shi'i activism as a transnational Islamic movement promoting a culture of resistance against various forms of injustice.[3] The cross-border migration of Shi'i clerics during the twentieth century helped to foster this notion of a shared religious ideology that is also political. Shi'i activists historicised Islam by viewing religion through a lens that reflects and responds to modern-day structures of oppression. This, in turn, helped to transform Islamic ideas and practices. Therefore, the rise of Shi'i activism in Lebanon is not wholly intelligible without an understanding of the historical narratives of the injustices that Shi'is have experienced throughout the region that link them to a wider transnational movement, as well as to other post-colonial revolutionary movements also confronting imperialism.

But despite the fact that Shi'i political identity is shaped by this rich history, all of these developments are still new and incredibly modern. In fact, many scholars argue that Shi'is had been politically quiescent throughout much of Islamic history precisely because they were margin-alised minorities,[4] focusing on the divine rule of the Twelve Imams, those descended from the Prophet Muhammad, as something above everyday politics (Algar 1980). According to Enayat (2011: 25), the return of the Mahdi, or Hidden Imam, was never imagined as a concrete possibility until the twentieth century. Still, according to Moussawi (2011), certain historical institutions in Shi'i Islam did help to create the framework for their later politicisation. For example, there is the practice of *ijtihad*, or interpretation, where any religious leader who reaches a certain level of authority and is at least a recognised jurist, or *mujtahid*, can use reason to interpret religious laws.[5] Moussawi (2011: 29) suggests that through this institution, Shi'i religious leaders are able to cultivate a unique relation-ship with the faithful by connecting their authority to the Hidden Imam.

Furthermore, when the Safavid dynasty declared Shi'ism to be the official religion of Iran in the sixteenth century, this was a political decision to curtail the expansion of the Ottoman Empire. Moussawi (2011: 30) explains how, ever since then, many interpretations of Shi'ism have become increasingly politicised, with two schools of

Shi'ism eventually emerging: political passivists who suggest that the faithful should wait patiently for the Mahdi to return to liberate them, and activists who believe that Shi'is themselves have a role to play in paving the way for the Mahdi's return. The latter are currently active in mobilising Shi'is in the fight against oppression.

Over the years, key religious concepts also started to adopt political hues among Shi'is. For example, Moussawi (2011: 15) suggests that the Islamic notion of *fitra*, or fine instinct, helped to foster among many Shi'is an individual commitment to liberty, as well as resistance against tyranny. There is also the concept of *faraj*, or freedom from grief, which supports the belief in the Mahdi, who will come to 'redeem the Shi'is when the world is consumed by tyranny and injustice' (Moussawi 2011: 27). Additionally, scholars note that by remembering the Umayyad rule that delayed Imam Ali's leadership and the subsequent martyrdom of his son Imam Hussein at the Battle or Karbala, this politicised Shi'i culture (Enayat 2011; Moussawi 2011; Norton 2005; and Rahnema 2005).[6] Hussain (2005) explains how this story of a brave young man marching to certain death gained traction almost immediately among the minority Shi'i populations, especially as the Umayyad dynasty outlawed any written account of the battle, almost ensuring that it would be rearticulated in oral and ritual practices.

Over the following centuries, Ashura and other Islamic rituals came to be expressed in new ways, depending upon the political circumstances. For example, after Sunnis started joining in the Ashura commemorations, Hussain (2005: 85) suggests that Shi'is wanted to be able to differentiate themselves, thus politicising their religious practices. Subsequently, the myth of Imam Hussein evolved hagiographic connotations and new rituals involving more dramatic forms of practice, including the *taziyeh*, or re-enactment of the battle, as well as *latm*, or chest beating. These public performances were instituted in Safavid Iran to distinguish the newly identified Shi'i empire from its Arab and Sunni Ottoman neighbours.

Hourani (2006) explains how a number of respected Shi'i *ulama* from southern Lebanon, as well as from Iraq and Bahrain, migrated to Iran during the Safavid period to help spread the new state religion. While the transition was slow, Shi'ism was quite widespread in Iran by the nineteenth century. The Iranian cities of Qom and Mashad eventually became known as important religious centres of learning, in addition to Najaf, Iraq's main holy city for Shi'is. The frequent cross migration of clerics meant that the politicisation of Shi'ism in Iran, Iraq and Lebanon had already created a regional movement by the mid-twentieth century. During the 1950s and 1960s, senior Shi'i clerics from these three countries all studied together in the region's holy cities, moving from one to the other to expand their learning.

For example, Iraqi-born Ayatollah Fadlallah of Lebanon studied in Najaf with Ayatollah Baqir al-Sadr of Iraq and Ayatollah Khomeini of Iran; and the Iranian-born Imam Musa al-Sadr studied with clerics in both Iran and Iraq before settling in Lebanon. These four clerics created vast networks of grass-roots institutions in their respective communities with the aim of empowering marginalised Shi'is through a highly polit-icised religious ideology, refashioning the martyrdom of Imam Hussein in the seventh century as a 'revolutionary exemplar' for the oppressed (Norton 2007: 50). As Behdad points out, contemporary Iranian intellec-tuals such as Ali Shari'ati also contributed to the politicisation of Shi'ism by referencing Frantz Fanon, Karl Marx and Jean-Paul Sartre to 'present Islam as a religion of liberation' (2005: 5). What follows is a brief overview of these five scholars' life and work: Ali Shari'ati and Ayatollah Khomeini of Iran; Ayatollah Baqir al-Sadr of Iraq; and Ayatollah Fadlallah and Imam al-Sadr of Lebanon, focusing mainly on their intellectual contri-butions to the mobilisation of Shi'i communities across the Middle East.

Ali Shari'ati and Ayatollah Khomeini in Iran

Although Iran was never officially colonised, the country still suffered from a long history of Western interference (Abrahamian 2008 and Sick 1985). Even before oil was discovered in 1908, foreign powers wanted Iran's resources. For example, in 1890, the Qajar government granted a monopoly over the production, sale and export of all Iranian tobacco to a British subject. Ayatollah Mirza Hassan Shirazi responded by issuing a *fatwa*, or legal injunction, against the unpopular tobacco concession. The Iranian *ulama*, or clergy, then urged a national boycott of tobacco that eventually pressured the Qajar government to cancel the unfair agreement. However, foreign interest in Iran's affairs soon intensified, with allied forces occupying the country during both world wars. Shortly after the Iranian government nationalised Iranian oil in 1951, the CIA and MI6 orchestrated a coup against the popularly elected Prime Minister Mohammad Mosaddegh, reinstalling the authoritarian regime of Shah Mohammad Reza Pahlavi. Throughout the 1960s and 1970s, American petrodollars helped the Shah to fund an increasingly repressive police state. His brutal security service known as SAVAK created what Kazemi (1996: 121) calls a 'hyper-autonomous' state.[7] To offer a visual metaphor of the gap between the ruler and his people, Graham describes an official photograph of the time depicting the Shah 'as though he was waving from the top of a mountain, the nation out of sight somewhere below' (1980: 60).

During this time, the Shah instituted a series of controversial policies that challenged popular sentiment in Iran; for example, the package including the land reform bill in 1963. Although land redistribution was long overdue, the reforms mostly helped selected elites acquire even more capital, undercut the power of rural landowners to the benefit of the central government and challenged Islamic charitable institutions like *awqaf*, which supported a wide range of social services to the people. According to Abrahamian, the reforms also neglected to grant land ownership to about 40 per cent of the peasant population, who were not given any rights to the land.[8] Despite opposition from both the *ulama* and *bazaar*, or shopkeepers, the government passed the package of reforms in 1963. The overall programme was called the 'White Revolution' and publicly promoted as 'the Shah-People Revolution' by the regime (Keddie 2003: 145).

As the government's latter name for the reform package illustrates, the Shah desired a connection to the Iranian people; however, at the same time, the regime did not shy away from flaunting the state's vast opulence, further widening the gulf between the state and the society. For example, in October 1971, the Shah ordered a month-long celebration to commemorate 2,500 years of Iranian history with lavish displays of wealth, power and pageantry. Furthermore, during his reign, the government's economic liberalisation policies mainly benefitted those connected to the state, rather than the people. And with so much oil wealth flowing into Iran, the ruling elite could simply import luxury goods instead of investing in local markets. According to Salehi-Isfahani (2006: 26), the Gini index, which measures income inequality, in Iranian cities rose from 0.4 in 1972 to 0.5 in 1977, a dramatic widening of social stratification over the space of only five years. At around the same time, Halliday (1978: 13–16) reports that a mere 45 families controlled 85 per cent of Iran's firms, with only one-quarter of them paying any taxes to help contribute to the public welfare. Ordinary Iranians were increasingly marginalised, both politically and economically. The critical intellectual

Jalal Al-e Ahmad famously called this post-colonial predicament *ghar-bzadegi*, which is difficult to translate from the Persian but generally means something akin to 'plague from the West', 'Weststruckness', or 'Westoxification'. Describing this term, Al-e Ahmad suggested that there was a paralysis of identity when those in developing countries were struck with the West, because their infatuation with Western society and its economic model created a dependency while precluding the possibility of local modernities emerging. Al-e Ahmad noted that while countries like Iran did not have machines and could not make them, they were still 'compelled to use machines because of the market and economic constraints on [them] to use machines' (1997: 20).

In the years leading up to the 1979 Islamic Revolution, other intellectuals, including Ali Shari'ati, adopted a religious lens to critique what was happening in Iran. Shari'ati's ability to synthesise a diversity of ideas was an important contribution to the modern Islamic revival in both Shi'i and Sunni communities throughout the region and beyond. Indeed, he is frequently referred to as the ideologue of the Iranian revolution (Abrahamian 1982). Born into a religious family in 1933 in a village near the holy city of Mashad in Iran, his father was a reformist cleric and teacher, and the son followed in his father's footsteps. It was during his own teacher's training that Shari'ati came into contact with the working class – by primary school he had read the Persian translation of Victor Hugo's novel *Les Miserables* (Rahnema 2005: 210). In the late 1940s, both father and son joined the first Iranian movement that attempted to reconcile Islam and European socialism, called *Nahzat-e Khoda Parastan-Sosiyalist*, or the Movement of God-Worshipping Socialists. After completing his religious and teacher's training, he taught for four years before pursuing a master's degree in foreign languages at the University of Mashad. Upon graduating, he was awarded a scholarship to continue his studies in Paris, working towards a PhD in hagiography at the Sorbonne. While in Paris, Abrahamian (1982: 25) describes how Shari'ati became immersed in political activism to support the post-colonial movements in Algeria and Cuba, as well as his native Iran, while also philosophically engaging with the writing of contemporary radicals, including Jean-Paul Sartre, Che Guevara and Frantz Fanon, translating many of their texts into Persian. Shari'ati learned from the latter 'the need for the Third World to create "a new man" based on "a new idea" and "a new history"' (Rahnema 2005: 221). But he also exchanged letters with Fanon while translating his work, arguing that religion should play a role in post-colonial struggles where societies are traditionally pious.

When Shari'ati eventually returned to Iran in 1964, he was arrested at the border. After spending six months in prison, he was released and taught in Mashad and then at *Hosseinieh Ershad*, a religious meeting hall in Tehran. Shari'ati was often critical of traditional Islamic scholars, particularly the *marja'*, who interpret God's law for the laypeople. Instead, he suggested that religion is socially constructed and thus proposed an 'understanding of Islam as a human, historical and intellectual movement, not as a storehouse of scientific and technical information'.[9] He thought that religion needed to be engaged with openly and not approached as something predetermined or merely written. He also argued that according to Islam, reason and religion were identical (Rahnema 2005: 230), as well as critiqued Western scientists, who by adopting the mantel of objectivity and neutrality refused to acknowledge how ideology shapes their understandings of science and removes them from the possibility of social commitment. Indeed, Shari'ati believed that modern science is itself an ideology, and one that destroys the human spirit and reproduces the status quo.

In a work titled 'Islamology: The Basic Design for a School of Thought and Action', Shari'ati maintained that Muslims should view the entirety of life through an Islamic lens. By suggesting that Islam is an ideology as well as a culture, he conceptualised Islam as a living religion with revolutionary potential. He suggested that faith is something that Muslims feel as much as they know, and as such, faith provides a framework for understanding all aspects of life, including science. To further clarify his ideas, Shari'ati characterised two different kinds of knowing: scientific facts, and the spirit or meaning that is hidden in an idea. He believed that the latter is deeper than the former and that our ideologies help us make sense of both. He proposed that Muslims combine them to realise a third kind of Islamised knowledge, a raised level of awareness and a commitment to movement, because viewing scientific knowledge through this kind of Islamic lens can support a progressive politics.

Shari'ati believed that it was possible to realise the Islamic concept of *tawhid*, or the unity of God, in human relations and socio-economic systems. But despite his progressive intentions, his conception of ideology, what he called a *maktab*, or school of thought, as something harmonious limits the possibilities for human interpretation and political contestation:

When I say 'maktab' ... I mean a harmonious collection of philosophical concepts, religious beliefs, ethical values and practical methods which, through a rational relationship, create a moving, meaningful, directed and united body which is alive, all parts of it being nourished by one spirit.[10]

Shari'ati also offered the metaphor of a galaxy, which he said fosters coordinated movement and social awareness – one spirit or one movement is thus important for Muslims to realise social change. The problem is that power is not factored into this framework, because in reality, ideology is never unified but instead is always multidimensional and replete with internal contradictions, as is Shari'ati's work. This means that ideas are always subject to interpretation, leading to particular constellations of meaning that empower some more than others. Furthermore, while Shari'ati was critical of de-historicising Islam, he sometimes appealed to divine universals in problematic ways. In his work titled 'Red Shi'ism: The Religion of Martyrdom and Black Shi'ism: The Religion of Mourning', he called upon all Shi'is to move in a common direction by embracing the marja' leadership, which will centralise the movement to effectively rebel against the oppression of orthodox Sunnism.[11] He even called for enlightened Islamic intellectuals to lead the unknowing masses, a project that he referred to as the Islam of the warrior intellectual (Sadeghi-Boroujerdi 2011). Thus, when it came to laying out a plan of action, Shari'ati disregarded his own critique of the marja' to realise his political goals, which may not always be in alignment with those religious leaders holding positions of power. His romanticised conception of a coherent ideology, especially in the form of Islam, does not leave enough space for internal disagreement, choice and negotiation, potentially laying the foundations for the same kind of repression that he critiqued under communism (Shari'ati 1980).

Nevertheless, these selected criticisms should not outweigh Shari'ati's extraordinary contributions. He realised that, 'Capitalism was not only unjust, inequitable and exploitative, but [also] immoral, destroying all real values and perverting the viceregents of God on earth. According to Shariati, capitalism prevented man from becoming God-like' (Rahnema 2005: 241). As Abrahamian (1982: 24) points out, his blending of religious ideology, Western philosophy and post-colonial activism was ground breaking. His work illustrates that the Islamic Revolution was based not only on native developments in Iranian Shi'ism, but also on a reflection of wider historical and philosophical movements in the East and West. Other Shi'i scholars would subsequently do the same, weaving together Western scholarship with Eastern scholarship, religions and histories to take understandings of Marxism and faith to new levels.[12] Shari'ati's unorthodox approach to religion and politics was a challenge to both the secular government of the Shah as well as to the established religious clerics. After the religious meeting hall in Tehran closed, he was arrested again and remained in prison for 18 months; he was only released after concerted pressure from the international community.

However, the Shah's government kept him under house arrest, also preventing him from publishing any of his work, until in 1977 when he was permitted to visit London. It was only one month later that Shari'ati died of a heart attack, at the age of 43. Following his death, his writings were instrumental in mobilising opposition to the Shah, but his theories declined in popularity after the revolution for various reasons, including his critique of traditional religious scholars and the misappropriation of many of his ideas, for example by the widely criticised *Mujahideen-e Khalq*, an Islamic movement initially inspired by Marxism that fought on the side of Saddam Hussein during the Iran–Iraq War (1980–1988). Still, Shari'ati's theories have remained influential among some Iranians as well as Arab Shi'is and Muslims outside the Middle East. More recently, the Islamic Republic has been trying to reclaim his legacy, for example, by marking the 2007 anniversary of his death by unveiling statues in his likeness at the Ershad Cultural Complex in Tehran (Press TV 2007). The following year, the government also organised an event where his son was invited to speak.[13]

While Shari'ati is considered to be the ideologue of the 1979 Islamic Revolution, Ayatollah Sayyid Ruhollah Musavi Khomeini is known as its political and spiritual leader. Khomeini was born to a modest family of learned Sayyids, or those descended from the Prophet Muhammad, in the small Iranian city of Khomein in 1902. He was raised by his more prosperous aunt, his father dying before he was even born. During his youth, he was thought to be a promising scholar, especially in the field of Islamic law (Al Jazeera 2009). Khomeini was also known to be a talented poet (Moin 2005: 66). He first moved to Isfahan and then to Arak to advance his studies, subsequently settling in the religious cities of Qom in Iran and Najaf in Iraq. He quickly gained knowledge and earned the respect of his peers to rise as a religious scholar. Khomeini studied the more mystical aspects of Shi'ism and, according to Moin (2005: 70), one of his key teachers emphasised the importance of asceticism and education, encouraging students to simplify difficult subjects to reach wider audiences. Khomeini also showed an interest in the role of the Shiʻi clergy in politics and was an activist from the early days of his youth, speaking out against the brutal authoritarian rule of the Pahlavi dynasty, a position that earned him both trouble and popular support.

In 1963, Khomeini joined other clerical leaders in the protest of the Shah's unpopular White Revolution package of reforms. Khomeini called attention to the poverty and suffering of the poorer classes and asserted that the Shah's government was acting in the interest of foreign forces to destroy Islam, a view that resonated at a time when government policies were undermining the social activities of Islamic institutions. Shortly after the reforms of the White Revolution were ratified, young seminary students in Qom rallied in non-violent anti-government protests. The army responded by attacking the protesters, killing one student while injuring many. In response, Khomeini continued to protest and was arrested and jailed. He was released ten months later only to protest once more, this time against the Status of Forces Law that was passed in 1964. The law granted immunity to personnel of American advisory missions to Iran, including their staff and family. Because the *majles*, or parliament, approved a US$200 million American loan for arms purchases immediately after the law was ratified, it was widely assumed by Iranians at the time that the two were connected, and that the government had made a humiliating concession to the United States. Khomeini issued a declaration after the vote, stating that the *majles* had 'acknowledged that Iran is a colony; it has given America a document attesting that the nation of Muslims is barbarous' (quoted in Bakhash 1984: 34). Shortly afterwards, he was once again arrested and then exiled to Turkey, eventually finding refuge in Najaf until Saddam Hussein ordered him to leave Iraq in 1978, when he went to Paris.

While exiled, Khomeini was finally able to freely speak out against the Pahlavi regime. Tape recordings and transcripts of his declarations against the Shah and the United States were smuggled back into Iran, and the Shah knew that, despite living abroad, Khomeini was still a popular figure in Iran. So, in order to challenge his influence, somebody inside the Shah's government published an article in 1978 that cast aspersions on his character.[14] Seminary students in Qom took to the streets in protest, and confrontations with SAVAK led to a number of deaths. Protesters responded with a series of mourning ceremonies, processions and riots over the following twelve months. On 8 September 1978, the Shah's army opened fire on demonstrators in Tehran and many were killed. This event came to be known as 'Black Friday', and is seen to mark the start of the Islamic Revolution.

By politicising religion, Khomeini had helped to create a permanent resistance to the Shah, who was ultimately forced to leave the country in January 1979. As Khomeini recounted (2002: 326), every time somebody was killed, the faithful would recite a *fatiha*, or the opening chapter of the holy Qur'an, during which time another person would be killed, requiring the recitation of another *fatiha*. In this way, the struggle continued organically without any interruption. Like Shari'ati, Khomeini's intellectual approach was dialectical. He suggested that secular governments were only concerned with preserving order in the natural realm rather than upholding divine justice and morality. And according to him, this criticism extended to both the Sunni Umayyad and Abbasid dynasties, because even though they incorporated both, they focused more on the rule of the natural realm than the spiritual. Instead, Khomeini believed that divine governments foster a dialectic between the natural and the divine, helping humans to realise their true potentials by also guiding their morality and behaviour in personal or private life. As such, Khomeini reasoned that everyday life is inseparable from the divine, because according to the prophets, this 'world is merely a means, a path to achieve a noble aim' (2002: 331).

After the revolution, Khomeini established in Iran a *wilayat al-faqih* (Arabic), or *velayat-e faqih* (Persian), meaning government of Islamic Jurists. While this particular system of Islamic government ultimately empowers the *faqih*, or Supreme Leader, there is also a complicated system of checks and balances among a number of state institutions,[15] including an extensive network of charities and foundations that focus on supporting the health, education and welfare of Iranians, especially the families of the martyrs who were killed during the long war with Iraq. Although the idea of *wilayat al-faqih* was not new to Shi'ism, Arjomand (1988) suggests that the concept and practice, which Khomeini conceived of and developed through *ijtihad*, or interpretation, was very different from other leading Islamist arguments, because most of the previous conceptions separated political and spiritual authority. However, according to Khomeini's interpretation, the *faqih* is absolutely qualified to 'to lead the community and to serve as a *marja' al-taqlid*, or source of emulation, because of his long and arduous training in Islamic jurisprudence and his expertise in Islamic law' (Bakhash 1984: 95). According to Moussawi (2011: 31), Khomeini's *wilayat al-faqih* is based on the belief that the Mahdi's absence made it necessary to establish a just Islamic government in the here and now.

While he is known more in the West as a religious and political leader, Khomeini was also a respected intellectual. His mastery of using reason to articulate religious concepts is evident in his essay 'The Same Thing in Different Languages'. In this short work, he suggested that humans have different languages to express the same concepts, thus we must always use our reason in interpreting what others say. In the same way, humans must use rationality to understand the meaning of religious concepts. So, while we can use metaphors to speak about God, none of these metaphors will ever 'fully correspond to the sustaining embrace of all beings, for that embrace means that there is no place in creation where He does not exist' (Khomeini 2002: 418). Within such an understanding, Khomeini argued that some contradictions are to be expected in religious texts because any linguistic expression is only an attempt to communicate the relationship between God and humans, and as such should never be interpreted literally. Indeed, based on this logic, he suggested that literal interpretations of religious texts are irrational, rather than the religious concepts therein.

Nevertheless, much like the work of Shari'ati, Khomeini's statements sometimes veered towards the absolute and it is here that we can see the dialectic breaking down. He always insisted on the purity of Islam, which he believed embodied justice and democracy. Therefore, he reasoned that the phrase a 'democratic Islamic republic' was an insult to Islam because it presumed that democracy and justice are extrinsic to Islam (Khomeini 2002: 339–340). However, this way of thinking prioritises the divine over the natural, presupposing a universal human commitment to the divine, even at the expense of democracy. Also, Iran's revolutionaries inherited a corrupt and authoritarian regime from the Shah, a historical legacy that meant the project of Islamising Iran's government was always at risk of reproducing the structural oppression of the past. The daughter of Mehdi Bazargan, the Islamic Republic's first prime minister who resigned in protest over the 1979 American hostage crisis, explained the situation to me with the following metaphor: Iranian religion is water falling down a mountain, starting at the peak as something holy and unadulterated, however becoming tainted as each person thrusts her hand into the water to purify herself.[16] Here, religion is both pure and contaminated, illustrating the dialectic at work.

But even though Khomeini is often maligned in the West, his political and intellectual legacy is extremely important and remains strong in Iran, as well as in Lebanon, not only among Shi'i activists, but also among religious conservatives and political reformists alike. After the Islamic Revolution successfully toppled the Shah, Khomeini ruled for ten years as the Supreme Leader of Iran until his death in 1989, shortly after agreeing to a ceasefire that ended Iran's long and bloody war with Iraq. Today, his picture appears throughout Iran as well as Lebanon, especially in Hizbullah strongholds like the area known in Arabic as the Dahiyeh, or the southern suburbs of Beirut, as well as in the Bekaa Valley and southern Lebanon.

Ayatollah Baqir al-Sadr in Iraq

Similar to their Iranian counterparts, the Shi'i *ulama* in Iraq were also becoming increasingly politicised by the turn of the twentieth century. After the collapse of the Ottoman Empire, the League of Nations demarcated the borders of modern Iraq and placed the new country under British mandate. The population consisted of a majority of Arab Shi'is and a minority of Arab Sunnis, with a sizeable community of Kurdish Sunnis in the north and much smaller numbers of Arab, Assyrian and Armenian Christians, as well as Arab Jews, throughout. Although Iraq officially gained independence in 1932 under the Hashemite monarchy, the British presence remained in the country, to the dismay of many Iraqis. As a result, the short-lived Kingdom of Iraq was marred by political instability and eventually the Iraqi army overturned the monarchy in a *coup d'état* in 1958, establishing an authoritarian and secular Baathist regime that privileged the Arab Sunni minority and oppressed the Shi'i majority. Furthermore, the socio-economic status of Shi'is in Iraq tended to be much lower than that of the Sunnis. And while the Shi'i *ulama* played a pivotal role in Iraq during the 1920 revolt against the newly established British mandate (Sankari 2005: 29), after that, Iraqi Shi'i activism largely declined until the 1950s and 1960s, when the rising popularity of communism coincided with increasing migration of impoverished Iraqi Shi'is to the urban centres, which helped to create slum-like conditions for many Shi'is living in Iraq's cities. According to Mallat, 'the combination of suspicion towards central rule and the spectre of communism turned direct involvement in politics into a condition for [their] survival' (2005: 253).

Although Ayatollah Muhammad Baqir al-Sadr's life was cut tragically short, his religious scholarship and political work have played a significant role in the Shi'i revival, both in Iraq and throughout the Middle East. One volunteer for Hizbullah explained to me that he was the kind of man who appears only once every century.[17] Born in the Iraqi city of Kadhimiyya to a Sayyid family of respected Islamic scholars, but living in relative poverty (Mallat 2005: 258), Baqir al-Sadr progressed quickly through his religious education, reaching an advanced stage before even finishing his secular studies. According to both Araki (2003) and Sankari (2005), Baqir al-Sadr developed a radical ideology that conceived of Islam as a total life system – a programme for a social, political and economic way of being that is based on both scientific methods and religious texts. Araki suggests that this new way of Islamic thinking served to protect Muslim societies from foreign ideological invasions, as well as to 'prepare the ground for organised political action' (2003: 12). Indeed, Baqir al-Sadr played an active role in mobilising the grassroots through education by politicising religious seminaries and organisations throughout Iraq, especially in Najaf. In addition to giving lectures and writing letters, he also took advantage of contemporary technology, using cassette tapes to distribute and communicate his message. As Araki (2003: 13) points out, these ideas and practices helped Baqir al-Sadr to create a religious relations network that connected the popular base with his religious authority.

Baqir al-Sadr was concerned that the Islamic religion had been removed from the contemporary lives around him. Therefore, he sought a total rethinking of Islamic ideology that was historicised, using inductive logic to bring Islam into the here and now. Araki (2003: 18–19) explains how Baqir al-Sadr set about the realisation of this vision by the following means: he reinterpreted canonical texts in light of new scientific and philosophical developments; introduced contemporary methods of research into theological schools; portrayed Islam as a comprehensive system with the support of philosophical proofs and logical evidence; deconstructed Western hegemonic ideas and practices to expose their deficiencies; and prepared religious intellectuals who were actively engaged with contemporary developments in Islamic culture and who were able to confront alternative ideologies. This project would help to create an ideological base that purposefully related to the traditional religious authorities in Shi'ism known as the *marja'*, thus laying the foundations for the establishment of an Islamic state.

Through his intellectual work, Baqir al-Sadr became a respected social and legal theorist. According to Kuran (1997: 325), he engaged with the social sciences in an effort to prove the superiority of Islam over communism during a time when Arab socialism was becoming increasingly popular. His book on the *Principles of Islamic Jurisprudence* outlines a logical approach to interpret Islamic law that is based on scientific methods. This may appear contradictory to those who conceive of religious texts, like the holy Qur'an or the Bible, as the immutable word of God. However, Baqir al-Sadr (2003: 54) reasoned that while the *shari'ah*, or Islamic law, is an instance of legislation issuing from God, the interpretation of the components of the *shari'ah*, including the Qur'an and the *Sunnah*, or the sayings of the Prophet, are not necessarily religious rulings in themselves – they merely shed light upon religious rulings. Thus, Baqir al-Sadr (2003: 52) concluded that everybody has the right to question any interpretation of law by a *mujtahid*, or recognised jurist, because any interpretation is only the result of an interpretive procedure and the *mujtahid* is not him or herself the source of the law, even after he or she has followed a correct procedure. At the same time, he recognised that the interpretive procedure itself is extremely important, since it comprises one part of the proof. Here evidence for any ruling is based not only on the actual texts themselves, including the Qur'an and the *Sunnah*, but also the rational evidence that guides the logic of interpretation. Accordingly, he focused on outlining a rigorous framework to arrive at a reasoned interpretation of religious law that is based on logic. As Baqir al-Sadr maintained, 'logic studies are the general procedures of reasoning, irrespective of the subject and discipline involved' (2003: 44). Therefore, it was not a contradiction to consistently apply a rational logic to both religious texts and practices.

Baqir al-Sadr also provided a framework for an Islamic economic system in his book titled *Our Economics*. While he embraced some of the leading ideas about political and economic liberalism, he was mostly concerned with adopting a reformed capitalist system that would preserve an acceptable social balance. Wilson (1988: 47) suggests that Baqir al-Sadr provided a moral justification based on the principles of Islam for an economic system that embraced a conception of private property as one form of ownership among others that were more communal. A strong moral framework guided his vision of property rights, because he believed that 'ultimately property is held in trust for God' (Wilson 1988: 51). As such, he reasoned that property has a relational value as well as an objective value in and of itself.[18]

By weaving together critical readings of Western political theories into an Islamic framework, Baqir al-Sadr's intellectual project was quite radical – he longed for the transformation of Iraqi society. But it is important to note that he did not view sectarianism as the biggest problem in Iraqi society; instead, he perceived the major problems to be foreign domination, capitalist exploitation and political oppression. Thus, he was not looking to simply reform the Baathist sectarian system, but to liberate the lives of all Iraqis from this system of subjugation. Baqir al-Sadr stressed that it was the duty of every Muslim, including himself, to do all that was necessary to wage a *jihad*, or the struggle against oppression, even if it cost him or her their lives. This applied to all Muslims in Iraq, including 'Arabs and Kurds alike, Sunni and Shi'i alike' (quoted in Araki 2003: 16). In his last appeal to the Iraqi people before his death, he explained that,

> I have spared no effort to sacrifice my well-being for the sake of the Sunnis and Shi'is in equal measure, as well as for the sake of Arabs and Kurds equally. This stems from my belief in defending the message that unites them all and their faith which unites them all.
>
> (Araki 2003: 16)

Baqir al-Sadr then cited the example of Imam Ali, the Prophet Muhammad's cousin and son-in-law, whom Shi'is remember as the first Imam and Sunnis revere as the fourth Caliph. He explained that Ali 'fought during wars waged against the apostates under the standard of the first Caliph Abu Bakr', the original successor to the Prophet Muhammad who was chosen by consensus and favoured by the Sunni community (Araki 2003: 16). By pointing to a central figure in Islamic history that both Sunnis and Shi'is honour, Baqir al-Sadr was attempting to unite all Muslims in Iraq.

Baqir al-Sadr was one of the founders in 1958 of the Iraqi Shi'i movement known as Hizb al-Da'wa. Sankari (2005: 77) describes how this name literally means the Party of Islamic Call, referring to the proselytising paradigm of the Prophet Muhammad, a peaceful mode of spreading the word of God. Several leading Shi'i *ulama* came together to form the party, with Baqir al-Sadr emerging as the group's leader.[19] Following the same approach of his intellectual work, Sankari explains how Hizb al-Da'wa's main 'goal was the comprehensive transformation of human society by the fundamental alteration of existing patterns of social relationships and political regimes' (2005: 80). While the religious inspiration of the proposed transformation that Hizb al-Da'wa was calling for may not have pleased Marx (1844), it was quite similar to his recommendation to rearrange the 'relationships to *man himself*', which is necessary for true emancipation.

Hizb al-Da'wa also borrowed from Sunni radical thinkers like Sayyid Qutb, the Egyptian scholar and activist whose ideas helped to inspire the Muslim Brotherhood in Egypt. Qutb regarded modern society as morally corrupted and *jahili*, referring to the ignorant state of traditional society before the Prophet Muhammad revealed Islam. But while Qutb's thinking sanctioned the struggle against a society of infidels, Hizb al-Da'wa altered this concept to focus on the moral corruption of secular political regimes rather than modern society more generally. Because the post-colonial secular state had strayed so far away from Islamic principles, Baqir al-Sadr believed that this struggle should take a revolutionary form, in the sense that only a radical reimagining of the state could achieve social justice. And yet although both Qutb and Hizb al-Da'wa shared similar transformative goals, according to the latter, the struggle should not be focused on society, but only on the political establishment and other material manifestations of modern-day structures of oppressions.

Baqir al-Sadr's intellectual work was both influential as well as politically subversive, and he was arrested by the Baathist regime in the late 1970s. His followers in Najaf, led by his sister Bint al-Huda, responded by organising demonstrations and even armed violence. But while this popular uprising led to his release, the regime still confined him to his home. After demonstrating his support for the emerging Islamic Revolution that was beginning to unfold in neighbouring Iran, he was arrested once again, this time along with his sister. In 1980, under the rule of Saddam Hussein, Baqir al-Sadr was executed. Several Lebanese told me that before he died, the Baathist security forces raped and killed his sister, forcing him to watch. This grotesque behaviour likely added to his follower's sense of grievance over both his treatment and their persecution, whether in Iraq, Iran or Lebanon.

Imam Musa al-Sadr and Ayatollah Fadlallah in Lebanon

Much like their brothers and sisters in Iraq, Shi'is in Lebanon also suffered from various forms of persecution throughout much of the twentieth century. Lebanese Shi'is were given an inferior status that was institutionalised by the sectarian framework of Lebanon as a modern nation state in 1943. The origins of the sectarian framework can be traced back to the French colonial project, which constructed a Phoenician narrative attempting to link the idea of a 'Lebanese people' to European Christians rather than Arab Christians and Muslims, despite the fact that Lebanon was for a long time a part of *bilad al-Sham*, or historic Syria, and was also grouped together with Syria under the French mandate. Traditionally, Lebanese society had primarily been organised around class rather than sect, with divisions cutting across sectarian lines. Ussama Makdisi (1996: 24) explains that while the villages were of mixed sects, the elites and the common people generally did not interact very much. And for those who lived in the cities along the coastline, Leila Fawaz (1984: 490) describes how shared economic interests were often more important than sectarian ones.

However, all of this changed as a result of the colonial encounter with France. As Asher Kaufman (2001) explains, the Phoenician narrative started to emerge during the nineteenth century when France was looking to legitimise its colonial project in the Middle East. He argues that the French started to embellish its historical connections to the Phoenicians of Lebanon and Syria to justify the colonial relationship and to discourage the Lebanese from identifying more with their Arab and Muslim neighbours. At the same time, many Lebanese Christians, and particularly the Maronites who already shared a strong religious connection to the Catholic Church in Rome, were happy to embrace this newly constructed narrative because it supported their own call for a separate political entirety in Lebanon.

At the turn of the twentieth century, elites from the most powerful sects also started to construct competing national narratives that adopted sectarian characteristics. By the time Lebanon was declared a republic in 1926, a logic of sectarianism was already systematically interwoven into the newly formed state. The unwritten national pact agreed in 1943 set the conditions for an independent government based on a confessional system where public offices are allocated along religious lines, thus institutionalising religious differences. And there are many religions in Lebanon – altogether there are 18 recognised sects, the dominant three being the Maronite Christians, Sunni Muslims and Shi'i Muslims. The newly formed state largely favoured the Maronites and the Sunnis, while discriminating against Shi'is and the other sects. As Walid Khalidi further explains:

> The Sunni–Maronite partnership in the formulation of the Covenant gave rise to a situation in which the leaders of the two communities at the highest level and with few exceptions looked upon the entire Lebanese scene through a bisectarian prism. This prism tended by the same token to be exclusivist and somehow able to block from view the existence of other sects, Christian and Muslim alike.
>
> (Khalidi 1989: 380)

The arrangement ultimately privileged Maronite Christians because the French directed census in 1932 construed the Christian populations to be larger than the Sunni or Shi'i populations combined, and as a result the subsequent government was divided in a manner favouring the Maronites, who always hold the office of the president. The next position of power is the prime minister, which is always allocated to a Sunni. And finally, a Shi'i serves as speaker of the parliament. At the time, parliamentary representation was allocated as a 6:5 proportion favouring Christians to Muslims. According to figures quote by Ahmad Nizar Hamzeh (2004: 12), the early bureaucracy also reflected sectarian bias, with Shi'is holding only 3.2 per cent of government posts. Over the years, this power sharing agreement became even more unequal as the Lebanese society experienced a demographic transformation. Although Lebanon has not conducted an official census since the one carried out in 1932, Norton (2007) and Deeb (2006) both suggest that the demographic changes since then have led to relative declines in the Christian populations and an increase in the Shi'i population. Dona Stewart (1996: 491) argues that by 1975, Shi'is had likely become the largest minority group in Lebanon, even though the system favouring the Christians and Sunnis did not change.

In addition to the inequalities enshrined in a disproportionate sectarian political system, income in Lebanon was unevenly distributed as well. In the years following independence, the economy was mainly controlled by what Fawwaz Traboulsi (2007: 115) calls 'the consortium', comprising 30 families related to the Maronite president (24 Christian, five Muslim

Figure 2.1 These picture souvenirs illustrate how sectarian elites are idolised in Lebanon alongside religious saints. From left to right: in the back row Rafik Hariri, former head of the Future Movement (14 March), Jesus and General Michel Aoun, head of the Free Patriotic Movement (8 March); in the middle row Ni'mat Allah Kassab Al-Hardini, a Maronite Saint, Sayyid Hassan Nasrallah, head of Hizbullah (8 March), Rafik Hariri and Samir Geagea, head of the Lebanese Forces (14 March); and in the bottom row various Maronite saints, Jesus and Michael Sleiman, former President of Lebanon (14 March). Photograph taken in Jbeil during summer 2009.

and one Druze). According to him, it is estimated that these families owned around 40 per cent of the national revenue (Traboulsi 2007: 117). Furthermore, Hamzeh (2004: 13) points out that most of the country's wealth was located in the urban centres and around 85 per cent of Shi'is were living in the rural areas in the south or to the east in the Bekaa Valley, regions that the Lebanese state has historically ignored in terms of providing services. Even today, these areas are often still excluded by the centralised political system. For example, Judith Palmer Harik (2005: 18) describes how the state did not provide sewage networks or potable water to many rural communities at the turn of the twenty-first century. Lebanese Shi'is suffered from extreme social marginalisation in the greater society as well. One Lebanese scholar explained to me how when he was growing up, being a Shi'i was almost comparable to being an untouchable under the caste system in India.[20] He said that it was simply not an identity that he or any other Shi'is would dare to publicly embrace. In popular parlance, Shi'is were called *Matawila*, referring to people who lived in misery (Weiss 2010: 1).[21]

To make matters worse, the Shi'is living in southern Lebanon found themselves in the middle of a de facto war between Israel and the Palestinian refugees in Lebanon, who were forced to flee their lands en masse in 1948 and again in 1967. Israel's retaliatory measures against the Palestinian resistance fighters caused high levels of insecurity for all those living in the south, including Christian and Shi'i Lebanese. To escape the conflict, Hamzeh (2004: 14) explains that many Shi'is in the southern areas moved to the cities during the 1960s and 1970s, with the majority residing in squatter settlements in the southern and eastern suburbs of Beirut, a destitute region that came to be known as 'the belt of misery'. Meanwhile, the Maronites resided mostly in the affluent neighbourhoods to the east of the capital city, and the Sunnis in the less prosperous west.

One of the most important persons to impact the Shi'is of Lebanon during this time was Ayatollah Baqir al-Sadr's cousin Imam Musa al-Sadr. Although born in Iran in 1928, Imam al-Sadr traced his family origins to southern Lebanon. Several members of his family were respected religious scholars and were also politically active at a time when most Iranian clerics still avoided getting involved in contemporary politics. For example, his father Sadr al-Din was the spiritual leader of a revolutionary armed group called the *Fedayeen-e Islam*, which loosely translates as Devotees of Islam (Al-Manar 2005). Imam al-Sadr spent most of his formative years in the religious capitals of Qom and Najaf. As a youth, he decided to pursue both a secular education as well as an Islamic one. At the time, this was an unusual step for an Islamic scholar in Iran, because the Western-influenced state school system was established to compete with the religious school system. However, according to Chehabi and Tafreshi (2006: 142), Imam al-Sadr made the decision to study in both systems in an effort to understand why some Iranians were choosing secularism over religion. After graduating with a degree in economic law from the University of Tehran, he pursued further religious study in Najaf. While living there, he was also the editor of a progressive journal that fused together modern ideas about rationality and religion. The intellectual focus of his work at this time was on the distributive capacity of Islamic economics (Chehabi and Tafreshi 2006: 148).

After immigrating to Lebanon in 1960, Imam al-Sadr made an extraordinary impact by mobilising the Shi'is of southern Lebanon. Chehabi and Tafreshi argue that, 'he exemplified the Shi'i cosmopolitanism that blurred the lines between Arab, Persian and Turk' (2006: 130). But due to political differences, he maintained an uneasy relationship with the Shah after leaving Iran. At the time, the Shah was allied with the United States and held close ties with Israel. Although Imam al-Sadr accepted development aid from his home country throughout the 1960s, by the 1970s, he had started to actively support critics of the Shah, activities that generated animosity in his home country. He also experienced some political problems in Lebanon because he expressed a degree of ambivalence towards the Palestinian resistance that was destabilising life for so many Lebanese Shi'is and Christians in the south. Although Imam al-Sadr was steadfast in his support for the Palestinian struggle against Israel, 'his relations with the Palestine Liberation Organisation were tense and uneasy at best' (Norton 2005: 200). Furthermore, he was concerned that the Palestinian refugees who were forced from their lands would settle in the southern areas and take local jobs away from Lebanese, encouraging even more Shi'is to migrate to the cities,[22] leaving the southern areas more vulnerable to Israeli occupation or even annexation. Some believe that these inter-Arab tensions may be what later on cost him his life.

Imam al-Sadr reached out to the secular and religious alike by viewing Islam and science as complementary.[23] Indeed, he believed that religion and science 'were born twins' and suggested that:

between science and religion there is an infallible bond and they determine the standard by which to measure humans' destiny and level of perfection. For science, in short, is an illumination to view reality and discover the truth; the truth being Allah's creations and demands.[24]

Imam al-Sadr suggested that during the Middle Ages, religion enslaved science and humanity suffered; however, he argued that after the Enlightenment these roles were reversed and science began to overpower and undermine religion. He believed that developments during the twentieth century offered an opportunity for humans to reconfigure a more enlightened balance between religion and science:

> Science has sobered up, has come in touch with reality, has realised that it alone cannot bring about human happiness. Science has felt alienated and estranged; it sees with greater clarity man's happiness, the ravages of war and oppression ... Sciences in all its branches are instruments of creation ... Man who created the machine, who created science, cannot kneel before his own creations, and worship these creations to the exclusion of God. Science begins with man and relies on man.
>
> (quoted in Ajami 1986: 92)

Much like the other leading Shi'i activists of his time, Imam al-Sadr often employed religious imagery as a metaphor for empowerment. Ajami (1986: 142) points out that he reworked the tragic story of the Battle or Karbala to stress the importance of Imam Hussein's courageous choice to take political action and refashioned the story of the Twelve Imams to be one of inspiration rather than imitation. During the 1974 commemorations of Ashura, he said:

> This revolution did not die in the sands of Karbala, it flowed into the life stream of the Islamic world, and passed from generation to generation, even to our day. It is a deposit placed in our hands so that we may profit from it, that we may extract from it a new source of reform, a new position, a new movement, a new revolution to repel the darkness, to stop tyranny and to pulverise evil.
>
> (quoted in Norton 2005: 197)

That said, Imam al-Sadr's approach also appealed to non-religious Lebanese as well. Ajami (1986: 136) describes how he also successfully incorporated a discourse evolving from the themes of disinheritance and deprivation to inspire Marxist-oriented Lebanese and post-colonial activists worldwide. Indeed, Imam al-Sadr strove to create a new post-colonial reality because he believed that contemporary 'politics, administration, markets and construction were not built on the basis of faith, they drifted from its path and turned into colonialism, looking for new markets, cold war periods ... etc' (1975). One Lebanese Shi'i scholar who was active in the socialist movement during the 1970s noted with some frustration that the Communists had failed to reach the same communities that Imam al-Sadr was able to mobilise by employing a religiously inspired Marxism.[25]

Similar to Marx and Engels (1970), Imam al-Sadr supported the idea that humans made their own history even though he rejected a purely materialist conception of the world. For him, Islam offered a dialectical approach, because Islam provides the basis for not only an economic movement, but also 'a moral one with implications for the economy and civil society' (quoted in Ajami 1986: 95). And it was through civil society institutions that Imam al-Sadr spread his message of empowerment. During the 1960s, he launched extensive social institutions for the Shi'is of Lebanon, and these institutions continue to deliver important services to the community today. In 1962, he founded the Imam al-Sadr Foundation, which works mainly with children and disseminates the types of knowledge that give Lebanese Shi'is control of their own lives. He also established the Supreme Islamic Shi'i Council in 1969, the first political institution to directly represent Shi'i populations in Lebanon.

In 1974 Imam al-Sadr, together with Gregoire Haddad, a Greek Catholic archbishop, created a social movement called the Party of the Deprived to provide services to the needy throughout southern Lebanon regardless of sect (Moussawi 2011: 210–211). Later on, Imam al-Sadr also launched a Shi'i resistance militia to retaliate against Israeli incursions into Lebanon, which is known as Amal (the Battalions of the Lebanese Resistance), an anagram that means 'hope' in Arabic.[26] The powerful Amal movement splintered after Imam al-Sadr disappeared on a trip to Libya and secularist lawyer Nabih Berri took over the party as leader. When Israel invaded Lebanon in 1982, three young Shi'i clerics formerly of Amal, Subhi al-Tufayli, 'Abbas al-Musawi and Sayyid Hassan Nasrallah, launched a new movement together that they would later call Hizbullah, meaning the Party of God. To aid the new resistance movement against the Israeli occupation of Lebanon, Ayatollah Khomeini immediately deployed about 1,000 members of the Iranian Revolutionary Guard Corps into the Baalbek region of Lebanon under the leadership of Mohsen Rafiqdoost (Wright 1990: 109).

A volunteer for Hizbullah explained to me how Imam al-Sadr opened up the space for Shi'is to empower themselves and resist against oppression.[27] Until the 1960s, the Shi'i dominated southern and eastern areas of Lebanon were under the leadership of autocratic leaders known in Arabic as *zu'ama* (in the plural and *za'im* is singular). Historically, all sects were governed by *zu'ama*, but for various reasons, including their rural location and exclusion from centralised politics, Shi'is remained more prone to their influence. The volunteer explained to me that while under the leadership of the *zu'ama*, religion played only a marginal role in the ordinary lives of Shi'is in southern Lebanon. The religious class was tied more to the ruling elites rather than the people, thus there was a separation between the people and the clergy, or *ulama*, and the latter's energies were dedicated to continuing the status quo rather than empowering the masses. As a result, religion was not important for most Shi'is and they were largely unreligious or at least unobservant in their daily lives. However, soon after Imam al-Sadr arrived in Lebanon in 1960, he began to play a vital role in politicising Shi'is through religious ideas and practices. He regularly travelled through the south in order to speak to people on the ground, listening to and connecting with them. This grass-roots activist work helped to politicise Shi'is as a community for the first time. One Marxist Shi'i activist pointed out the irony that somebody from Iran was able to mobilise Lebanese Shi'is based on their religious identity, because these were the same Shi'is who had been ashamed of their untouchable status for so many years.[28]

Although his language resonated mostly with Lebanese Shi'is, Imam al-Sadr also employed a post-colonial discourse that included the disinherited and deprived worldwide. Furthermore, he made frequent and bold overtures to Christian leaders in Lebanon, even establishing the Shi'i Islamic Supreme Council in Hazmieh, a Christian area just south-east of Beirut, as a model of coexistence. The journalist Robert Fisk quotes a Palestinian Islamic scholar in Lebanon as saying that Imam al-Sadr 'took on the Christians of Lebanon in an extraordinary manner. He revived Islamic interest in Jesus and Mary. He was an extraordinary performer. He almost embraced Christian theology. He would lecture in churches with the cross right behind him!' (2014). I was told on several different occasions about how Imam al-Sadr once led a congregation after prayer to a Christian ice cream vendor who was being boycotted by Muslims. Before anybody in the congregation could realise what was happening, he ordered an ice cream from the vendor and, in the end, his followers did the same.[29] Unfortunately, Imam al-Sadr's political pragmatism sometimes displeased his polarised contemporaries and he disappeared during a trip to Libya in 1978 under circumstances that are still shrouded in mystery. The official Libyan story is that he went to Tripoli accompanied by Sheikh Muhammad Yaacoub and journalist Abbas Badreddine to meet with Colonel Muammar al-Qaddafi and from there he allegedly boarded a flight to Italy, where all three of them disappeared. But the Italians have never verified this claim, saying instead that only the travellers' baggage arrived in Rome, luggage that was checked in by two Libyans.

There are several popular explanations for Imam al-Sadr's disappearance and each blames various foreign actors. One story is that he and al-Qaddafi had some sort of dispute over several passages in the Qur'an, resulting in the Imam's death (Al Jazeera 2012). Another account claims that al-Qaddafi removed Imam al-Sadr from the scene because he was not pro-Palestinian enough during a time of increasing Israeli aggression. I was also told that the PLO, which was then based in Lebanon, killed him for the same reason. And yet another story is that the Shah of Iran and Saddam Hussein of Iraq both feared him enough to have him killed because he was so popular and politically powerful in Lebanon that they were concerned this could potentially lead to a wider pan-Arab and Iranian Shi'i revolution. Alternatively, some even suspect that it was the revolutionaries in Iran who disappeared Imam al-Sadr because he potentially posed a challenge to the authority of Ayatollah Khomeini. One of Sheikh Yaacoub's nieces believes strongly that the Iranians, in one way or another, are the ones responsible for her uncle's death;[30] however, her family has not been able to gather the appropriate legal evidence to support this position.

Since Imam al-Sadr spent most of his time working with Lebanese at the grass-roots level, giving speeches and working directly with the people rather than writing books, his intellectual contributions have not been widely disseminated. However, in recent years, his daughter Maliha has been cataloguing his work to be published by the Imam al-Sadr Research Centre in Beirut.[31] The untimely departure of Imam al-Sadr has had vast consequences for Lebanon and especially the Shi'is. Parallels of his disappearance to the Twelfth Imam, or the Mahdi, have been drawn by some of his followers. As a result, Imam al-Sadr has achieved an almost saint-like status and is rarely ever criticised. His picture appears on many street signs in the Dahiyeh and throughout southern Lebanon.

Ayatollah Sayyid Muhammad Hussein Fadlallah was another charismatic Shi'i activist in Lebanon who emerged at around the same time as Imam al-Sadr. While he came from a Lebanese family, Ayatollah Fadlallah was born in the holy city of Najaf in 1935. As a youth, he formally undertook a religious education, but like Imam al-Sadr he also pursued a parallel education, studying to become a radical poet and writer. He moved to Lebanon in 1952. Sankari (2005: 52) suggests that Ayatollah Fadlallah's engagements with secular Lebanese activists encouraged him to become familiar with Marxist concepts, becoming especially concerned with praxis. According to Sankari, in the 1960s, Ayatollah Fadlallah saw 'an alarming discrepancy in the role of religion in the ideal sense, and the actual present-day Muslim character and way of life' (2005: 138). Here, he was construing the ideals of Islam in the same empowering way as other liberation theologians discussed in more detail below, where the true believer is an active agent for individual (spiritual) as well as collective (social) change. In fact, one of his translators told me that in the past, some analysts have even called Ayatollah Fadlallah a liberation theologian himself.[32]

In his book, *Islam and the Logic of Force*, Ayatollah Fadlallah suggested that, 'salvation in this world and in the next is directly linked to the way society conducts its life and the relations within society' (2001: 103). He explained how, 'God's relation with man is one of the sources of his strength that continues to charge him with the power to grow and develop, to renew life around him and move it forward' (2001: 23). It was Ayatollah Fadlallah's belief that Islam approved of rebelling against injustice and oppression in everyday lives. Furthermore, he suggested that those who adopt a position of neutrality 'in the case of oppression in political systems where the weak are dominated or persecuted in the name of preserving an effective rule of law,' or in systems 'founded on monopoly, manipulation, cheating, usury or corruption and built through stealing, bribing, depriving oppressed people of their rights' would be subject to God's punishment when positive or conclusive actions could have been taken instead (Ayatollah Fadlallah 2001: 53). These qualifications clearly show that Ayatollah Fadlallah was only supporting violence when humans are being subject to deeply oppressive systems of injustice and direct action could effectively alleviate the suffering.

Ayatollah Fadlallah was also deeply critical of how today's hegemonic system of knowledge replicates injustice, especially the hegemonic research, studies and 'selective use of statistics' that focus attention on Western superiority and thus reproduce the colonial and imperial framework (2001: 64). Similar to Al-e Ahmad's idea of 'Weststruckness', Fadlallah also argued that those in developing countries often internal-ised feelings of frustration and inferiority, a situation that encourages them to seek assistance from the colonisers, saying that this develop-ment only helps the frustrated peoples to cultivate 'distorted images of their own civilisation', where they end up losing their cultural identity (Ayatollah Fadlallah: 2001 64–65).

Sankari (2005: 147) argues that Ayatollah Fadlallah aspired towards gradual change from the ground up with the goal of supporting the entire *umma*, or global collective of Muslims. In the years leading up to the Lebanese civil–international war, he saw the benefit of trying to maintain unity with the Sunni communities in Lebanon. After analysing the largely secular curriculum at Ayatollah Fadlallah's charitable schools, Shaery-Eisenlohr (2008: 76) concludes that even today his institutions are promoting a scientific approach to religion that breaks down sectarian boundaries, especially within Islam. Another example of this was his effort to promote an astronomical approach for calculating the start of Ramadan, the holy month of fasting for all pious Muslims (Dick 2011), which would synchronise the *umma* regardless of sect. His approach to the relationship between religion and science was also pragmatic, reasoning that being knowledgeable in *fiqh*, or Islamic law, does not nec-essarily mean that one is qualified in society and politics. In fact, he so strongly believed that a *marja'* ought to make an effort to be qualified in the social sciences that he deemed this essential knowledge to have in order to become an effective religious leader (Moussawi 2011: 35).

During his life, Ayatollah Fadlallah was revered as a *marja' al-taqlid*, or source of emulation, for the Shi'is of Lebanon and beyond. While he shared sympathies with Hizbullah, he did not embrace the concept of *wilayat al-faqih* in Iran, which distanced him politically from its official line. He established al-Mabarrat Association in 1978, which is a vast network of social service institutions funded by charity, including *zakat* and *khoms*, as well as income generating projects. Today al-Mabarrat Association includes dozens of schools, hospitals, orphanages and religious centres. Many Lebanese whom I spoke with considered Ayatollah Fadlallah to be a humanitarian, including Christians and Sunnis. Indeed, leaders from all of Lebanon's main sects were present to commemorate his death in 2011.[33]

However, because of Ayatollah Fadlallah's political connections to Hizbullah, the Americans and Israelis both attempted to assassinate him. According to several intelligence analysts, after the 1983 bombing of a US marine barracks in Lebanon, the CIA wanted to retaliate (Schwartz 2007). While there was never any publicly presented evidence connecting Ayatollah Fadlallah to the attack, his convoy was the target of a subsequent car bomb in 1985 that killed 81 people. His life was only spared because he had stayed behind to consult with an elderly woman on the street. During the July 2006 war, the Israelis also bombed his home, but he was not there at the time of the attack. When he eventually did die, it was from illness in the summer of 2010, and he was mourned throughout Lebanon and across the region. His son Ali now oversees both his network of charities and the administration of his office, although nobody has taken over his status as a religious authority.

Liberation theology in Latin America

To further understand the revolutionary goals of Shiʻi movements in the Middle East, it is helpful to look at the many parallels between Shiʻi activism and other theologies of liberation in post-colonial contexts, including Christian liberation theology in Latin America. Like many countries in the Middle East, Latin American countries were also colonised by Western powers. And much like the situations in Iran and Iraq, many of the post-colonial dictatorships that emerged in Latin America oppressed indigenous revolutionary movements. Indeed, much like Shiʻi activism, liberation theology is a post-colonial response to entrenched systems of dependent capitalism, where ruling elites benefit from local peoples being economically and technologically reliant upon the West – precisely what Al-e Ahmad had called Weststruckness. Both religiously inspired movements hold that radical change is necessary. As Leonardo Boff and Clodovis Boff argue, 'the relationship of dependence of the periphery [or the colonised] on the centre [or the colonisers] had to be replaced by a process of breaking away and liberation' (1987). Thus, both Shiʻi activism in the Middle East and Christian liberation theology in Latin America are revolutionary projects that seek to empower the poor and oppressed through religious ideas and practices, where a commitment to God is imagined as the means to realise radical social change.

Liberation theology also incorporates Marxist theories, but like Shi'i activism takes them in new directions. While there are many interpretations of Christian liberation theology in Latin America depending on the country specific context, and diverse historical influences have shaped the various movements, many point to the Second Vatican Council (1962–1965) as a precursor to the Christian liberation theology that emerged in Latin America. Along with an indigenous 'church movement', Christian liberation theologians in Latin American worked together with the poor to develop a more historicised understanding of religion. The Second Vatican Council was launched to respond to the Roman Catholic Church's increasing disengagement with its worldwide followers, a move that was also responding to the larger social and intellectual developments in the West, where the hegemonic church doctrine started to embrace the notion that belief is a state of mind and not an activity. This removes Christianity from everyday lives by focusing on the other-worldliness of the Kingdom of God, whereas liberation theology makes a radical break from this framework.

According to Mulholland (1987), liberation theology does not start with scripture, but with the situation of poverty and exploitation in Latin America. As such, liberation is something that happens not in heaven but in the here and now (Herndl and Bauer 2003: 567). Hence, liberation theology seeks praxis on earth for contemporary Christians. Hinkelammart explains that the question is not about,

> orthodoxy, but *orthopraxis*. The problem of liberation theology is to find the appropriate praxis for a given situation. Therefore, it is in a continual state of gradual development, in which the problems change and new knowledge must be acquired for confronting them. It is living theology.
>
> (Hinkelammart 1997: 26)

Before the Second Vatican Council, most Christian theologians were not accustomed to confronting historical problems. Hinkelammart (1997) explains how liberation theologians chose to embrace Marxist concepts, including class struggle and historical determinism, in order to offer new possibilities in a capitalist global system that oppressed the poor. Marx's critique of human rights pointed out how liberal democracies are based upon a conception of individual rights where the individual is abstractly separated from the society, rather than focusing on a rights-based approach that also considers the relations between man and man (Arthur 1970: 9), ultimately taking into account questions of power. Marx believed that the liberal framework's imagining of rights 'makes every other man see in other men not the realisation of his own freedom, but the barrier to it' (1844).

Nevertheless, protecting individual rights is also essential. So, while Hinkelammart accepts that capitalism is dominant and reasons that it will always exist, by focusing on the relational nature of society, he believes that we can offer mutual recognition as well. To illustrate how this might work, the Peruvian theologian and Dominican priest Gustavo Gutiérrez (1997: 78) recounts a passage in the Gospel where Jesus asks of a poor man, 'What do you want from me?' to point out that we must listen to the poor, ask them what they want and not impose our ideas of what we think they want. And when Jesus tells the man, 'your faith has saved you,' Gutiérrez suggests the participatory potential here: the man is free to choose his faith and thus participates in his own salvation.

Gutiérrez is considered one of the founders of liberation theology in Latin America. Other leading proponents include: Leonardo Boff of Brazil, Jon Sobrino of El Salvador and Juan Luis Segundo of Uruguay. As Nickoloff (1996) recounts, Gutiérrez was born on 8 June 1928 in Lima, Peru and lived humbly as a child, later suffering from a serious illness that kept him bedridden throughout much of his youth. After recovering, he went to university to study as a psychiatrist, before turning to religious studies in Peru and Europe. Gutiérrez attended a meeting of Latin American theologians in Rio de Janeiro in 1964 as well as the fourth session of the Second Vatican Council, and during this time he began to outline the framework for a historical approach to theology based on pastoral concerns and committed action (Boff and Boff 1987). Over the following years, he continued to develop this concept with other theologians and local communities. In 1969, Gutiérrez presented the lecture 'Towards a Theology of Liberation' at a conference in Switzerland, and published a ground-breaking book on the same subject two years later.

Gutiérrez and other proponents of liberation theology employ a religious framework which engages with the social structures that cause poverty in developing countries to call for political action to address these global and local injustices. Much like Shari'ati did, Gutiérrez critically engages with the ideas of many different Western philosophers in his writings, including Georg Hegel, Karl Marx, Jean Paul-Sartre and Albert Camus (Nickoloff 1996: 3). He then systematically weaves together the ideas of these and other Marxist writers, the methods of the modern social sciences and Christian theology, synthesising materialism and ideology to understand relational structures of power in a way similar to the Italian Marxist Antonio Gramsci. For example, in a lecture on 'Announcing the Gospel', Gutiérrez reasons that,

> traditionally we have this saying to change ourselves first and then society. That is why society has not changed ... it is a bad question and a bad answer. Both happen at the same time. To change the heart of [the] person and to change [the] social structures also.
>
> (Gutiérrez 1995b)

Here the person and the social structures are mutually conditioned.

Gutiérrez (2003) suggests that sin is evident in oppressive social structures and the exploitation of man. Much like Ayatollah Fadlallah, he admonishes those Christians who accept the status quo and fail to act against injustice and the suffering of the poor (Nickoloff 1996: 12). And similar to Shi'i activists who turn to religious historical figures like Imam Hussein as a model of resistance, Gutiérrez and other liberation theologians suggest that Jesus is a revolutionary figure because he fought against Roman domination and was involved with class struggle (Piedra 1985: 152). In the same way that Jesus sacrificed his own life, many proponents of liberation theology also acknowledge the need for armed struggle to realise social transformation today. They believe that Christians must pave the way for the Messiah in a similar fashion to how Shi'i activists frame the return of the Mahdi. As Gutiérrez urges, only when we are struggling 'for a just world in which there is not servitude, oppression or slavery' are 'we signifying the coming of the messiah' (1996: 27).

Gutiérrez enhances the Marxist theory of praxis with his notion of religious praxis, which he beautifully explains in a lecture called 'Doing Theology' (1995a). He says that theology is two moments. The first is contemplation, prayer and worship as well as a commitment 'to put into practice the Will of God in our lives. It is a moment of silence.' The second moment is a historical reflection. Theology only comes after that, not before. Gutiérrez also says that charity is theology in action. Thus, theology is not just faith but a living expression of that faith, a historicised faith, because it is a response to the questions of those who are poor and marginalised because of present-day structures of oppression not of their own making. As Gutiérrez elaborates, 'if faith is a commitment to God and human beings, it is not possible to live in today's world without a commitment to the process of liberation' (1996: 25), because our contemporary social structures create oppression and suffering that needs to be resisted by all. It is only when these two moments of theology meet, the moments of commitment and reflection, that Gutiérrez believes there is praxis.

Hence, according to Gutiérrez, 'theology is always a confrontation, a dialogue, between faith and common reason' (1995b). As he further explains:

In the old times, philosophy was the expression of common reason. Today this is not the case. Today we have science, and the social sciences. For liberation theology, philosophy is relevant. But social science is also relevant, because of poverty. We need to know something about social sciences to understand the causes of poverty. Social science is a means to understand poverty – we need social science to know the social economic dimension of poverty.

(Gutiérrez 1995b)

At the same time, and similar to both Shari'ati and Ayatollah Fadlallah, Gutiérrez remains critical of constructing the kind of social scientific knowledge that reproduces Western superiority by claiming the mantel of universalism or objectivity, stressing that, 'The last systematic obstacle for any theology committed to human liberation is a certain type of academicism which posits ideological neutrality as the ultimate criterion,' because this 'levels down and relativises all claims to absoluteness' (quoted in Esack 2002: 72).

Through embracing a dialectical approach and historicising theology, Levine suggests that liberation theologians 'see the church itself in historical terms, as a community of believers living and changing over time and space' (1988: 244). And by enabling Latin American theologians to translate ritual and liturgy into local languages, it turns out that more people have ended up participating in religion, generating more interest and concern with Bible study (Levine 1988: 244). This is because liberation theologians view all Christians as creative participants in the process and were themselves deeply transformed by unique historical developments. The same can be said of religious activism in South Africa, as is addressed next.

Theologies of Liberation in South Africa

At around the same time that liberation theology came to the fore across Latin America, similar kinds of Christian and Muslim theologies of liberation were empowering those struggling against apartheid in South Africa. According to Renick (1991: 133), under the British colonial system, Dutch Afrikaners had used religion to justify their apartheid project, saying they were 'following in the footsteps of the ancient Israelites'. However, the indigenous peoples of South Africa also ended up using Christianity to oppose apartheid, thus reclaiming the religion in the name of justice and liberation. While Christianity was introduced to South Africa largely through missionaries, Peter Walshe notes that, 'African traditions among the Bantu-speaking peoples emphasised communal and egalitarian values' (1991: 29). Therefore, the egalitarian values of Christianity politically resonated in these communities, and by the beginning of the twentieth century, black leaders were employing a Christian discourse to critique racial segregation in South Africa.

Influenced by other revolutionary movements in post-colonial societies, as well as the civil rights movement in the US, Christian liberation theology in South Africa really started to gain momentum in the second half of the twentieth century. Walshe (1987: 301) describes how church leaders began to argue that any social system of apartheid, or separation, is like dismembering the Body of Christ – it is a sin and a travesty of the Gospel. By the 1970s, liberation theology had mobilised much of the black community and a growing number of white South Africans started to join the movement. In 1976, church leaders called for international sanctions against the South African apartheid regime, internationalising the struggle. The General Council of the World Alliance of Reformed Churches issued a declaration in 1982 stating: 'apartheid (separate development) is a sin, and that the moral and theological justification of it is a travesty of the Gospel and, in its persistent disobedience to the Word of God, a theological heresy' (News24 2012). Finally, in 1985, amidst rising state repression, South African church leaders released the Kairos Document, urgently calling for those churches complicit in apartheid to repent and embrace liberation theology, and for the entire world to act now against injustice. The word *kairos* is from the ancient Greek and means the right or opportune moment.

However, it is important to stress that liberation theology was opportune not only for the Christian community in South Africa, but also for Muslims, who played an important role in the struggle against apartheid as well. Farid Esack, a South African Sunni Muslim scholar, writer and political activist, known for his opposition to apartheid and for co-founding the activist organisation the Call of Islam, discusses the history of the South African Islamic liberation theology, explaining that:

> In South Africa, liberation theology was manifested in the growing numbers of religious figures and organisations who confessed the sin of silence in the face of oppression, acquiescence in the face of exploitation and power in the face of want. They sought a God who is active in history, who desires freedom for all people and the simultaneous conversion of hearts and social structures, a God whose own unity was reflected in the oneness of people.
>
> (Esack 2002: 8)

In *Qur'an, Liberation and Pluralism*, he provides a history of the South African context and analyses the religious justifications in Islam for pursuing a progressive and pluralist politics. He suggests that a new reading of scripture is required to realise human solidarity, reasoning that: 'The Qur'an, in order to be socially meaningful, is in need of moments within history,' and 'one such moment was now being forged within a context of oppression and [the] struggle for liberation, a struggle shared by others outside the house of Islam' (Esack 2002: 36).

Furthermore, Esack points out that Islamic liberation theology in South Africa draws on the work of both Christian liberation theologians in Latin America and Shi'i activists, among others. He describes how, 'Just as South African Christians committed to justice derived inspiration and guidance from liberation theology emerging in Latin America and elsewhere, Muslims were inspired by a theology of revolt against neo-colonialism and dictatorship' (Esack 2002: 33). These theological sources of inspiration included the work of not only the Latin American liberation theologians discussed above, but also the work of influential Sunni thinkers like Sayyid Qutb and Abul A'la Mawdudi, the Pakistani Islamist philosopher who founded the Jamaat-i-Islami party, as well as Shi'i revolutionary activists, such as Ali Shari'ati and Ayatollah

Mahmood Taleqani of Iran. In his follow up chapter on Islamic liberation theology in South Africa, Esack (2004: 291) cites the following passage from a pamphlet issued by Qibla, a revolutionary Islamic movement in South Africa:

> The centrality of justice as the objective of *jihad*, rather than the estab-lishment of Islam as a religious system, was common in virtually all the public pronouncements of the Islamists. The purpose of *jihad* is to … destroy and eradicate injustice and not to replace one unjust system with another. *Jihad* is, therefore, a ceaseless, continuous, super conscious and effective struggle for justice.
>
> (Arise and Bear Witness, n.d.)

Esack then compares this to a Call of Islam pamphlet, which argues that for Muslims,

> the struggle for freedom and justice in South Africa is a sacred one. Any Muslim who abandons the struggle in South Africa, abandons Islam. *Jihad* in the path of God is part of the *iman* [or faith] of a Muslim (We fight on, September 1985).
>
> (Esack 2004: 291)

However, Esack (2004: 290) also warns that the conflict in South Africa was not averted with the dismantlement of the apartheid state, arguing that: 'it has merely assumed another character', citing the country's high rape statistics and gun violence, not to mention gross economic equalities. He is critical of the reconciliation process in the post-apart-heid era, where the desire to attain peace and stability superseded the fight against injustice, reminding us that, 'Whatever benign gloss peace activists and Muslim apologists may want to apply to *jihad*, we cannot escape the fact that [the Prophet] Muhammad consciously provoked conflict – disturbed the peace, if you will – because the peace was based on injustice.' He notes that: '*jihad* is intended to transform both one's self and society,' therefore 'one may say that *jihad* is simultaneously a struggle and praxis' (Esack 2004: 291). Esack is also critical of the dominant Christian narrative of the Truth and Reconciliation Commission that played out in South Africa, as well as Muslims' indifference to the process. He concludes that South Africans 'have become victims who have internalised the cheapening of the human spirit which the apartheid system had so desperately sought' (Esack 2004: 293).

But although the struggle against injustice in South Africa continues today, the country's experience of fusing together these various religious and intellectual traditions, as well as Esack's analysis of the progressive and pluralistic foundations of the Qur'an, are remarkable. In Chapter 3, I deconstruct the dominant conceptions of terrorism and resistance in the West, and discuss the conflicts that have transformed contemporary Lebanon, as well as propose a decolonial research method that responds to my own research experiences in Lebanon, including the various difficulties that I encountered while in the field.

3

Deconstructing Terrorism and Resistance

Understanding terrorism

By deconstructing contemporary understandings of terrorism and contextualising Lebanon's history of conflict, my goal in this chapter is to decentre Western narratives of the Islamic resistance movement and to tease out some ideas of decolonial research methods in light of the psychological impact that hegemonic narratives have had on supporters of the resistance. While terrorism should be far removed from any discussion of theologies of liberation, lest we forget, the African National Congress was portrayed as a terrorist organisation during the struggle against apartheid in South Africa. The US has also framed Christian liberation theologians in Latin America and Shi'i activists in the Middle East as terrorists.[1] To understand these developments, I first turn our focus to how the interests of empire and capital have worked to transform the concept of 'terror' in recent history.

The modern notion of terror emerged during the French Revolution (1789–1799). Maximilien de Robespierre, one of the leaders of the revolution and an architect of the ensuing violence, explained to his peers during the infamous 'Reign of Terror' that: 'If the basis of a popular government in peacetime is virtue, its basis in a time of revolution is virtue and terror – virtue, without which terror would be barbaric; and terror, without which virtue would be impotent' (quoted in Grahlfs 2009: 190). According to Robespierre, what differentiates terror from barbarism is that the former is inherently political in nature; terrorist violence is committed to achieving particular political objectives. In the case of the French Revolution, the revolutionary government terrorised reactionaries and the wider population with the aim of radically reimaging and restructuring contemporary French society and culture in the name of liberty and equality, however brutal the intermediate results. In the following two centuries, authoritarian states and revolutionary movements both practised acts of terror to achieve political ends that have ranged from emancipatory to fascist. It is only in the last two or three decades that the hegemonic discourse on terrorism has become increasingly divorced from politics, not to mention the state.

As a result, the contemporary field of terrorism studies has been subjected to widespread criticism (Hoffman 1992; Smyth, Gunning, Jackson, Kassimeris and Robinson 2008; Miller and Mills 2009; and Stampnitzky 2011). As I explain elsewhere (Marusek 2017a), the critical research shows that terrorism is poorly defined and fails to properly account for state terror. So-called terrorism experts in the West are often self-appointed, and a significant number of them have some kind of affiliation with either the intelligence or defence sectors, with the vast majority promoting orthodox views on the 'War on Terror'. Furthermore, Kevin Toolis (2004) points out that many Western academic centres dedicated to counter-terrorism studies are closely linked to Israeli institutions, such as the International Institute for Counter-Terrorism (ICT), which is housed at the Interdisciplinary Center (IDC), Herzliya, a private Israeli university that has close ties to Israel's military and intelligence (see Rettig Gur 2007).

In recent decades, Israel and its Western allies have also started designating non-military groups that are anti-imperialist and/or oppose Israel's occupation of Palestine, including humanitarian non-governmental organisations (NGOs), as terrorists. Even before 11 September 2001, right-wing researchers affiliated with the RAND Corporation, a defence think-tank based in California, were preparing the intellectual ground for this paradigm shift. From the mid-1990s, John Arquilla and David Ronfeldt began articulating what they call the 'new terrorism', now reduced to 'Islamic terrorism', claiming that it is dual in nature: 'waged on the one hand, by terrorists, criminals and ethnonationalist extremists; and by civil-society activists on the other' (2001: 14). The thrust of their argument is that so-called 'Islamic terrorists' exploit charities and NGOs that are humanitarian, simply because they service particular Muslim communities that are challenging Western hegemony (Jackson 2007: 410). Consequently, contemporary Western discourses about Islam and terrorism dehumanise Muslims by denying them the right to be political. Edward Said explained that when:

> the assumption about Hizbullah is that it is primarily a terrorist, militant Shi'i group backed by Iran, a whole set of other, not explicitly

stated views about Islam as enraged against modernity, as addicted to gratuitous violence, and the like, comes into play, and these confirm the carefully engineered Israeli view during the invasion of Lebanon … that the Lebanese guerrillas more or less deserve what they got. By calling guerrillas 'Iran backed Shi'i militants', resistance is both dehumanised and rendered illegitimate.

(Said 1997: xlvii)

A number of well-funded, well-connected, right-wing organisations have subsequently been established across the United States, Europe and Israel to campaign against groups perceived to be affiliated with overtly Islamic political movements, including Hizbullah, Hamas and the Muslim Brotherhood. These groups usually peddle an Islamophobic discourse and support charities working in Israeli settlements (Marusek 2017b). Their work reflects the fact that the 'War on Terror' is an attempt to concentrate power in the centres of global capital. Jonathan Turley (2014) argues that the 'War on Terror' has created a vast industry linking American foreign policy together with multinational corporations, foreign governments and a growing government bureaucracy that sustains the US economy by employing millions. He adds that: 'The core of this expanding complex is an axis of influence of corporations, lobbyists and agencies that have created a massive, self-sustaining terror-based industry' (Turley 2014). Furthermore, the US has exported its discourse of terror so successfully that both its allies and foes now embrace this hegemonic framework, ultimately empowering a neoliberal axis of militarist elites who financially benefit from the world being in a perpetual state of war.

Today, the US Treasury Department lists many of the charities affiliated with the Islamic resistance movement as 'Specially Designated Nationals' or SDNs. This means that: 'their assets are blocked and US persons are generally prohibited from dealing with them.'[2] Charities and organisations affiliated with Hizbullah that are listed as SDNs include: the Martyr's Foundation, assisting those wounded in wars as well as the families of martyrs;[3] Emdad Committee, assisting children, mainly orphans and the poor; Jihad al-Binaa, building social and humanitarian infrastructure; Waad Rebuild, managing the massive reconstruction efforts after the 2006 war against Israel; al-Nour Broadcasting, the party's radio station; and finally al-Manar, the party's television channel. While the Imam al-Sadr Foundation is not listed and works with the United

States Agency for International Development, World Health Organization and United Nations Children's Fund (Al-Hajal 2009), until his
death the US State Department listed Ayatollah Fadlallah as a terrorist.
He once told an American delegation about former US President Jimmy
Carter's efforts to try to remove his name from the terror list, efforts that
appeared to be very important to him.[4] Indeed, when he spoke about
being called a terrorist his face expressed great pain. Sadly, he died only
one month after this meeting, before any such de-listing could happen.

While none of the charities affiliated with the al-Mabarrat Association have ever been listed as SDNs, on the first day of the 2007 trial
against officials at the Holy Land Foundation, an Islamic charity based in
Texas,[5] federal agents raided the offices of the Michigan-based branch of
al-Mabarrat Association, as well as the Michigan offices of the Goodwill
Charitable Organization Inc. (Egan 2007). The US Treasury Department
accused the latter of having ties to Hizbullah's Martyr's Foundation,
already on the SDN list. Subsequently, the Goodwill Charitable Organization Inc. was shut down and listed as an SDN; however, the FBI allowed
al-Mabarrat Association's Michigan offices to remain open. These coordinated efforts have had a chilling effect on Muslim charitable giving
across the United States.

Although the UK has not designated the political wing of Hizbullah
as a terrorist organisation, the Israel lobby has been pressuring the
London Mayor Sadiq Khan to call for the British government to make
'all factions of [Hizbullah] illegal in Britain' (Weich 2017), not because
of any terrorist threat, but because the party is popular among British
Muslims. The UK Charity Commission has taken similar politicised
actions against Islamic NGOs in recent years. Under the leadership of
Conservative William Shawcross, co-founder of the right-wing Friends
of Israel Initiative, 'more than a quarter of the statutory investigations
that have been launched by the Charity Commission since April 2012
and remain open have targeted Muslim organisations,' with a significant proportion focusing on Muslim charities associated with running
mosques, providing humanitarian relief and aid to Syria (Ramesh 2014).
The Claystone report, *Muslim Charities: A Suspect Sector*, found that a
disproportionate number of charities under investigation were Muslim,
with 55 being 'labelled with the "radicalisation and extremism" issue code
without their knowledge,' not to mention any transparency about the
criteria used (Belaon 2014: 6). However dangerous the current political
climate in the United Kingdom, the Charity Commission is spending its

resources on repeatedly scrutinising organisations like InterPal, which delivers humanitarian assistance to Palestinians in the occupied West Bank and Gaza (Delmar-Morgan and Oborne 2014). As a result of these developments, the 'War on Terror' has transformed Western conceptions of terrorism from being politically motivated violence to a form of collective punishment against particular people who are struggling for autonomy and social justice.

Frantz Fanon, the Afro-Caribbean psychiatrist, philosopher and revolutionary, argued that violence is a justified response to oppression, calling it 'a cleansing force' that 'frees the native from his inferiority complex and from his despair and inaction; it makes him fearless and restores his self-respect' (2008: 74). This kind of liberation also delivers equality. But violence for Fanon is a diagnostic of colonialism; 'for Fanon, it is a world of alienation (in all senses of the word) created by colonial violence, an abstract violence that provokes responses which initiate a mutually destructive escalation' (Caygill 2013: 101). Lebanese Shi'is understand this point very well, many grieving for the families of conflict. On the other hand, many in the West are unable or unwilling to understand how violence can be a response to oppression, and instead view it as a provocation. They do not get beyond their visceral reaction to violence and mistranslate the discourse of resistance into hatred and intolerance in order to justify harsh policies against those resisting oppression. I believe that effectively challenging this kind of mistranslation is key to decentring knowledge.

Lebanon's history of conflict and occupation

Lebanon is a country that has suffered frequent bouts of violence, and the many scars of conflict are still visible across Lebanese society today. Thus, any discussion of contemporary Shi'i movements in Lebanon must account for this history to contextualise their ideas and practices. The unwritten national pact agreed in 1943, the year of Lebanon's independence from French mandate, set the conditions for an independent government based on a 'confessional system' where public offices are allocated along religious lines, thus institutionalising religious differences. As already noted, there are many different religions in Lebanon. All together there are 18 recognised sects, the dominant three being the Maronite Christians, Sunni Muslims and, more recently, the Shi'i Muslims.

The political and social disparities resulting from institutionalised sectarianism were further aggravated after the influx of Palestinian refugees into Lebanon in 1948 and again in 1967, resulting in an increase in tensions between Christians and Muslims. When the Palestine Liberation Organization (PLO) was expelled from Jordan in 1970, the group transferred its base of armed resistance to Lebanon. As the social disparities and labour unrest increased, Lebanese parties started to form sectarian militias to protect their interests. According to Makdisi, 'the militias took sectarian politics to their logical and destructive conclusion' (1996: 26). When Christian militias started clashing with Palestinians in central Beirut on 13 April 1975, this marked the start of a long and bloody civil–international war in Lebanon. Two powerful Shi'i militias emerged during this time: Imam Musa al-Sadr launched the Amal movement in 1975; and after the Israeli invasion of Lebanon in 1982, a new Shi'i movement was created that adopted the name Hizbullah in 1985.

Despite the religious-based identity of the different militias, Lebanon's civil–international war was not always clearly sectarian. In fact, both cross-sectarian allegiances and inter-sectarian conflicts shifted throughout. As Suad Joseph explains, most Lebanese,

> continued to have relationships across religious sects. With the government non-operational during parts of the war, it was often necessary for social and political survival to maintain extensive networks with members of different militias, many of which constructed themselves in religious sectarian terms.
>
> (Joseph 1997: 84)

Some of the fiercest clashes took place among the various Christian factions or among Muslim militias; for example, the War of the Camps involving Palestinians and Amal in Beirut's Palestinian refugee camps. Also, regional and international actors often contributed to prolonging the hostilities in Lebanon, including the displaced PLO and Palestinian refugees, Syria's intervention in 1976, the disastrous American and French presence and pull-out,[6] the incursion of Israeli forces across Lebanon's southern border in 1978 and their occupation from 1982, and Iran's support for the Shi'is in the Bekaa Valley, who were strongly allied with the Palestinian resistance against Israel.

External forces and the sectarian militias continued Lebanon's civil–international war for almost 15 years, inflicting innumerable casualties on all sides. Around 150,000 Lebanese perished and the damage to the capital city of Beirut was estimated at approximately US$25 billion (Stewart 1996: 494). The city's infrastructure was in tatters: the airport, sewage system, electrical grid and telephone lines were all seriously damaged. Homes and businesses were ruined. Countless numbers of Lebanese emigrated, breaking up families and communities. The war also destroyed the national economy. The International Monetary Fund estimated that Lebanon's real GDP dropped from Lebanese £8.1 million in 1974 to Lebanese £4.1 million by 1993 (Stewart 1996: 495). Even today, the fear experienced during the civil–international war is still palpable, especially after sectarianism began to dominate the unruly conflict in Iraq following the US-led invasion and occupation.

The fighting in Lebanon officially ceased with the signing of the Taif Accords in 1989. Hizbullah was the only sectarian group allowed to maintain its arms because the new government classified its military wing as a resistance movement, a decision that Joseph Elie Alagha (2006: 41) says was controversial among some Lebanese since it gave the party, rather than the government, a monopoly on resisting Israeli forces. The peace agreement transferred some power away from the Christian president to a cabinet comprising Christians and Muslims. Also, an equal number of parliamentary seats were allocated to Christians and Muslims, but ultimately, Lebanon's disproportional sectarian system was preserved. Currently, almost all aspects of the Lebanese state and society are confessional. For example, institutions like the central bank distribute key positions along sectarian lines, with a Maronite Christian always at the top. Many Lebanese claim that non-governmental organisations also abide by this logic. And while sectarianism has always influenced where populations choose to settle in Lebanon, the trend is becoming more pronounced today. According to Mouhamad Wehbe (2011), mixed neighbourhoods are now on the decline, and traditionally diverse regions, including the southern city of Saida, are becoming more homogenous, or 'pure'.

Rafik Hariri, a Sunni Muslim and self-made millionaire, was appointed prime minister in 1992 and his government orchestrated the national post-war reconstruction effort. Although he was immensely popular, some Lebanese still criticised him for promoting grand commercial and public works projects, which his family profited from, while other segments of the population continued to live in squalid conditions. One of his major initiatives was the creation of Solidere,[7] a joint stock

Figure 3.1 A bombed out building in the Shiʻi neighbourhood known as Bosta near downtown Beirut. This building is located on a residential street that is under Solidere's jurisdiction, but had not yet been reconstructed. Posters of Imam Musa al-Sadr appear on the inner wall. Photograph taken in Beirut during summer 2009.

company responsible for reconstructing downtown Beirut as a luxury commercial centre – a project which many claim has been carried out at the expense of preserving historical Beirut.[8] While Solidere is in some ways a private company, it is often referred to as governmental as it is granted special privileges by the state and is responsible for public works. The Hariri family also owns a majority stake in the highly profitable company. Because of all this, Solidere remains quite controversial among many Lebanese, as it is widely perceived to only benefit the rich and not the masses.[9]

Figure 3.2   The owner of the Hotel Saint Georges argues that Solidere had no right to sell the beachfront land by his hotel to a private company and protests by draping signs against the company on the bombed-out frame of his hotel. Although Lebanese law considers the coastline public land, ever since the civil–international war, a majority of the beaches in Lebanon have been privatised and charge considerable entrance fees. Photograph taken in Beirut during summer 2011.

Sectarianism, Lebanese Shiʿis and resistance

Israel's involvement in Lebanon's civil–international war had tragic consequences for the entire country, and its role is one of the most important to consider in relation to Lebanese Shiʿis.[10] After Israel's 1982 invasion of southern Lebanon, populated mostly by Shiʿis, almost 18,000 Lebanese and Palestinians perished trying to resist its military occupation within the first three months. Perhaps the most well-known tragedy to occur during the civil–international war was the 1982 massacre of Palestinian civilians living in the Sabra and Shatila refugee camps in Beirut, when thousands were brutally killed by a right-wing Christian militia that was supported by Israel. The Israeli army retreated from Beirut shortly afterwards, but remained an occupying force in a large swathe of southern Lebanon for the next 18 years.[11] During this time, a strong culture of resistance developed among many Lebanese Shi'is. In 1996, another tragedy struck when an Israeli rocket hit a United Nations compound in Qana, a small city in southern Lebanon. Reportedly, 106 Lebanese civilians who had taken refuge in the compound were killed by the attack and 116 were injured (Fisk 2001: 676). The Israelis continued their occupation of southern Lebanon until 25 May 2000, only retreating after being pressured for years by Hizbullah's forces.

Israel's withdrawal from Lebanon signalled the first major victory of an Arab army over the Israeli army. As a result, Hizbullah's 2000 victory was widely celebrated across the country and is now commemorated every 25 May as a national holiday called Liberation Day. Hizbullah also claims victory for the outcome of the July 2006 war against Israel. However, not all Lebanese would agree.[12] The war started directly after Hizbullah captured two Israeli soldiers along the border, an action viewed by the party's critics as an unnecessarily provocation. Dr Ali Fayyad (2010), one of Hizbullah's representatives in parliament, explained to a group of foreign journalists that the party's intention was to create greater leverage when negotiating the release of Lebanese prisoners held in Israeli jails. But the response from Israel was immediate, asymmetric and catastrophic. The conflict lasted for 34 days and devastated significant areas of Lebanon. The primary targets of Israeli strikes were Hizbullah strongholds, especially in southern Beirut and the south. Qana – the site of the 1994 massacre – suffered another blow when an Israeli air strike targeted a building killing at least 60 people, many of them children (Steele, McCarthy and Tisdall 2006).

After the war was over, the BBC (2006a) reported that 1,287 Lebanese had died in the conflict, nearly all civilians, and 4,054 had been wounded. The war also inflicted severe damage to civilian infrastructure, including: the Rafik Hariri International Airport; various ports; a lighthouse in trendy Ras Beirut; bridges, roads and factories throughout the country; ambulances and relief trucks; mobile telephone and television stations; as well as fuel containers and service stations. Despite the passage of UN Security Council Resolution 1701 calling for an immediate halt to hostilities, during the final three days of fighting, Israel dropped up to 4 million cluster bomblets in southern Lebanon, with over 1 million

Figure 3.3 The Islamic resistance movement established this memorial to honour those killed by Israeli forces in the 1994 and 2006 massacres in Qana. The images of Imam Musa Sadr and Nabih Berri appear on the poster, as well as the Amal movement's logo. Photograph taken in Qana during summer 2011.

remaining intact and not exploding, prompting charges from the UN's humanitarian chief that Israel employed a 'completely immoral' use of cluster bombs during the conflict (BBC 2006b). According to Lebanon's Foreign Affairs Minister Adnan Mansour, as of 2011 more than 400 Lebanese had been victims of these unexploded cluster munitions since the ceasefire (*Daily Star* 2011a), 115 of them under the age of 18 (Mahdawi 2011).

On the other side, 116 Israeli soldiers were killed as well as 43 civilians, with Israel suffering severe damage to civilian infrastructure, including a post office and two hospitals (BBC 2006a). The two tallies do not balance out, and according to a commander in the Israeli Defense Forces, Israel's use of disproportional force was intentional. Gadi Eisenkot, the head of the army's northern division, later proclaimed that Israel has and will continue to pursue what he calls 'the Dahiyeh Strategy' to deliberately target civilian infrastructure and wreak collective punishment on Shi'i civilians living in southern Beirut. In 2008, he threatened Hizbullah by saying that, 'What happened in the Dahiyeh quarter of Beirut in 2006 will happen in every village from which Israel is fired on' (Reuters 2008). The same strategy was employed only two and a half years later in 'Operation Cast Lead' against Palestinians in the Gaza Strip. In an op-ed for *The Jerusalem Post*, one journalist vowed that in the next war Israel would extend the Dahiyeh Strategy to all of those living among designated enemy areas, because:

> the Palestinians in Gaza are all Khaled Mashaal [the exiled leader of Hamas], the Lebanese are all [Sayyid Hassan] Nasrallah [the Secretary General of Hizbullah], and the Iranians are all [Mahmoud] Ahmadinejad [former President of the Islamic Republic of Iran].
>
> (London 2008)

In 2012, the former head of Israel's intelligence, Danny Yatom, threatened that, 'Israel may need to destroy parts of Lebanon and Gaza', if Hizbullah or Hamas responded to an Israeli strike on Iran (Keinon 2012).

During the 2006 war, Israeli strikes targeted many Shi'i charitable institutions, whether officially tied to Hizbullah or not, including orphanages, hospitals and schools managed by Ayatollah Fadlallah's al-Mabarrat Association and the Imam al-Sadr Foundation. This is discussed in more detail in Chapters 4 and 5. While on the one hand such attacks damaged key infrastructure and disrupted essential social services in Shi'i areas, on the other hand, they also mobilised and strengthened community relationships. According to Yaakoub Kasir, the head of the media department at the Emdad Committee for Islamic Charity (affiliated with Hizbullah), 'In 2006, after the [July] war, donations went up to 50 percent more than any other year. During the war itself, it reached 70 percent' (Patterson and Raustol 2011). But even with these increased donations, many charitable Shi'i institutions faced difficulties serving traumatised communities both during and after the war.

Beyond occupation and war, Shi'is have also continued to face social discrimination in Lebanon. Roschanack Shaery-Eisenlohr (2008), a German-born Iranian scholar, candidly recounts the prejudice she repeatedly encountered against Shi'is during her fieldwork in Lebanon. Although from a completely different background, I too experienced a similar dynamic. As one Sunni taxi driver complained to me, 'Shi'is are simply not good and they should all go away.'[13] Another Lebanese colleague complained to me that the Shi'is were uneducated and they wanted to replace all the educated leaders with their own uneducated people. She spoke about 'them' with disgust.[14] Furthermore, there is an insidious discourse about Shi'is that frames them as foreigners, or even invaders. As Salloukh, Barakat, Al-Habbal, Khattab and Mikaelian note, both '14 March and Saudi Arabia labelled Hizbullah's intervention in Syria as an "invasion" orchestrated by Iran to shore up the beleaguered Alawi regime in Damascus and protect Tehran's strategic interests' (2015: 30). During my fieldwork, Lebanese (even critical Shi'is) often referred to members of Hizbullah as foreigners or invaders from Iran.

The loving stranger as a decolonial method

As the above experiences illustrate, global interference and the sectarian system in Lebanon encourage divisions that are very hurtful to try to understand, making it a difficult place to live as a researcher. My own research approach is to embrace a critical ethics of love, seeking to understand 'the Other' in her full humanity. However, love is deeply emotional and can at times be overwhelming. According to Persian theologian al-Ghazali, love 'emerges from the sixth sense of man, which is instinct (*mata-hati*) or also known as *aql* or *nur*. Its understanding (*idra'*) is stronger than what can be defined by the physical senses of man' (Masri 2013: 69). Because the force of love can be so emotionally strong, I believe that critical researchers require some distance from their beloved. In fact, this critical distance can actually strengthen genuine love. The Sufi mystic, poet and philosopher Ibn Arabi argued that:

> The Beloved keeps Himself absent from the lover for the sake of imparting knowledge and teaching courtesy in love. For, if the lover is truthful in his claim when God tests him by the absence of what he loves, a movement of yearning to witness Him will appear in him, and thereby he will display his truthfulness. Then he will rise up in station, and his reward of bliss in his Beloved will be multiplied.
>
> (quoted in Chittick 2011: 192)

Writing about women's interpretations of the Bible in the context of Latin America, Elsa Tamez also believes 'in the importance of gaining distance from the text,' meaning that when she picks up the Bible, she actively ignores 'the interpretations that almost automatically come to mind even before reading the actual text' (1995: 54). Tamez further explains that, 'to distance oneself means to be new to the text (to be a stranger, a first-time visitor to the text), to be amazed by everything, especially by those details that repeated readings have made seem so logical and natural' (1995: 54). Indeed, she adds that reading from a distance 'will help uncover keys to a liberation oriented reading. This is the process of coming closer to daily life, which implies the experiences of pain, joy, hope, hunger, celebration and struggle' (Tamez 1995: 54).

Still, Tamez argues that any new reading must be imbedded in a context (in her case Latin America) and understood 'within the framework that arises from the situation of the poor' (1995: 55). It might not be possible for Western-based scholars to fully achieve this, but the burden is always on us to try. Gail Davies and Claire Dwyer (2007: 259) argue for 're-enchanting' fieldwork through 'a range of emotional repertories', including fear, love, desire, grief and boredom, to name only a few. This is not a rejection of the Western episteme or ethnography, but a learning from them while moving towards new horizons imagined by others. In their edited collection, Joy Hendry and Laara Fitznor (2012) aim to reconcile the disciplines of anthropology and indigenous studies, thus transforming both ways of thinking and being. However, as Trina Ward notes on her work on Chinese medicine, the:

> literature is strewn with contradictory knowledge. This partly arises from the practice of retaining texts, or bodies of knowledge, rather than replacing them, as is the current practice in the biomedical 'scientific' literature. The latter approach eschews an epistemology that holds that this can be true as well as that, even when those truths contradict each other. Such a view holds that either this is true or that is, based on the assumption that there is one true reality.
>
> (Ward 2012: 128)

The point is that humans are contradictory by nature, therefore, our truths ought to reflect this. Decolonial epistemologies not only challenge the either/or conception of the world, but also the universality of Western frameworks, while retaining what resonates locally.

But while I recognise that a critical politics of love is key, I fear that political solidarity may sometimes go too far. Reflecting on my research years ago while still living in Lebanon probably pulled me too much in that direction. Genuine love requires absence, as Ibn Arabi argued. Additionally, social science is often about researching other people unlike ourselves. The Anglican Bishop, theologian and poet Rowan Williams argues that:

> By holding together love and understanding in speaking about God, we are reminded that what we want to say about the subject and the other always requires a complex interplay between doing justice to the 'participatory' element, the life of the other in the subject, and doing justice to the abiding difference, the exploratory element, the invitation of the other to the subject.
>
> (Williams 2001: 271)

Alan Jacobs elaborates that: 'the preservation of difference is absolutely central for a hermeneutics of love. I am to love my neighbour as myself, but this is a challenge precisely because the neighbour is not myself' (2001: 14). In trying to counter Orientalist stereotypes, liberal-minded Westerners have had a long history of trying to point out how non-Westerners are 'just like us', erasing their particular lives and histories, as well as their important political struggles. But, as Sarah Sentilles asks, 'What if instead of signalling the presence of an enemy, otherness signalled the presence of God?' (2017).

Since psychoanalysis reveals that there is strangeness even within the self, Hage (2009) calls for a more open embrace of the complexity and ambivalence of conducting ethnographic research on 'the Other'. What is known can still be foreign, and vice versa. Along this line of thinking, I want to unpack the idea proposed by Hardt (quoted in Schwartz 2009) that we need to think about the love for and of the stranger to critically reorient a politics of love within the context of ethnography and the social sciences. The modern intellectual history of the stranger is rich, but somewhat contested. Walter Benjamin argued that the *flâneur*, the French equivalent of the postmodern stranger, embodies the potential for resistance as she is 'still on the threshold'; neither the city nor the bourgeois class have engulfed her yet (1978: 156). Albert Camus described the stranger of his eponymous novel as absurd, but Jean-Paul Sartre pointed out that: 'in Camus's work this word takes on two very different meanings. The absurd is both a state of fact and the lucid awareness which certain people acquire of this state of fact' (1955: 108). In other words, there is the impossibility of reconciling what is irreconcilable and then there is our grasping of what this actually means.

In most accounts, the stranger herself is a contradiction: she transcends categories and is always excluded. Georg Simmel observed that:

> The unity of nearness and remoteness involved in every human relation is organised in the phenomenon of the stranger, in a way which may be most briefly formulated by saying that in the relationship to him, distance means that he, who is close by, is far, and strangeness means that he, who also is far, is actually near. For, to be a stranger is naturally a very positive relation; it is a specific form of interaction.
>
> (Simmel 1950)

The simultaneous nearness and distance of the stranger appeals to those doing social research; sociologists, anthropologists and others have developed the concept of the stranger as a methodological approach (Schütz 1944; Agar 1996; and Ybema, Yanow, Wels and Kamsteeg 2009). However, Simmel also noted the potential dangers that strangers can present to modern society; and Bauman (1990: 144) argued that the stranger is rebellious because she disrupts the binary of friend or enemy, a relation that is always asymmetric because the friend is the only subject with the power to name 'the Other'.

By focusing on those strangers whom Western secular modernity excludes, the stranger becomes a category that can also disrupt its artificial conceptual boundaries like order/chaos. According to Bauman, such boundaries lead to the societal 'establishment of a meta-order, thereby suppressing and excluding any individual or group that comes to symbolise disorder or ambivalence' (Marotta 2002: 38). As already discussed, Western secular modernity includes a number of imperialist projects that impose a meta-order of binaries, including West/East (the Rest), insider/outsider, knowledge/religion and rationality/faith. While utopian ideals (even love) can also impose exclusionary orders, Bauman believed that, 'The utopian function of the social project can be retained … only on condition that its critical edge is directed against *all* reality' (1976: 130). The same holds true for critical ethnographic research; our approaches must be critically self-reflexive and humble.

Disrupting the hegemonic binaries is key. While Kierkegaard also made the connection between knowing and loving, observing that: 'We see here, moreover; that to love and to know … are essentially synonymous' (quoted in Jacobs 2001: 108), we must not, however, fall into the trap that equates two lovers with becoming one. Doing so risks ignoring the power imbalances that reproduce an imperial dynamic. Although a transformation does indeed occur, something new – a third – is created, a challenge to binary relations.

There are countless examples in religion and culture that contradict or complicate the mind/body Cartesian dualism that is foundational to Western secular liberalism. The Christian doctrine of the Trinity, the Father, the Son and the Holy Ghost, is one example. Another is the southern African philosophy of Ubuntu, often explained as 'I am what I am because of who we all are'. In discussing charity in Islam, Thierry Kochuyt (2009) points out that sociological analyses of reciprocity do not factor in the importance of God, the third party to any charitable exchange. As a loving stranger, the scholar cannot lose her subjectivity vis-à-vis her research subjects or erase her distance from them; but in loving them, something new emerges, a new kind of knowledge. It is not her own knowledge, nor the knowledge of the researched, but something new that is co-constructed. But of course, the realities of field research are never that simple, as the next section illustrates.

Research obstacles in the field

As a non-Muslim American woman, my access to research partici-pants in Lebanon was severely restricted, because, as already noted, the US State Department lists Hizbullah, the leader of the Islamic resistance movement, as a terrorist organisation. This includes many of its affiliated charities; meaning that all its workers (including teachers, nurses, diplomats, academics and reporters) are considered terrorists. Throughout my field research, the political situation in Lebanon was also quite tense. In summer 2011, Hizbullah's General Secretary Sayyid Hassan Nasrallah publicly accused the US of using its embassy in Awkar, Lebanon to spy on the party for Israeli interests.[15] According to Hizbul-lah's subsequent investigative report into this matter, 'the CIA officers were active in recruiting agents from various segments of the Lebanese society: government employees, security and military personnel, religious, banking and academic figures' (Al-Manar 2011).

In December 2011, the party produced a television documentary accompanied by a press statement, revealing more details of these spying allegations. According to the press statement, the CIA agents asked questions about where the children of party members went to school, and they also requested detailed information about Hizbullah's extensive network of social and health institutions.[16] According to Nawwaf Moussawi, a Hizbullah member of parliament, one of the CIA agents was posing as a researcher (*Daily Star* 2011b). Although the CIA initially refuted the accusations, they turned out to be true; US officials eventually confirmed to Reuters news agency 'that some CIA informants assigned to gather information on Hizbullah and the government of Iran had been compromised, and that any such losses are considered damaging to US intelligence collection efforts' (Hosenball 2011). My own reaction to this difficult situation was to keep a respectful distance from Hizbullah members during this time and instead to critically reflect upon my research.

Being in the field for so long, I came to know several of my research participants very well. Having close relationships with research participants is contradictory for any researcher; while these relationships forced me to struggle over questions of my own subjectivity, such intimacy also added to my own understanding and analysis. Subjectivity can be described as one's sense of self in relation to others and the world, a position that is always in varying ways both consciously and unconsciously negotiated with, struggled over, and accepted or rejected. Caitlin Cahill proposes feminist inspired 'conceptualisations of subjectivity as unstable, multiple, contradictory and in process; continuously being shaped in discourse and other material social practices as we interpret and act upon the world' (2007: 269). However, I would nuance this by saying that our selves are also always over-determined. But I do agree with Cahill that participatory research can contribute to creating new subjectivities that challenge the hegemonic power of dominant discourses (2007: 270).

Recognising and communicating your subjectivity is not a simple task. Many feminist geographers call for a reflexive strategy, which involves making visible one's position vis-à-vis the research. Gillian Rose (1997) suggests that this can be a constructive process between the researcher and the researched, creating new spaces to situate knowledge that ultimately exists in relationship with existing forms of knowledge. Still, there are times when it is also necessary to try to transcend one's position and question oneself. During my own field research, I had to negotiate my position as a single American scholar critical of US foreign policy in the Middle East, who is as flawed as any other human. As a result, I often struggled to manoeuvre between an insider/outsider position, perhaps suggesting that this binary is another abstraction that we have yet to critically consider, and yet another reason for why the love for and of the stranger is such an appealing research method.

As a foreigner, you are usually an outsider; but when you are a single woman and have a certain kind of politics, many research participants, especially male, often grant you special insider privileges when it comes to certain behaviours, particularly those that are social (like hanging out) and political (like attending events). The latter was helpful to my research; however, the former sometimes made me feel uncomfortable. This probably has as much to do with the sensitivity of my gender as it does with the seductiveness of having an American passport (along with misconceptions about Western women). Some participants expressed a desire to visit or even live in the United States, despite being so critical of American politics and society; thus, at times I was not sure if they had certain expectations from our collaborations. To be honest, these pressures often made me even more sensitive, where I backed off immediately when sensing any expectations, rightly or wrongly.

I also wrestled internally over other aspects of my insider/outsider position throughout my fieldwork. Since I was trying to understand a marginalised community, I aspired to be an insider so that I could see the world from a different perspective, and interpret my surroundings accordingly. One of my field notes reflects this attempt to identify:

The other day I went to *Press TV* for another interview. The studio is located in Bir Hassan, a region of Dahiyeh that is a stronghold for the resistance. Most visitors to Beirut do not dare to visit this southern area. Indeed, many Christian, Druze and Sunni Lebanese do not even enter Dahiyeh either. Some of my friends think that the area is not safe, saying the Shi'is all 'hate us'. The southern suburbs of Dahiyeh also get ridiculed as backward and unclean, where the poor and uneducated Shi'is live. On this particular day, I saw a group of young Lebanese children walking down the little side street in Bir Hassan near the studio. They were probably between the ages of five and eight, maybe even nine or ten. All of them were boys, except for one little girl with dirty blonde curly hair who obviously commanded the attention of her playmates, laughing with one boy and then reprimanding another in succession. She was their leader, no doubt. The girl was thin and her skin was pale. She was wearing jeans and a tee shirt that were already old friends with the outdoors, obviously a child comfortable in her own skin and still unaffected by gender norms. She reminded me so much of myself at that age.[17]

Of course, there is a real danger in approaching your research in this way, as your own subjectivity can over-determine your interpretation of what you see. Humanising people does not necessarily mean that they look or act like you; as noted above, when it does so, this can easily become an imperialist dynamic, where one particular type of human is preferred, consciously or not (in the case of the above field note, the preference is for one who is revolutionary or radical). Furthermore, these children have all suffered from experiences of war and extreme social discrimination, something that I have never experienced – and these are both extremely important forces that shape the lives of all Shi'is in Lebanon.

There is also a tendency among contemporary scholars of 'terrorism' to humanise those who engage in armed struggle in an overly depoliticised fashion. Scholars, particularly from the West, search for rational explanations to explain why supporters of any given resistance movement are willing to sacrifice their lives for a greater cause; thus, we read rationalised accounts of the economic, psychological and cultural factors at work. Žižek suggests that when scholars abuse this kind of approach, it distorts the subjects' humanity:

> Although their aim is to understand the Other from within, they end up attributing to the Other the most ridiculous beliefs – including the infamous 400 virgins awaiting the believer in paradise as a 'rational' explanation of why he is ready to blow himself up. In their effort to make the Other 'like us', they end up making him ridiculously weird.
> (Žižek 2008: 71)

According to Žižek, this is another illustration of how our knowledge is biased; an example of Orientalist scholarship where researchers make claims to rational objectivity and end up distorting Middle Easterners' way of being. Ultimately, there needs to be a balance between understanding meaning-making and over-rationalising the processes that any society adopts in knowing. As Kate Crehan (2002) observes, Western anthropology has over-rationalised the culture of 'the Other' for decades, using standards that would ultimately fail when applied to the self. At the same time, as Mahmood (2005: 5) warns, we must be wary of mistranslating certain ideas and practices into liberatory terms just to make them more palatable for liberal audiences. Asad also points out how our prejudices can simply be reinforced 'if we translate potentially disturbing concepts from other cultures into terms palatable to the liberal world view' (2003b: 211). As somebody who feels confined by liberalism, I try to take my cue from Mahmood, who suggests that when we engage 'we leave open the possibility that our political and analytical certainties might be transformed in the process' (2005: 39).

Also, there were instances during my field research when I deliberately prompted myself to dis-identify from my participants to maintain a critical distance; as well as times when participants dis-identified from me. During my fieldwork, I participated in numerous activities related to Palestine solidarity, both because I support the right of Palestinian refugees to return to their homeland and also to build more relationships within the resistance community in Lebanon.[18] I thought that by participating in such activities on a regular basis that I would build trust within this community, and at one time I even felt that this was, in fact, 'my community' in Lebanon. After all, many of my comrades would explain to others that, 'she is one of us'. However, when I needed help to secure a residency visa, most Lebanese participants refused to help me. It could be that they were not in any position of power to offer me help; or it could also be because of where I come from. Being an American made me an outsider, no matter how much I wanted to be on the inside. Lebanese Shi'is, in particular, simply could not trust an American, and with good reason.

Misrepresenting Hizbullah

As one of my Arabic language teachers once joked, many Western students and tourists who come to Lebanon think that all members of Hizbullah wear black hoodies and are eternally hiding in dark corners waiting to attack them. They never travel to the southern areas, nor do they understand how the party is a living community supported by many different aspects of Lebanese society. Supporters include politicians, doctors, lawyers, teachers, social workers, shopkeepers, waiters and mechanics, as well as friends, lovers, brothers, sisters, mothers and fathers. As one supporter told a journalist, 'Hizbullah is us, from the smallest child to the oldest man' (Tavernise 2006). And while some Western researchers and journalists who stay long enough in Lebanon to witness the many breaches of Lebanon's southern borders do come to learn about the concept of resistance, surprisingly few seriously write about it. So, between Western stereotypes and Washington's listing of Hizbullah as a terrorist organisation, as well as naming the party's affiliated charities as SDNs, I always knew that access to informants for this kind of study would be very difficult.

This was especially so because immediately after the 2006 war against Israel there was a window open to many foreign journalists and scholars who came to Lebanon to research Hizbullah's vast reconstruction efforts. Some of these journalists and scholars were genuinely impressed with the party's ability to rebuild communities devastated by the war, and these visitors wished to communicate a more nuanced portrayal of the party. Indeed, there were quite a few articles in mainstream Western newspapers applauding the party's reconstruction efforts (see, e.g. Kifner 2006 and Gebauer 2006). However, most of these journalists and scholars never critically engaged with the Western conceptual framework that misrepresents the resistance, and thus often only interpreted what they saw to support already existing biases. For example, Thanassis Cambanis, a Greek journalist, said that he wanted to portray the human face of Hizbullah and he was initially granted access to party members for his research. And yet, in his best-selling book, *A Privilege to Die*, Cambanis ends up claiming that the party espouses an ideology of perpetual war:

> Hizbullah has shifted the norms of Middle Eastern politics with its fast-spreading ideology of perpetual war. Hizbullah has inculcated millions – including many beyond Lebanon's borders – into its ideology of Islamic Resistance. The credo is catchy and thoroughly thought out; and it is coupled to an unusually effective program of militancy and mobilization. That recipe has put Hizbullah in the pilot's seat in the Middle East, steering the region into a thicket of wars to come. And it has made Hizbullah dangerous not only in the short term, as a military threat to Israel and to the pragmatic, compromise-seeking Arabs in its neighbourhood, but over the long term as the progenitor of an infectious ideology of violent confrontation against Israel and the United States, which is vilified as the ultimate backer of the Jewish State.
> (Cambanis 2010: Kindle edn)

Cambanis is overwhelmed by his visceral reaction to subjective violence, and thus fails to recognise objective violence, including the ongoing occupation of Palestine that inspired Hizbullah's culture of resistance. Instead, he observes that Hizbullah takes the offensive on every level: 'against Israel, the regional military bugbear; against poverty; against immorality; and against ignorance,' as if these were not responses to real historical conditions (Cambanis 2010: Kindle edn). He portrays Hizbullah as being committed to a confrontation, whereas those Arab neighbours willing to accept the occupation are pragmatic. And even when Cambanis does acknowledge how, over the decades, Palestinian negotiators have failed, which is why resistance is viewed as a more attractive option than diplomacy, in the following sentence he claims that Hizbullah 'also draws on a deep well of hatred of Jews, knowingly and cleverly intertwining it with the bubbling vein of anger at Israeli policy' (Cambanis 2010: Kindle edn). The party's rationality becomes completely overshadowed by its deviousness and hatred.

Indeed, Cambanis portrays Hizbullah as being totally unreasonable, arguing that the party's 'entire vocabulary [is] delusional' and claiming that it 'has thwarted any attempt to organise alternative Shi'i parties, either religious or secular,' by not allowing any 'competing organisation to provide social services' (2010: Kindle edn). In reality, the avowedly secular Amal movement currently has more seats in parliament than Hizbullah and al-Mabarrat Association runs the largest network of Shi'i charities in Lebanon. Nevertheless, Cambanis (2010: Kindle edn) does recognise the importance of Hizbullah's social programme and portrays some party supporters in a thoughtful and human manner. And yet, he becomes confused because most of the Shi'is he meets do not 'sound like extremists when they talked about their faith and their personal goals; they considered their piety a work in progress, refrained from judging others, and accepted their own sins as faults to be repaired' (Cambanis 2010: Kindle edn). The reason why Cambanis struggles to understand why Lebanese Shi'is support Hizbullah is because he never really tries to step out of his own world-view and into theirs.

Like Cambanis, most foreign journalists and scholars who compliment certain aspects of Hizbullah's military and social programmes do not critically assess them, but instead find it necessary to make denunciatory judgements – a visceral reaction. And, of course, after the war, there were also plenty of scholars and journalists working for Western mainstream media who were only too eager to dismiss the party altogether (see CNN 2006; and Foroohar 2006).

In his book *The Road to Fatima Gate*, the American journalist Michael Totten (2011) writes condescendingly about his meeting with a representative of Hizbullah's media relations department before the 2006 war, recounting his own antagonistic behaviour when he is refused an interview with the party's current Secretary General, Sayyid Hassan Nasrallah. Totten brags how he later posted on his blog that: 'the goons picked me up at my hotel. They stuffed me in the back of the car, blindfolded me, drove me around in circles, then took me (I think) into the mountains to a "safe house" to talk to the sheik [sic]' (2011a). Only afterwards did Totten admit that this was a lie, remarking that: 'Hizbullah was not amused' (2011a). When somebody in the party's political bureau does finally agree to sit down with him for an interview, he dismisses almost everything that the official tells him, which was quite similar in content to the party's second political platform.

Although it is reasonable for any journalist to doubt official narratives, Totten insists that: 'those suckled on Hizbullah schooling and weaned on Hizbullah media were bombarded with hysterical bigotry, conspiracy theories and warmongering' (2011b). He then quotes an earlier conversation, which appears to reveal his true mission in Lebanon:

> 'People in the United States find it hard to understand how people in Hamas and Hizbullah think,' veteran Middle East reporter Jeffrey Goldberg told me when I met him in Washington. 'It's alien. It's alien to us. The feverish racism and conspiracy mongering, the obscurantism, the apocalyptic thinking – we can't relate to that. Every so often, there's an eruption of that in a place like Waco, Texas, but we're not talking about ninety people in a compound. We're talking about whole societies that are captive to this kind of absurdity.'
>
> (Totten 2011b)

Goldberg goes on to tell Totten that: 'it's very important – and you know this better than almost anyone – to go over there yourself and tape it, get it down on paper, and say, "This is what they actually say".' Nevertheless, Totten admits that, 'I never published most of what' the official 'said to me … because it was too slickly packaged and disingenuous. I wanted to let Westerners know what the Party of God really believed, but', the official 'was smart enough not to tell me.' As a result, his account of Hizbullah is speculation, and one which, according to Paul Cochrane, 'lacks historical insight and glosses over inconveniences such as "facts" that would run counter to the agenda Totten is pushing' (2011).

I was told second-hand about other negative experiences with Western scholars and journalists that have had a very powerful political impact on the psychology of supporters of the resistance. Several research participants told me how they had welcomed different foreigners, inviting them into offices and even into their homes, only to find themselves betrayed in what was subsequently written. The press officers of al-Mabarrat Association explained to me how they had recently welcomed a scholar researching Shi'i charities. They showed this scholar everything about al-Mabarrat Association and were extremely hurt when they discovered that the research report misrepresented this information. Somebody who works with Hizbullah had a similar experience. He invited an eager student to visit the offices of Al-Manar television, only to later read how the student called the station terrorist television. I even heard one story about how a journalist showed up unannounced at the house of a Hizbullah politician in southern Lebanon, and then later penned a biased and stereotypical description of the politician's brother to insinuate he was gay.[19]

A critical analysis is always necessary, but when so many Western-based journalists and scholars are not honest about their political motivations, these abuses have serious personal consequences. The field note below captures some of this dynamic:

The other day a research participant who works with Hizbullah explained to me what he means by boredom. What he related to me was both sad and profound. He recounted how exhausting it was to face so many threats in his everyday life. Daily challenges included making a living. It is difficult in Lebanon, especially for those who are members of marginalised communities, to find ways to meet the economic needs of their families. But then of course, some communities are also globally marginalised. He said that he is never able to escape this sense of threat. Every time he watches the news or reads the newspapers, he is reminded that the US and its allies want to isolate his people. And threats against the party's friends, like Syria, are also perceived to be existential. He seemed, in some ways, resigned, as if he is managing the struggle but not authoring it. When I asked him whether his people or countries like Iran are providing an alternative way of being to challenge this unjust global system he seemed to imply they were, but that it was quite futile. The struggle is against too much: uncontrollable capitalism, all encompassing imperialism and unchecked settler colonialism. He also explained that after living through so many years of internal war, the Lebanese have not been able to move forward. Lebanon is polarised. He smiled and explained that perhaps the world needs a messiah, whether it is in the form of the Mahdi, Jesus or the Buddha. He then explained how Shi'is are able to take from their religion to help them manage their daily lives. He himself looks to Imam Ali as compassionate and just, as well as to Imam Hussein, who nobly sacrificed his life. He finds that if he tries to live through these religious figures on a daily basis, then they help to provide his foundation.[20]

As this field note expresses, the psychological traumas of being labelled a terrorist play out on multiple levels. The culture of resistance in Lebanon may often be a defensive strategy, but it does help Shi'is to understand and cope with everyday injustices, and can sometimes also provide them with the hope that they need to create a better tomorrow. Chapter 4 provides a detailed overview of the charities affiliated with Hizbullah and al-Mabarrat Association, and then analyses how faith and rationality combine to further their socio-political project to create a culture of resistance in Lebanon.

4

Lebanon's Resistance Charities

The rise of the resistance in Lebanon

As discussed in Chapter 2, a transnational culture of revolutionary Islamic activism developed among Shi'is across the Middle East starting in the mid-twentieth century, with scholars like Ayatollah Fadlallah of Lebanon studying in Najaf with both Ayatollah Baqir al-Sadr of Iraq and Ayatollah Khomeini of Iran. The Iranian-born Imam Musa al-Sadr also studied with celebrated clerics in both Iran and Iraq before coming to Lebanon. Furthermore, in the case of Lebanon, these religious scholars often worked with and inspired many Lebanese revolutionary thinkers, who would later become prominent leaders of the resistance community. For example, Sayyid Hassan Nasrallah, the current secretary general of Hizbullah, is actually connected to all four of these religious scholars.[1] As a child, Sayyid Hassan prayed in the same mosque as Ayatollah Fadlallah. He then joined Imam al-Sadr's Amal movement as a teenager, taking on considerable organising responsibilities at a very young age. Later on, he studied under Ayatollah Baqir al-Sadr in Najaf. And as an adult, he would become a religious follower of Ayatollah Khomeini and a proponent of the concept *wilayat al-faqih*, or government of Islamic Jurists under a supreme leader.

Upon his arrival in Iraq in 1976, Sayyid Hassan met Sayyid 'Abbas Musawi, a senior student of Ayatollah Baqir al-Sadr, who would go on to become the first secretary general of Hizbullah. When the Baathist government in Iraq began to heighten its persecution of religious seminary students and their religious guides, Sayyid Hassan returned to Lebanon and, together with Sayyid 'Abbas, started a religious seminary in Baalbeck, in the eastern Bekaa Valley. Throughout this time, Sayyid Hassan was also an active member of the Amal movement. However, after the disappearance of Imam al-Sadr in August 1978, internal divisions started to emerge within the movement, with some members critical of how the leadership of Amal had fallen into non-clerical hands.[2] But the main source of division likely arose after the Israeli invasion of Lebanon in 1982, when several Amal members reportedly collaborated with Israeli occupation forces in their efforts to uproot the Palestine Liberation Organization from Lebanon (see Norton 2000; and Noe 2007). In any case, there was an internal split in the movement in the early 1980s, and Sayyids Hassan and 'Abbas, along with Sayyid Subhi al-Tufayli, Sheikh Muhammad Yazbek and Sayyid Ibrahim al-Amin, decided to form a new group, which would later call itself Hizbullah.

Many Western critics argue that Hizbullah is an Iranian creation. But according to Sayyid Hassan, the role of the Iranian Revolutionary Guards was generally 'limited to firing us with the spirit that prevailed on the front in Iran'. Although he admits that: 'we also benefitted from their advanced abilities in our training camps. On the organisational level, they helped us delineate the operational context, and form a new movement and political line all to ourselves' (Noe 2007: 126). So even though the revolutionary Islamic spirit that helped to successfully topple the Shah of Iran did ideologically inspire Shi'is across the Middle East to mobilise against their own oppression, it is important to remember that Hizbullah was ultimately a resistance movement that was created in response to a very particular history: the decades of marginalisation that Lebanese Shi'is suffered under a sectarian political and economic system, and more urgently the 1982 Israeli invasion of Lebanon.

Sayyid Hassan further explains the attitude that prevailed among the earliest members of Hizbullah, and how the party came to choose its name:

> There was a need for a *jihadi* spirit, for a sense of sacrifice, for giving without restraint, and for transcending all calculations, selfishness and personal temptations. People who are born with such tendencies and have such a spirit deserve the best name of all – a name that befits them best. A group of people who dedicate themselves to God Almighty and decide to become martyrs in the fight against the enemy, in spite of the obvious fact that there is no balance of power either militarily or in fighting abilities, these people deserve to call themselves Hizbullah – the Party of God.
>
> (Noe 2007: 127)

Hizbullah decided to publicly communicate its existence in 1985, when the party published its ideologically powerful 'Open Letter'. The party argued that this document was written on behalf of the 'downtrodden in Lebanon and in the world', emphasising the liberatory potential of Islam by citing the Iranian Revolution as an inspiration to action. According to a translation published by Norton, the letter addresses:

> all the Arab and Islamic peoples to declare to them that the Muslims' experience in Islamic Iran [has] left no one any excuse, since it [has] proven beyond all doubt that bare chests motivated by faith are capable, with God's help, of breaking the iron and oppression of tyrannical regimes.
>
> (Norton 1987: 183–184)

In addition to the party's vast network of social services, discussed in detail below, Hizbullah runs a professional media division that now includes *al-Intiqad* weekly newspaper, al-Nour radio station and al-Manar television station to help it achieve its revolutionary goals. The party also established several research organisations, including the Centre for Strategic Studies, Research and Documentation that organises conferences and publishes journals in both Persian and Arabic, and the Consultative Centre for Studies and Documentation that houses a library, which was targeted by Israel during the July 2006 War (Noe 2007: 15). According to one scholar who works there, Israeli shelling destroyed around 200,000 documents.[3]

From its inception, Hizbullah instituted a strong organisational structure and culture of discipline. According to Sheikh Naim Qassem (2005: 59–86), the current deputy secretary general of Hizbullah, the party is set up as a democratic hierarchy. Originally there was a group of elected leaders, called *al-Shura*, or the Council, at the very top of the pyramid, but it soon became apparent to members that Hizbullah also needed an official spokesperson, and so the party created the position of secretary general, to be elected by the Council. Five boards were also created to oversee specific duties: the *Jihad* Assembly is in charge of all military resistance activities; the Political Assembly is responsible for fostering relationships with the Lebanese government and other political parties; the Executive Assembly organises education, culture and other social activities; the Parliamentary Assembly oversees party allegiance and represents civic concerns; and the Judicial Assembly works on conflict resolution and enforces *shari'ah*, or Islamic law. Hizbullah membership requires the adoption of all party goals, including those that are religious, although Qassem describes how recommendations have reportedly been made to try to better accommodate individuals who are religiously excluded by creating parallel groups and granting peripheral memberships.

The three Pillars of Hizbullah communicate the mission of the party: the belief in Islam, *jihad* and the jurisdiction of the *wilayat al-faqih*. The First Pillar upholds a definition of Islam that incorporates notions of both social and political fairness. The *jihad* of the Second Pillar focuses primarily on the struggle for personal and national liberation. The Third Pillar of Hizbullah refers to the *wilayat al-faqih*, or government of Islamic Jurists, as innovated by Ayatollah Khomeini and discussed in Chapter 2. This belief gives ultimate political authority to a chosen religious leader. In Hizbullah's case, the Third Pillar means complete obedience to the Supreme Leader in Iran, currently Ayatollah Ali Khamenei. In return, party members can expect supervision, protection in terms of their 'independence from domination and subjugation', and care for 'the needy and the oppressed' (Qassem 2005: 56). However, mainstream Shi'i supporters of Hizbullah are free to follow other sources of emulation, including Ayatollah Fadlallah (until his death) and Ayatollah Ali al-Husayni al-Sistani in Iraq. Some choose to follow no religious leader at all.

Sayyid Hassan has been the charismatic secretary general of Hizbullah since 1992. He embodies the party's triumph in building a resistance community among a large portion of Shi'is in Lebanon. Over the last 25 years, he has been an effective spokesperson for the party and his oratory skills are celebrated throughout the region. According to a 2008 survey, Sayyid Hassan was the favourite leader among those living in the Arab states (Haaretz 2008). However, these attitudes have since changed because of the party's strong support for President Bashir al-Assad in Syria (Barnard 2012), a topic addressed at length in Chapter 6. Still, in Lebanon, his image appears on posters and billboards throughout the Dahiyeh, Bekaa Valley and south Lebanon, usually alongside images of Imam al-Sadr, Ayatollah Khomeini or Ayatollah Khamenei. More than anybody else in the party, Sayyid Hassan has become the voice of Hizbullah. One Shi'i student recalled to me a story about how her eleven-year-old nephew had recently been visiting a hospital in Beirut. When a nurse asked him whom he was with, meaning which family member, he misunderstood the questions and shouted out 'Hassan Nasrallah!'[4] She said the hospital staff all laughed.

Sayyid Hassan and other party members often employ a language of empowerment that is similar to the Islamic and Christian liberation theologians discussed in Chapter 2. The concept of resistance, in particular, is critical for any understanding of Hizbullah's ideology. As already noted, the Arabic word *jihad* means both an inward and outward struggle and comprises the party's Second Pillar. Hizbullah expands on this concept of *jihad*, because the party believes oppression refers to not only those suffering from political or religious marginalisation, but also economic exploitation. Mona Fawaz explains how according to the party:

> The victims of oppressive structures are not hopeless, desperate individuals but rather active subjects who are resisting oppression – they are only 'perceived as weak' (*mustad'afeen*). They therefore can enrol in organisations, and in doing so join a 'resistance society' which 'fights' the 'oppression' and misery heaped on them by unjust social structures. This new language is above all challenging people's perceptions and hopelessness consciously through rewording and redefining their position and role in the society.
>
> (Fawaz 2000: 25–26)

As Amal Saad-Ghorayeb (2002: 17) also points out, the party has Islamised its understanding of oppression, whereby the suffering experienced from exploitation and poverty become Islamic virtues. In practice, this encourages a discourse of empowerment, translating class struggle into religious terms. Accordingly, even though Hizbullah does not control the means of production, through its discourse the party articulates itself into the fight against capitalism, but without explicitly challenging the system because the resistance movement has higher goals. As Fawaz describes, resistance charity workers:

> speak of social justice, of dispossession and displacement. They have placed financial self-reliance in the context of challenging existing power relationships in the city and redefining the control of resources among residents. This definition of financial self-sufficiency as a means and not a goal, and the position of such projects in the context of strengthening the communities' capacities to stand for its rights is at the heart of [its] success … Islamic [organisations] have managed, in this context, to develop a more elaborate vision of self-sufficiency that

goes beyond an increase in financial means and have placed empowerment back in its original political context.

(Fawaz 2000: 19)

Islamising class struggle also allows for Lebanese Muslims to believe
that they can still assert control over their life – even when they have
no control over the means of production. This contradiction will be
discussed in Chapter 6.

And yet as Gramsci stressed, the means of production is only one
site in the struggle for hegemony. Culture is another, a space where the
Islamic resistance movement creates what I call a resistance subjectivity – a faith and commitment to the cause of revolutionary Islamic
activism. According to Khashan Hilal and Ibrahim Moussawi (2007: 15),
Hizbullah is a religious party with a total societal perspective, including
a comprehensive doctrine and practice. Fawaz writes that the party's
'organisations have built on their political ideology a sense of mission, an
aura, a culture, and a language all proper to them and capable of strongly
improving their services' (2000: 13). One Shi'i student told me that only
a certain kind of person could become a member of the party, rather
than just a supporter. She believed that one had to be a model human
being with a high moral standard and a strong sense of discipline.[5]
Another young woman I worked with, who was married to a Hizbullah
fighter, also frequently mentioned the importance of discipline.[6] In her
case, she chose not to abide by the same strict rules that her husband
embraced, sometimes secretly. Feeling that she had to, at times, break the
rules covertly also raises some critical questions.

Nevertheless, this self-disciplinary culture does illustrate what Hilal
and Moussawi suggest when they say that, 'Hizbullah has indeed created
its own Islamic society. Of course it is not ideal; yet, it is really discerni-
ble not only from Lebanese society at large, but also from Shi'is who are
not members of the party' (2000: 42). By Islamising everyday struggles,
the party has formulated its own, often contradictory, articulation of a
resistance culture that proves to be quite popular among many Lebanese
Shi'is, and is even respected by some – but by no means a majority of –
Lebanese outside the sect (Merhi 2012). Indeed, over the years Hizbullah
has effectively created a space for supporters who are not party members
to pick and choose which aspects of the resistance culture to embrace
or reject.

While Ayatollah Fadlallah was never officially connected to Hizbullah, he was an important leader of the wider resistance community and his network of charitable institutions continues to serve many supporters of the resistance as well as members of Hizbullah. Sayyid Hassan describes the relationship as follows:

> there is no organisational link between the leadership and decision-making process of the party and His Eminence. However, apart from the organisational aspect, Sayyid Muhammad Hussein Fadlallah has a very special position in what we call the 'Islamic scene' in Lebanon – a position he earned thanks to his high level of education, personality, broadmindedness, and his secular, social, and organisational activities throughout the years … Undoubtedly, there is a feeling of common fate between Hizbullah and Sayyid Mohammad Hussein, due to our common spiritual and intellectual way of thinking and the historical relationship that exists between us.
>
> (Noe 2007: 136)

Accordingly, when one speaks about the resistance in Lebanon, Ayatollah Fadlallah and his vast network of charities must also be included in any discussion about the production and reproduction of a resistance society – a resistance subjectivity. As one Lebanese Christian told me during my fieldwork, Hizbullah and al-Mabarrat Association are the only true resistance charities in Lebanon.[7]

The resistance as a social project

During my fieldwork, it was very difficult to get access to representatives of Hizbullah's charitable institutions to formally discuss my research. Fortunately, I was able to speak with many people informally. I asked one contact who works for the party about which literature would be the most informative for my research and he suggested the book *Resistance: The Essence of the Islamist Revolution* by Alistair Crooke. Crooke (2009) brilliantly argues that contemporary Western studies of 'Islamism' continue the Orientalist project, as well as misrepresent its critical potential vis-à-vis liberalism. Therefore, such studies ultimately say more about Western societies than they do about Islamic movements, because they fail to critically account for the historical failures of the

Western colonial project that have led to present-day understandings of liberalism in the West.

Crooke contends that only by recognising the failures and weaknesses of Western liberalism can one see that Islamism is not just a reactionary movement, but a,

> distinct view of human behaviour that posits an alternative method of thinking about the human being; his or her place in the natural order; his or her conduct towards others; his or her place in society; the ordering of his or her material needs. And the management of politics.
>
> (Crooke 2009: 29)

Integral to this revolutionary project is a conceptualisation of rationality and faith that diverges from the Western secular liberal framework and practice by interweaving the divine into everyday life.

Crooke (2009: 3) examines 'why the West has been so fixated in its denial of rationality in Islamism,' and suggests that one reason for this development is because Western conceptions of rationality have become overly instrumentalised. He thus not only presents an informed analysis of Islamism, but also an excellent critique of Western rationality today. Crooke quotes at length an Iranian cleric whose critical observations are worth further consideration:

> In Western thought, rationality has lost its position. Instead of being directed to perceive truth and values – rationality has turned into a tool to accomplish man's psychological and materialistic needs. Instead of seeking out the realities of society, Western thinking has been channelled into the construction of a desire-seeking and materialistic society. By eliminating God from society, they have eliminated also the values and structures which enable man to advance and to aspire to perfection. The separation of faith from reason was contrived deliberately – to eliminate from our minds the potential to know the values and realities of the world. This severance facilitated man's materialistic mind to dedicate itself to the 'management of society' – without any intrusion from God – and without ethical values. Faith then became confined only to the personal corners of man's solitude with his Lord. The omission of God from this universal view is an omission of the ladder of values and ethics that man was destined

to search out – in order to reach perfection. Rationality therefore assumed a materialist cast; and faith became no more than an individual's private connection with God.

(Crooke 2009: 14–15)

The cleric's focus on both the ethics of rationality and the communal importance of faith are key, allowing for the construction of a moralised conception of rationality that challenges the instrumental one while helping to complement the importance of conceptual rationality, which the cleric unfortunately overlooks by adopting a more binary approach that is ill-suited to challenge the coloniality of power. Still, his point is to show how self-interest can make way for more humanly based social interests. Thus, according to the cleric, the two goals of the Islamist project are,

on the one hand, we need to reinvest culture with its rationality; and on the other hand, to humanise politics; to make politics human. Only in this way can we limit [the] abuse of power, and prevent the domination of man over man, man over humanity.

(Crooke 2009: 6)

Although Crooke offers many philosophical insights into Islamism, and a wonderful critique of Western ideas and practices, unfortunately he fails to adopt a consistently critical lens throughout his writing. Thus, while his critique of the Western framework is excellent, he fails to offer a similar critique of Islamism. This could be forgiven considering his desire to challenge the dominant misrepresentations of Islamism. After all, he admits upfront that he is not offering a normatively 'balanced' account. But occasionally, his arguments about the 'essence' of Islamism come across like Samuel Huntington's 'clash of civilisations' thesis, presenting culture as a fixed monolithic geography rather than a diverse and interlinked set of processes, reifying divisions between peoples.[8] Crooke (2009: 4) even suggests that the conflict between Islam and the West is 'at core a religious one', although this statement actually undermines his subsequent focus on the historical evolution of Western philosophy, where the Christian influences are only implicit in his argument.

And while Crooke's critique of Western universalism is sound, he sometimes posits Western and Islamist ways of thinking as mutually exclusive, for example, regarding 'their fundamentally opposing views of the "essence of man", despite admitting that Islamists are also influenced by the work of non-Muslim thinkers such as Marx, Sartre and Fanon, while suggesting that Western thinkers should also find 'in some Islamist ideas the energy to revitalise their own activism' (Crooke 2009: 109).

Nevertheless, Crooke's study is an important contribution to understanding the Islamic resistance movement. He argues that Hizbullah's social programme is about capability and mobilisation, citing one supporter of the party who described the movement's flat social structures as creating 'communities of capability' that allow people to be linked by shared values and an ideology of resistance (Crooke 2009: 152–153). By developing a social system where supporters are self-reliant and resilient, he points out how this can foster politically mobilised communities where formerly marginalised individuals feel empowered. Accordingly, Hizbullah has formulated culture itself as a site of resistance. As Crooke further explains:

> Hizbullah uses its social and community activities precisely to re-politicise culture: by stressing the collective community as a set of values, norms and role models that can be emulated by Shi'i living their day to day lives, Hizbullah ... articulates the collective norms – Imam Hussein's martyrdom in pursuit of justice, for example – that politicise a collective culture as a site of resistance.
>
> (Crooke 2009: 180)

Hizbullah has created numerous organisations to promote cultural sites of resistance. For example, al-Manar is the party's commercial television station and offers news coverage and analysis, as well as many different kinds of social, religious and political programmes. One day when I was in the Dahiyeh, the southern suburbs of Beirut, I met a supporter of the resistance who told me that he only watches al-Manar television.[9] He explained that when you have children, until they are a certain age, as parents you must only watch al-Manar to show your children proper morals, correct behaviour and faith. When the children are older, of a certain age, both you and they can watch something else. For example, the father reasoned that since his own son is now 13 years old, he should be old enough to take care of himself and to make the correct choices, thus he is now allowed to watch whatever channel he wants.

The theme of Ashura in popular culture is also an extremely powerful way to mobilise supporters of the resistance towards various goals (albeit sectarian, as discussed in Chapter 6). As Crooke explains, a believer can draw strength from God's power and develop an inner strength to enable 'a person to contrive the willpower and spirit with which to confront and overcome disproportionate force used against him or her' (2009: 180). The story of Imam Hussein is a perfect illustration of this strength, and is often referenced through words and actions. Indeed, Sayyid Hassan's decision to appear in person during the December 2011 commemorations of Ashura in southern Beirut was a move symbolic of the Battle of Karbala and Imam Hussein's act of courage.[10] Because of security concerns, prior to this appearance, Sayyid Hassan had rarely appeared in public ever since the 2006 war with Israel. During a time when Washington and Tel Aviv were increasing their threats against Iran, Syria and Hizbullah, and when US and Israeli spy networks in Lebanon had been discovered, Sayyid Hassan's choice to appear in public during the Ashura commemorations was viewed as a remarkable act of leadership, as well as a political statement of strength and readiness to face external military and security threats.

Beyond Ashura, many Lebanese Shi'is view the Battle of Karbala as something that inspires social resistance all year round. During my fieldwork, Ashura music and videos were often played throughout the

Figure 4.1 Sayyid Hassan Nasrallah personally addresses the Ashura commemorations in southern Beirut on 6 December 2011.

year. Lara Deeb suggests that both Imam Hussein and 'the reinterpreted version of Sayyida Zeinab' as an activist community leader 'are held up as examples of ideal piety and public service, as specifically Shi'i models for living a moral lifestyle' (2009: 246). Deeb argues that these activist interpretations of Ashura symbolise different conceptions of time and space that challenge Western secular ideas. According to her, there are two main ways of approaching this complex notion of time and space. Some Lebanese Shi'is believe that the story of Imam Hussein was actually predicted in one of the *hadith*, or the sayings of the Prophet. This leads them to interpret Hussein's struggle as an ever-repeating battle that occurs throughout history, without beginning or end. Deeb quotes a young Lebanese Shi'i woman who further explains:

> In every era there is an oppressor and an oppressed. And this history always repeats itself, throughout all eras. Ashura reminds us of this, so we will never forget that there is a Yazid and a Hussein in every time, in every nation, in every government, and people should always have the spirit of revolution against oppression, in all its faces, no matter what its identity.
>
> (Deeb 2009: 247)

However, Deeb also encounters other Lebanese Shi'is who prefer to see Ashura as directly linked to the present-day emergence of the resistance in Lebanon. She describes how, according to this perspective, all previous struggles merely provided a bridge to today's battle against Israel, US imperialism, capitalist exploitation and other forms of oppression. Either way, in both interpretations, the theme of Ashura plays out daily in the social lives of supporters of the resistance.

The charities affiliated with Hizbullah

The charitable institutions affiliated with Hizbullah offer another site where the battle against contemporary oppression and injustice is waged, helping to produce and reproduce a resistance subjectivity. Over the past two decades, several scholars have raised awareness of Hizbullah's social institutions (Fawaz 2000; Harik 2005; Hamzeh 2007; and Cammet 2014), however, the most influential to my own research is Deeb's (2006) ethnographic study of women's involvement in the resistance charities. Through charitable work, Deeb shows how women participate in the

Figure 4.2   Young children celebrate the Ashura commemorations in southern Beirut on 6 December 2011.

construction and interpretation of religious discourses, a dynamic that is modern, cosmopolitan and pious. In her subsequent work, Deeb argues that: 'public activism [for both men and women] is a key way in which people strive to live Ashura on a daily basis,' where public includes the 'many types of work that are viewed as contributing to the common good, often, although not exclusively, through the institutional framework of a social welfare or community development organisation' (2009: 247–249).

The charities affiliated with Hizbullah are numerous and offer a wide range of programmes that are not only cultural, but also deliver important social and financial assistance, build infrastructure and provide education and health care. Shawn Teresa Flanigan and Mounah Abdel-Samad (2009: 15) categorise the party's social programme into four main organisations: Jihad al-Binaa, the Islamic Emdad Charitable Committee, the Martyr's Foundation and the Foundation for the Wounded.

Jihad al-Binaa was established by Hizbullah and licensed by the Lebanese government in 1988. It has since become one of the most important social institutions in the entire country. The organisation was founded in response to 'repeated Israeli assaults on different parts of Lebanon' (Atalla and Alleik 2008). This point is important, and contradicts the notion that Hizbullah and its social institutions are inherently violent organisations when they are meant to provide for the defence and self-sustenance of Shi'i communities. Indeed, despite its terrorist designation, Jihad al-Binaa is actually responsible for constructing infrastructure and providing essential services like potable water to underserved Shi'i communities, who as described in previous chapters comprise a population that the Lebanese state has long ignored. According to Fawaz (2000: 8), between 1965 and 1982, the Lebanese government did not initiate any major public project in the southern suburb of Beirut. As Hajj Kassem Alleik, the general director of Jihad al-Binaa further elaborates in an interview:

> To this day, the southern suburb does not receive potable water from the city, except in the quarters of Bourj al-Barajneh and Mraijeh where an antiquated network of pipes is in place. Today Jihad al-Binaa actually buys drinking water from the ministry in Beirut, stores it in large cisterns and distributes it to residents in the southern suburb. For political reasons, this part of the city – a human reservoir for the resistance against Israeli occupation – is evidently not allowed to access drinking water running through city pipes. The extent of political pressure and discrimination was starkly obvious when the city of Beirut constructed and ran a new water pipe from the Damour river right through the southern suburb in order to supply the city's water needs. At the time, the Hariri government refused to make that water source accessible to residents in the southern suburb and refused to install an extension from the main pipes that were built right through the suburb. In such an atmosphere of unofficial sanctions and neglect, Jihad al-Binaa's mission has been to fill many of the gaps where the national government is either unable or unwilling to provide basic needs to a good percentage of the population. In the past our volunteer work included garbage collection, sewage repairs and maintenance of electrical grids so residents may have a minimum of public services. At the end of the civil war when the national government reactivated the work of municipalities, our mission transitioned from service provider to developer of social capacities of the various communities where we operated. For instance, Jihad al-Binaa started building schools, hospitals, health clinics and cultural centres where none existed, as well as renovating damaged houses, mosques

and churches after every Israeli assault on our towns and villages. This year we are planting one million trees supplied by the Syrian ministry of agriculture, in collaboration with various Lebanese municipalities.

(Atalla and Alleik 2008)

This transition that Alleik refers to, from service provider to developer of social capacities, is key, and helps the party offer a total social programme committed to including education and health. In this way, a society's self-sufficiency is a quality of the resistance community.

It is also important to note that Jihad al-Binaa's role as emergency service provider never really ended. After the 2006 war, many international journalists and scholars focused on the pivotal role that Jihad al-Binaa played in assessing the damage and 'paying reconstruction compensation to residents of southern Lebanon and Beirut's southern suburb' (Flanigan and Abdel-Samad 2009: 17). More than 130,000 homes were reportedly destroyed (Foroohar 2006). Furthermore, Alleik points out that Jihad al-Binaa was also responsible for:

helping hundreds of thousands of the internally displaced return to their destroyed towns from the first day [after the] cessation of hostilities: rubble removal, road clearance, engineering the transportation for a massive return of people, collecting donations, recruiting volunteers for community services.

(Atalla and Alleik 2008)

In addition, it was 'closely coordinating relief efforts with local and international organisations, including the United Nations Development Programme, Economic and Social Commission for Western Asia and European Union, linking such groups with hundreds of municipalities and agricultural co-ops in the south' (Atalla and Alleik 2008).

The following year, the US government listed Jihad al-Binaa as a Specially Designated National, even though the organisation was quite obviously constructing things rather than blowing them up. When an interviewer asked directly about this terrorist designation, Alleik offered the following response:

Perhaps I am a terrorist because I am the executive director of a humanitarian and development organisation. Maybe because Jihad al-Binaa is concerned with social empowerment and the struggle for conditions of peace, security and a dignified social and economic life in Lebanon. Jihad al-Binaa provides engineering services and social support to hundreds of towns. As a result, Jihad al-Binaa is resisting Israel's insatiable and illegal appetite for our water resources and lands. Israel has had long-term plans to weaken, impoverish and ultimately expel our people from our lands. By protecting people's identity and livelihood, Jihad al-Binaa is diametrically opposed to such Israeli designs.

(Atalla and Alleik 2008)

While Alleik's tone is one of defiance, the interviewer also notes how 'there is a muted resentment and indignation in the air no matter how much this short and stocky man refuses to acknowledge the emotional brunt of being labelled a terrorist' (Atalla and Alleik 2008).

Another important Hizbullah organisation is the Islamic Emdad Charitable Committee, which is related to the Imam Khomeini Relief Foundation in the Islamic Republic of Iran.[11] The Lebanese Emdad was established in 1987 and licensed by the government in 1994. The purpose of the charity is:

to carry out its missionary role and to restore humanity and dignity in man and to stretch its hand without asking for anything in return, so the poor, the orphan and the disabled can lead a dignified and honourable life, whose culture is love, and whose manners are mercy.[12]

Emdad primarily serves the remote areas of southern Lebanon that have been subject to Israeli bombardment and regions where government services are scarce. According to the committee's official web site, charitable services include: financial aid, donations in kind, health care, education and recreation, caring for orphans, emergency response, income generating programmes and cash donations.[13] During the 2006 war, the charity provided help and assistance to more than 128,500 supporters.[14] Whenever possible, the charity offers these services as a total package because:

According to our social studies and experience, we found that the cause of most of the families' poor conditions is due to low educational standard and knowledge and the tendency to look for luxury items instead of fulfilling basic family needs. For this reason we provide a small financial aid per month for each family and we cover in return many other needs (education, health care, cultural awareness, food supplies and household goods).[15]

As one supporter of Hizbullah in southern Lebanon explained to me, while local mosques still provide food, shelter and some modest support for people in need, institutions like Emdad were in place to provide the bulk of social support.[16] Financial support for Emdad is largely thought to come from Iran, but also through placing collection boxes throughout areas in Lebanon that are strongholds for the resistance, and where anybody can make donations. A young Shi'i student I spoke with explained to me that she puts money into the charity's collection boxes because it is a way to give anonymously to the resistance, which she politically supports, but without the commitment required by adopting the party's strict way of life.[17]

The remaining two organisations of Hizbullah's social programme support communities directly impacted by the military struggle against Israel. The aim here is to socialise the care of those members who have dedicated their lives to the resistance. The Foundation for the Wounded serves those who have been injured in military operations. According to Hamzeh (2007: 133), the foundation was established and licensed in 1990, and is divided into separate committees focusing on health, social, educational, informational, cultural and development projects. Services include financial aid, health, housing, education and counselling. The official web site describes the goals of the foundation to be the following: to provide treatment and hospitalisation for the wounded immediately following the injury through recovery, either in Lebanon or abroad; to help secure comfort, stability and all conditions of a decent life; to rehabilitate and develop competencies, skills and talents; and to provide psychological care and help integrate the disabled back into society.[18]

And finally, there is the Martyr's Foundation, which was founded back in 1982 and licensed in 1988 (Hamzeh 2007: 133).[19] The foundation offers support to the families of those killed in military operations, including both civilians and fighters (Flanigan and Abdel-Samad 2009: 18). According to its official web site, the foundation was created to promote an Islamic vision of social solidarity and collaboration.[20] And similar to the other charities affiliated with Hizbullah, the Martyr's Foundation also offers a comprehensive service package, including: cultural assistance that provides educational and cultural programmes

Figure 4.3 A collection box for Islamic Emdad Charitable Committee. These boxes appear on the streets in Hizbullah strongholds as well as in private businesses, including pharmacies, sweet shops and telecommunications outlets. Photograph taken in the Bekaa Valley in July 2009.

to the children and their parents – the aim is to help them overcome life obstacles; educational support that helps the martyr's children with their scholarship from the first grade up to the highest level; healthcare assistance that offers comprehensive medical coverage for all the members of the family; and social assistance that includes a regular monthly contribution allocated to each family for daily needs, as well as special financial aid when needed.

In addition to Hizbullah's social programme, the party also has an Islamic health unit and an education unit. According to Flanigan and Abdel-Samad (2009: 19), Hizbullah plays an instrumental role in

Figure 4.4 Hizbullah supporters wave flags during a rally in southern Beirut to commemorate 'Martyr's Day' on 11 November 2010.

meeting public health needs throughout Lebanon by operating three hospitals, 12 health centres, 20 infirmaries, 20 dental clinics and ten health defence departments. Health care is offered at a reduced rate or low cost, and doctors work in partnership with local pharmacies to provide affordable drugs. One does not necessarily have to be a member of Hizbullah to access affordable care at these institutions – sometimes even foreigners can receive treatment.[21] The education unit consists of a number of primary and secondary schools that are free for the children of party members, and for others at a cost that is far less than most other private schools. It is important to note that this arrangement is not unusual in Lebanon because the public system of education is very poor, and so most Lebanese students are educated in private institutions run by the various sects. Flanigan and Abdel-Samad (2009: 22) report that Hizbullah schools serve approximately 14,000 students. Furthermore, the education unit offers 'low-income students with scholarships, financial assistance and books, buying in bulk and selling at reduced prices; it also operates lending libraries for students' (Flanigan and Abdel-Samad 2009: 23).

Rula Jurdi Abisaab (2006) argues that the *hawza* system adopted by Hizbullah schools in Lebanon is a more institutionalised and bureaucratised version of the traditional and religious-based *madrasa* school system that is common in other Islamic societies. Whereas the traditional educational system is hierarchical and organised around a learned cleric, the *hawza* system is more democratically run and offers a fixed curriculum where religion is political. Most of the students are from the poorer classes and although the courses are rigorous, entrance is not as selective as the more established religious schools in Qom and Najaf that also require a certain level of family means to sustain. Therefore, Abisaab reasons that Hizbullah's aim is to produce 'organic intellectuals' who are able to speak to the common masses. This was a term employed by the Italian Marxist Antonio Gramsci, who conceived of 'organic intellectuals' as those intellectuals who remain organic to the interests of the working class. Abisaab explains how the *hawza* system aims to 'nurture the "intellectual" as someone organically tied to the depressed Shi'i classes, and to spread the ideas of the party as effectively as possible' (2006: 241). She believes that the *hawza* seminaries provide an alternative modernity based on a revolutionary religious ideology that guides all aspects of life. Indeed, the comprehensive services provided by all of Hizbullah's charitable organisations listed above help to reproduce this revolutionary ideology and sustain resistance communities.

The charities affiliated with al-Mabarrat

Ayatollah Fadlallah founded al-Mabarrat Association in 1978 as a charity and social service organisation to care for the orphans of the civil–international war. The first social institution launched was the Imam Khouie Orphanage in southern Beirut, which was later relocated further south to Dawha-Khalde. According to a publication released by the association after the 2006 war against Israel, its 'efforts later widened to include the care of the disabled and people with special needs, in addition to the poor and needy. It also provides education (both academic and vocational) and healthcare for all people.'[22] Today, the charities affiliated with the association reach all regions of Lebanon, and according to its press officer, the association is the largest charitable institution in Lebanon.[23] Indeed, thousands of students have 'graduated from the association's schools, institutes and orphanages, and the number of people who have benefitted from its humanitarian, social and education services' over last three decades has reached into the tens of thousands. The association was able to provide a measure of stability to communities in southern Lebanon during the Israeli occupation and immediately after Israel's withdrawal in 2000, helping internally displaced peoples return to the region by opening additional orphanages, schools, health centres, cultural centres and mosques to assist the redevelopment of local communities.

The goal of the association is to develop the community 'using all means to help the people hold fast to their homeland.'[24] To achieve this, the association aids in the resistance by building sustainable communities through the following:

1. building orphanages that help children to 'become active members in the society in order to participate in building and developing it';
2. founding schools that employ 'the most modern scientific techniques';
3. constructing rehabilitation centres for the handicapped (mental, physical and psychological) to secure 'a sound and stable society';
4. ensuring 'access to scientific development in academic programmes and curricula, by establishing training centres for the teachers and a scientific research centre, so as to achieve self-sufficiency in the association's development of its academic and educational performance';
5. promoting the message in the community through holding seminars, founding public libraries and Islamic research centres;
6. providing medical care to the community;
7. building houses of worship 'that achieve a balance and stability in the individual's relationship to God, a relationship that reflects itself on his respect of his fellow human beings, his preparedness to help them and his appreciation of their difficult circumstances'; and finally
8. providing other special services.

The press officer for the association told me that the charity has nine institutions for orphans throughout Lebanon that serve between 3,000–4,000 children each year.[25] The services provided by these orphanages are comprehensive and include: education, cultural upbringing, religious study, artistic development and medical care, as well as proper nourishment that builds healthy bodies to provide orphans with total well-being; 'physical, psychological and social welfare' to 'develop all their potentials and capabilities that they will in turn make use of to enrich and enhance their society.'[26] The focus here is on both personal and social development. The orphanages are set up so that every group of orphans is living as a family with a pastoral guardian. In other words, the orphans sleep and eat together with the pastoral guardian like a traditional family. The association also launched an orphan sponsoring project in 1985 'that creates a direct and even personal link between the benevolent sponsor and the sponsored' child. According to the association:

> the orphan's need is not limited to the material aspects but surpasses it to entail the spiritual and moral aspects that are embodied in the feelings of security, love and belonging, the association has tried to provide him/her through this project with the moral sponsorship that could be best realised through the personal relationship between the sponsor and the orphan, a relationship that is established through exchanging gifts, letters, postcards and visits (if possible).[27]

These programmes suggest that community support for the orphan is not only beneficial for the orphan, but also for the cohesion of the community.

In addition to the orphanages, the association runs many other institutions in order to achieve stability and development on multiple levels for the communities in the south and the Bekaa Valley. For example, the association constructed the al-Hadi Institute, which is comprised of al-Nour (Light) School for the blind, al-Raja' (Hope) School for the deaf and al-Bayan (Statement) School for those with language and communication disabilities, all of which give the disabled 'an opportunity to learn and develop their potentials, boosting their confidence in themselves and in their believing community and enabling them to become active members of society.' The association has also built several cultural centres and mosques throughout Lebanon, as well as a library in southern Beirut. In addition to its other medical centres in southern Lebanon, in 1999 the association built Bahman Hospital in the Dahiyeh, which offers either free or subsidised care,[28] is equipped with all modern facilities and has a capacity for 250 beds. According to its social media, the hospital's mission:

> is to provide quality medical care that values the human life and dignity, and through offering medical services for every patient regardless of race, sex, and beliefs with the help of highly specialised medical and nursing teams; while it aims at presenting a bright picture about the practice and implementation of quality health programmes.

Bahman Hospital ... continuously develops its human resources who will strive to spread and plant the seeds of good under the slogan: 'Doing good for health'.[29]

Furthermore, the association 'has built several modern and model academic schools, as well as vocational institutes for both boys and girls, to provide the coming generations with a high level of education and a profound sense of values'.[30] According to the association's press officer, the charity runs 21 schools throughout Lebanon, serving about 35,000 students.[31] During my fieldwork, I learned that the association's education system is highly esteemed by the community; for example, many Lebanese boast that family members are teachers at these schools. Furthermore, despite the fact that Hizbullah schools are free for the children of party members, many choose to send their children to al-Mabarrat Association schools instead, and at a considerable cost.[32]

In addition to these social service institutions, the association runs a number of income generating projects, including a café-restaurant, two gas stations (one of which was destroyed during the 2006 war) and Assaha Traditional Village complex. All profits from these projects are donated to the association's charities. Initially constructed in 2001, the original Assaha is located in the southern suburbs of Beirut and consists of a restaurant, hotel, market, library, playground, prayer rooms and event conference hall.[33] One night, while eating dinner in Assaha restaurant with a delegation of Americans, we were introduced to the architect, Jamal Makki, who explained that the inspiration for the structure of the building was an epistolary novel about a father's recollections of rural life to his son who was now living in a city.[34] The structure of the complex recreates the rural landscape of nineteenth-century Christian Mount Lebanon interwoven with contemporary Islamic ideas and communal practices, Assaha (al-Sahah) meaning 'the square' in Arabic. Mona Harb argues that Assaha offers pious entertainment – a place providing an 'environment complying with pious Muslim practices' (2006: 10). In her interview with Makki, he further 'explains that the challenge was to translate the concepts of history and tradition into elements that materialise their meanings to people' (Harb 2006: 10). During our own meeting, Makki pointed out that the theme of the then recently opened hotel on the second floor is dialogue of civilisations and he even invited us to take a tour.[35] Each of the rooms has a cultural theme from a different part of the world and is elegantly decorated.

Similar to the situation with the charities affiliated with Hizbullah, my research on al-Mabarrat Association's charities was also restricted. From what I could gather, the reasons were mostly to do with the following: (1) the designation of several Hizbullah-affiliated charities as SDNs at around the same time as the FBI raided the association's Michigan-based offices in 2007; (2) negative experiences with other researchers; (3) my request coincided with the unfortunate passing of Ayatollah Fadlallah; and, most importantly, (4) the destruction of many of the association's charitable institutions during the 2006 war against Israel. Indeed, the association claims that Israel intentionally targeted various charitable institutions in an attempt to 'cause social collapse by targeting the educational, social and developmental infrastructure.' During and immediately after the war, the burden on the association to provide services was especially immense because of the increased numbers of orphans and disabled, not to mention the psychological consequences on children and adults. Furthermore, the dead included students, orphans and staff.

According to one of the association's publications, numerous institutions in southern Beirut and throughout southern Lebanon were damaged and required immediate reconstruction.[36] One of the institutions completely destroyed was the Isaa bin Marian School in al-Khiam, southern Lebanon. Established in 2002, the school served 560 pupils and comprised three four-story buildings; all were completely destroyed. There were 40 classrooms and 13 activity rooms, including a library, chemistry laboratory, art gallery, theatre, prayer hall, music room, audio-visual room, indoor and outdoor sports halls and a sand playground. Also in al-Khiam, the association's al-Nabi Ibrahim Orphanage was destroyed. Established in 2004 to care for 150 orphans and poor children, the two four-floor buildings housed 18 dormitories and 16 halls for activities, including a kitchen, restaurant, clinic, prayer room, information technology laboratory, library and leisure rooms. The Imam Ali bin Abi Talib mosque in Bint Jbeil, southern Lebanon, was also destroyed. This mosque had been constructed using sandstone collected from several demolished houses with over 100 years of history. In addition to many other orphanages, schools and mosques that were damaged or destroyed by Israel, other institutions were also attacked, including hospitals, medical centres and even a centre for youth scouts.

Despite the wide-scale destruction, the association remained defiant:

By standing up in the midst of the wreckage of the war to rebuild what has been destroyed, we demonstrate our belief that care, education and knowledge has the priority in people's lives, and we are determined to restore these civilised establishments so that they become a witness to the strength of the will of knowledge over destruction.[37]

However, the losses from the war exceeded the association's financial capacity and outweighed the costs of the original building of the institutions. The UN Human Rights Council recommended that Israel be made to compensate Lebanon for the widespread damages that the Israeli military inflicted during the July war. But, thus far, Israel has not been held accountable for the damages caused, and the possibility of renewed conflict continues. In January 2014, the Israeli air force chief Major-General Amir Eshel threatened that in any subsequent war, Israel will intentionally target civilian homes and infrastructure because it believes that Hizbullah has established bases in residential buildings, citing the areas of Beirut, the Bekaa Valley and southern Lebanon. Speaking to a think-tank near Tel Aviv, Eshel explained that:

Above and below live civilians whom we have nothing against – a kind of human shield. And that is where the war will be. That is where we will have to fight in order to stop it and win. Whoever stays in these bases will simply be hit and will risk their lives. And whoever goes out will live.

(Reuters 2014b)

Faith and religious rationality in the resistance charities

The vast networks of charitable institutions affiliated with both Hizbullah and al-Mabarrat Association are modern and dynamic, interweaving rationality and faith into a resistance subjectivity that positions the believer within the social peripheries to struggle with the marginalised. Although at times these charities conceive of and practise rationality differently from the dominant standards in the West today, these ideas and practices are nevertheless still perfectly rational. Furthermore, there are also occasions when the charities' ideas and practices of rationality overlap with the dominant expressions of rationality elsewhere, especially liberal conceptions, and these intersections will become even more apparent in the analysis of the Imam al-Sadr Foundation in Chapter 5.

So, in order to fully appreciate the different expressions of rationality as all being rational, instead of relying upon a conception of rationality as something neutral or objective, we can refer back to the Iranian cleric's critique, and conceive of rationality as a set of interrelated processes and outcomes informed in various ways by conceptual, substantive, instrumental and systematic concerns. As such, rationality is an unstable concept that is mediated by competing sets of ethical commitments and which is always in between the individual and the community. In the West today, most forms of rationality are mediated by mathematical and scientific commitments in the abstract, whereas the Shi'i movements in Lebanon also deliberately incorporate faith-based rationalities alongside the scientific and systemic ones.

Furthermore, Western conceptions of rationality prize continued existence above dignity. But for the Islamic resistance movement, a commitment to dignity also strongly mediates its conception of rationality. Thus, resistance can be seen as a more rational choice to make than self-preservation when the latter requires humiliating negotiations with the occupying or imperialist forces, as Sayyid Hassan explains:

> The developments and events in the last three decades – at least since 1982 – proved that the correct realistic, rational, logical, fruitful and effective choice that leads to the achievement of goals is the popular armed resistance and the unrealistic, absurd, irrational, maddening choice which does not lead to any goal but rather leads only to depression, frustration, humiliation, degradation and begging on the doors and thresholds is the choice of negotiations.[38]

Although there are multiple forms of rationality in today's world, they are not always competing and can often coalesce. Indeed, as Dr Ali Fayyad, a Lebanese member of parliament for Hizbullah who also once served as the head of one of its think-tanks, pointed out to me, conceptual rationality has always been embraced in Islam:

> There is a du'a, or prayer, by the Prophet Muhammad. He said, 'my God help me to see reality as it is.' That's pretty important. And you know it's been an historical and philosophical challenge throughout the history of humanity. It's one of the most important theoretical challenges, to get the methodology, to understand the facts or the reality. And you know the philosophical relationship between ideas

and facts. This prayer of Prophet Muhammad – he asked for God to be, to get the ideas, the methodology, the perspectives to understand the realities and facts around him.[39]

Accordingly, Dr Fayyad believes in the importance of religious rationality. As he explained:

I believe in God, I believe in Islam, and the values of Islam control my behaviours; but at the same time, I have to respect the mind, I have to respect logos and I have to be based on logic, the rules of logic. And I think the values of Islam are not in contradiction with the rules of logic.[40]

Remember the discussion in Chapter 2 of how Ayatollah Baqir al-Sadr used logic to historicise and transform Islamic ideology. To help further illustrate his own position, Dr Fayyad described the work of an influential Iranian philosopher:

His name is Mustafa Malakian and he's very important – he has a book about religious rationality. He separated between traditional religiosity and rationalistic religiosity. He said the main difference between the traditional and the rationalistic is like the difference between a person who is swimming and a person who is standing up on a boat. The traditional one is like the person standing up on the boat: he's praying, he's reading … he can do everything, he feels safe and he's standing up in the boat – he's going. But the rationalistic religiosity is like the person who is swimming. He needs his arms and his mind at every moment, and he has to do his best and he has to have a great will. He has to fight. And he is insisting to swim, to reach a safe place. And any time he feels that it is not necessary to swim, he will sink to the depths and will finish. The people who are belonging to the rationalistic are like the swimmers. They need their mind and arms at every moment. They are suffering. They are in a challenging situation.[41]

While the one swimming and the one standing in the boat are both believers, the swimmer is always questioning his belief as a rational subject. Thus, the challenge arises for her because she must question while always being committed to swimming. Dr Fayyad elaborated on this point, saying that: 'He believes in God surely; but he needs every moment to think about this issue. It is not exactly a doubt, but it is the right of thinking, the right of asking, the right of progressing towards … forward.'[42] This is a rational approach to faith, as well as a religion that is rational.

In fact, religion and morality always mediate our ideas of rationality; however, some are just more upfront about this role than others. A journalist who is a supporter of Hizbullah explained how for him, faith is rationality. One can see this perspective in a 2009 urban policy campaign conducted by Hizbullah called 'Order is part and parcel of faith'. The campaign was focused on treating drug addiction, as well as 'regulating traffic and unregistered vehicles and de-cluttering sidewalks' in the southern suburbs of Beirut (Al-Ahed 2009). According to both this campaign and the journalist I interviewed, faith is how you live.[43] The journalist further described faith as something that mediates one's personal and social behaviours towards the just and the good, saying that he ultimately believes faith gives meaning to life. Dr Fayyad referred to a message from the Prophet Muhammad that stated that the best people are those who are working to help their societies or communities, and not those who are more believing, because religious practices, like fasting and prayers, only express one's relationship to God on the individual level, whereas faith also requires a human commitment to express one's relationship with God on the social level:

What about our feelings, our treatment towards society – the poor people? To help any people who are in need for me; to be ready to sacrifice myself if my country needs that; to face the offenders; to refuse injustice … I feel in my faith that I have to be useful, a constructive person towards my society. And I think it's more than just to our societies, I feel a duty towards humanity in general. Even the people who belong to other religions – if they need me to help them, I have to help them.[44]

For many Lebanese Shi'is, faith is both a belief in humanity and a belief in the resistance – a resistance subjectivity. The journalist explained that when 'you listen to people from your community, like Sayyid Hassan or others, without that faith you probably would not believe a word they said.' You believe because you have faith in the resistance despite all the odds, and you have faith in their honesty. Here faith is politicised and one's commitment to the cause leads one to make choices on behalf of the resistance over other material concerns. The journalist suggested that this also explains why so many people volunteer for the various charities affiliated with the resistance project, including his mother-in-law who distributes money for al-Mabarrat Association. Or why his wife's brother, who is currently studying journalism, recently decided that he wants to work with Hizbullah's media department because he thinks that the $1,000 monthly salary he would receive from the party would have more blessings to him than maybe a $5,000 salary from somewhere else. However, the journalist also admitted that not everybody thinks this way. So, for example, he said that many people who work at al-Manar television complain about their low salaries. He himself is critical of Lebanon's overly materialistic society, including among many Shi'is. This concern is addressed in more detail in Chapter 6.

Another party supporter explained how faith is not just belief, because it also requires a certain kind of relationship with God.[45] When you open yourself up and God fills you, this gives you a purpose and a passion for humanity, so you no longer feel alone or unhappy. He said that you could love your enemies if they are being oppressed and challenge your brother even when he is being the oppressor. He spoke about Sayyid Hassan, explaining that he is not necessarily a genius, but somebody who through his relationship with God can speak to the people. This relationship with God is key, because any system that does not focus on the soul can lead to corruption. In this way, communism can lead to the same sort of moral and social corruption as capitalism. He also explained that this connection to God is what makes the resistance so successful. For example, the result of the 2006 war against Israel was proclaimed as a divine victory because Israel was by far the stronger military power. He concluded that the connection to God is what inspired the victory.

Faith in God connects humans to other people and faith in the cause unites all supporters of the resistance. In an interview with Fawaz, Hajj Kassem Alleik, the general director of Jihad al-Binaa, describes how: 'The resistance society is our vision. It is the task to build a society that will refuse oppression and fight for its rights. All the rest – water provision, garbage collection, agricultural training – is only a working strategy' (2000: 63). Here the strategy, or methodology, is based on rationality, but the motivations, or values, are deeply influenced by faith. Dr Fayyad also made a similar distinction:

The institutions of these charities – the hospitals, medical centres and schools, as well as the other institutions to help the wounded or poor people – if you want to study or analyse the construction of these religious institutions, you will find it completely modernised. They depend on administration, computer systems, and evaluating models like the ISO (International Organisation for Standardisation) and the other [international] sources of evaluating. You will never find aspects of religion in these things. And then you have to ask: where is the religion in these institutions? You will find it in the values, which are leading the ways. The values are the cause, and where to aim. But about the rules, about the procedures, about the systems, these are rationalistic.[46]

Some examples of how al-Mabarrat Association stresses rationality can be seen in its literature, where much attention is paid to the scientific standards that the various institutions embrace.[47] The orphans are expected to be 'mature and efficient in society' and both the pedagogical and pastoral domains are guided by 'expertise and specialisation'. The academic programme for the girls at the orphanages includes a management programme to help the students be self-reliant and problem-solving, as well as a system to make sure that 'he or she comprehends information and scientific concepts provided on a daily basis'. And 'for this purpose, a detailed set of definite rules have been laid for precise application'. The association also uses workshops and training in a non-stop process to help the students learn self-management, self-assessment and self-esteem at al-Mabarrat Schools.

Because Shi'is have faith in the values and the aims of the resistance, as well as the rational way that these institutions are managed, there is a strong level of trust in the social service work that Hizbullah and al-Mabarrat Association offer. Flanigan and Abdel-Samad (2009: 53) point out how the opposite is true when it comes to the Lebanese government. Indeed, many Lebanese think that the government has a corrupt bureaucracy with a reputation for cronyism, whereas Hizbullah services are often presented as gifts – a reward for those loyal to the resistance. While this can become cronyism, it can also express the concept of charity as love. As Tavernise (2006) explains, supporters do not always know how these gifts are determined and by whom, relating the experience of a new father who was having difficulty paying the bills. He had complained to some neighbours about his financial woes and a few days later, men arrived at his door with groceries. Of course, some will argue that the party can expect votes in return for giving gifts and so this instrumental calculation may play a role in its decision to provide services; however, Flanigan and Abdel-Samad find that many charity workers believe that more people in the community trust Hizbullah because they provide services more broadly and do not misuse the government bureaucracy to serve only their supporters. As one worker describes to the authors:

> We started the resistance in 1982, and from 1982 to 1993, we were not able to send one wounded person to hospital on the government's tab. We didn't care. When leadership has morals and provides services in the right way, it will be respected and loved. Finally, with all this corruption and waste, we don't want anything from the government.
> (Flanigan and Abdel-Samad 2009: 53)

The charities affiliated with Hizbullah and al-Mabarrat Association are so effective in their delivery of services because the workers and volunteers are from the communities they serve, and this kind of effectiveness is also a standard of Western rationality. As Flanigan and Abdel-Samad (2009: 56) point out, these grass-roots networks in the community allow the charities to locate the needy and react quickly. This was especially true after the 2006 war against Israel, when Jihad al-Binaa sent hundreds of workers and volunteers to assess the damage in locations that were difficult for other humanitarian organisations to access. As a result, they ended up coordinating with these other organisations to efficiently deliver the necessary aid.

But in addition to benefitting from local knowledge, the resistance charities are also effective because of the faith of their workers, as the journalist explained to me. Supporters of the resistance want to work for the cause because they believe in it, according to the research findings of Flanigan and Abdel-Samad (2009: 56). So, one reason why Hizbullah is so efficient is because 'of the motivations of its social-service employees. Many of them are volunteers with a strong belief in the morality of their work'. Therefore, they are inspired to work to the best of their ability not for money, but rather the cause. The website for al-Mabarrat Association's Bahman Hospital also describes that: 'Armed with a strong faith in God, the Almighty, we have continued materialising Sayyid Fadlullah's dream by continuously developing our human element to present distinguished hospital wide services that cater to your specialised needs.'[48] This beautifully articulates the importance of both rationality and faith, and how they can be seamlessly woven together.

It is important to point out that for Lebanese Shi'is, charitable work is also seen as an act of resistance – an idea that is reinforced when Israel deliberately targets the charitable institutions. A publication issued by al-Mabarrat Association after the 2006 war against Israel vows that, 'Our will of benevolence shall prevail!.'[49] And after the war, Ayatollah Fadlallah insisted that successfully rebuilding the institutions would 'represent a triumph of knowledge over the desire to destroy' (Bathish 2007). Flanigan and Abdel-Samad (2009: 63) find that the resistance culture is also evident in other charity and service publications. For example, they cite this quotation by Hizbullah's Islamic Health Society Minister Dr Karam Karam:

> The services provided by the Islamic Health Committee strengthen the heroic efforts of fighters and reduce their worries about who will take care of those who support them. This network is a shield that protects the resistance fighter and assures those in need and protects those fighting for dignity, for the country and for sovereignty.

The authors also find that for many Hizbullah supporters, working for the charitable institutions is thought to be similar to military resistance, or I would argue closely aligned with the same political struggle. One of the staff members that Flanigan and Abdel-Samad interviewed explained to them how:

> A medical doctor is a resister. Helping sick people and fighting microbes and other maladies is resistance. And when you give social services, you are saving a kid from ignorance or from going to prison.
>
> (Flanigan and Abdel-Samad 2009: 65)

Strengthening the community is viewed as an act of solidarity and resistance. The authors noted that a volunteer quoted in an Islamic Health Committee publication also views charitable work in a similar way:

> I found in the Islamic Health Committee, which heals the wounds of the *mujahedeen* of the Islamic Resistance on one hand and also helps

the oppressed in our society [on the other], a place where I can help people and reduce their suffering and build a healthy society.

(Flanigan and Abdel-Samad 2009: 65)

Social development and building a healthy society seems to be an extremely important goal for all the resistance charities, and this mission is deeply influenced by a faith in God, the community and the resistance. Revisiting the power of the story of Ashura, Deeb's research finds that:

> For women, in particular, volunteering (or, more rarely, working) for a social-welfare organisation is perhaps the most common way of bringing Zeinab into the present. Zeinab's example translates as thousands of women volunteering their time and energy in Islamic social-service organisations, often taking on a third shift, in addition to paid employment and their household work, to do so. In addition, more Shi'i women are formally employed than ever before, and the types of employment have diversified widely. Much of this volunteerism or employment is described by pious women as their contribution to the development of their community – whether by providing goods and services for the poor, facilitating girls' education, or working as a doctor in a clinic.

(Deeb 2009: 250)

However, rationality also influences the mission of these charities because their aim is to establish sustainable communities that will not abandon the land, a passive resistance in the form of *sumud*, and the comprehensive package of services they offer is an illustration of this. There is a systemised approach to the development of the individual and the community, both of which are always linked.

For example, this linkage was apparent during an event I attended at al-Mabarrat Association's Lady Khadija Orphanage in the southern suburbs of Beirut to commemorate the birth of the Prophet Muhammad.[50] During the ceremony, prayers were recited, the young orphans performed several dance routines and Ayatollah Fadlallah's son Sayyid Ali read a sermon. These kinds of performances help to link the children to the community and are also common at other charitable events, including an *iftar* I attended that was organised by the association in 2011 during Ramadan to raise funds.[51] After the ceremony at the orphanage, the audience was ushered through an exhibition of sculpted scenes of the Prophet Muhammad's life, featuring life-like papier-mâché figures. Upon exiting the exhibition, there was a giant paper wall and people were encouraged to write personal messages to the orphans, another community building practice where members of the audience could express their solidarity with the orphans so that these children would later be reminded that they belong to the resistance community. By rationalising social services through the lens of faith and resistance, this decolonial move helps to continuously reinforce the importance of maintaining a resistance subjectivity in everyday lives. In Chapter 5, I broaden the scope of our discussion of the resistance charities by focusing on the work of the Imam al-Sadr Foundation in southern Lebanon.

5
The Imam al-Sadr Foundation

It was Imam al-Sadr who woke up the sleeping giant that is the Shi'is of Lebanon.
— Aql Hamiyah, former military commander of the Amal movement

We plant the seeds of hope.
— Imam al-Sadr Foundation

The legacy of Imam Musa al-Sadr

As discussed in Chapter 2, Imam Musa al-Sadr had an enormous impact on the Shi'is of Lebanon, and his untimely disappearance in 1978 deeply affected the population. Despite spending only 18 years in the country, he inspired a marginalised and oppressed community to take control of their own lives by calling their situation what it was: destitute. Rebab al-Sadr, Imam al-Sadr's sister, explained to me that before his arrival, the Shi'is of southern Lebanon did not have any important social institutions like the other sects did, and had to live amidst constant military strikes by Israel.[1] According to a 1972 report, the monthly income for Shi'is was less than $50 and half of the population was illiterate, with the number achieving a high school education at only 6.6 per cent. Another report from that same year found that Shi'is comprised at least 20 per cent of the population but had a mere 0.7 per cent share in government (al-Manar 2005). Only after Imam al-Sadr started calling attention to this collective poverty did Shi'is become politicised. He was able to instil courage and dignity among Shi'is through sermons, grass-roots work and an array of social and political institutions, including the Party of the Deprived, the Imam al-Sadr Foundation, the Amal movement, the Technical Institute of Jabal Amil, the Shi'i Islamic Supreme Council and the Imam al-Sadr Research Centre. And, of course, some of his followers went on to develop more social institutions under the programme of Hizbullah.

However, Imam al-Sadr's disappearance also impacted Lebanon more generally. In the years leading up to the civil–international war, he had spent much of his time delivering sermons in Christian churches and working with different religious leaders to promote coexistence. A former aid, Abdullah Yazbek, recalls one time when Imam al-Sadr visited a Christian village in southern Lebanon to give a talk. When the Christian congregation saw him, they chanted in Arabic 'Allahu akbar', or 'God is great'. Yazbek remarked that, 'the way people treated him, it was as if he was Jesus Christ' (Blanford 2011). When war finally broke out, Imam al-Sadr delivered a remarkable speech against sectarian violence, telling all Lebanese:

> I declare that if a bullet is fired at a Christian neighbourhood, it is as if it was fired at my house, at my bosom, at my own child. If any well-wisher tries to stop this calamity, tries to extinguish this fire of war, it is as if he has extinguished the fire in my house, on my door, on my pulpit.
>
> (Al-Manar 2005)

He also went on a hunger strike that lasted for five days, trying to persuade Lebanon's various leaders to negotiate a political solution, leading to the formation of a national reconciliation cabinet. Nevertheless, Lebanon's civil–international war continued to spiral out of control.

When Israel invaded southern Lebanon in 1978, Imam al-Sadr met with neighbouring Arab leaders to mobilise support for his people. The Libyan leader Muammar al-Qaddafi extended an invitation to meet Imam al-Sadr in August of that same year, and so Imam al-Sadr travelled to Libya. Tragically, he would never return to Lebanon again. After he disappeared, diplomatic relations between Lebanon and Libya soured. When officials failed to provide any resolution to his mysterious disappearance, some Lebanese took matters into their own hands. According to Camelia Entekhabifard (2011), a delegation of around 200,000 Lebanese Shi'is travelled to Syria during one of al-Qaddafi's visits to ask him about the Imam's whereabouts, however, they were coolly rebuffed. Blanford (2011) also writes that Aql Hamiyah, a former military commander of the Amal movement, carried out 'six hijackings of Middle Eastern airliners in the years that followed' Imam al-Sadr's disappearance to publicly pressure Libya into revealing the truth about what happened to him. However, none of these attempts were successful.

When Libyan demonstrations against al-Qaddafi erupted in 2011, many Lebanese were quick to support the rebel movement, even though this meant indirectly siding with the NATO coalition led by France, United Kingdom and United States. The subsequent fall of the al-Qaddafi regime rekindled hope among many Lebanese that they would finally discover the whereabouts of Imam al-Sadr. His family issued a statement, appealing 'to those who will take over in Libya after the collapse of the tyrant to give special attention to this case' (Dehghan 2011). Some Lebanese believe he was killed back in 1978; but others are still holding out hope that he is alive. However, while rumours abound, at the time of writing the truth about what really happened to Imam al-Sadr is still unknown.

Several interesting dynamics have emerged as a result of Imam al-Sadr's sudden and mysterious disappearance. As discussed in Chapter 2, he is often compared with the Twelfth Imam, or the Mahdi, who is also known as the Hidden Imam. According to Twelver Shi'is, the Mahdi went into hiding in the ninth century and is supposed to return to save mankind when injustices overwhelm the earth and its inhabitants. As Imam al-Sadr's cousin, Ayatollah Muhammad Baqir al-Sadr, described:

faith in the Mahdi is faith in the removal of injustice and tyranny even if it darkens the entire world, and is an inexhaustible source of strength and resistance, as it is a ray of hope which removes despair from the human spirit by keeping the flame of hope lit in gloomy times when injustice assumes monstrous dimensions. This is because the promise of such a day affirms the possibility of justice defying a world filled with injustice and oppression, by pulling down the foundations of injustice to rebuild a new structure in its place. It implies that when injustice becomes monstrous and worldwide and [is spreading] its tentacles over human destiny, that is an unnatural condition, which is bound to terminate. This great and inevitable defeat of injustice, at a time when it is at its zenith, gives a great hope to every victim of injustice and reassurance to every oppressed nation of the ability to tilt the scales and build a new order.

(Baqir al-Sadr 1990)

This rendering of the Mahdi is another example of Shi'is historicising religious myth in a way that mobilises them into action today. According to Baqir al-Sadr, while this new socio-political structure of justice may only be realised in the next world, a person's faith in the Mahdi requires her to strive for justice and liberation in the here and now. As he stressed, this interpretation shifts the concept of salvation 'from the plane of transcendence to that of concrete reality, from the future to the present' (Baqir al-Sadr 1990). Here, the Mahdi is always ever-present. Furthermore, according to Baqir al-Sadr, the Mahdi will also one day appear as a human, closing 'the gulf of transcendence between the oppressed and their awaited saviour' (Baqir al-Sadr 1990).

So, while Imam al-Sadr's body is no longer physically in Lebanon, many Shi'is still feel his presence. His image appears on signs and billboards throughout Beirut's southern suburbs and the south of Lebanon, and sometimes even on buses, a daily reminder of Shi'is socio-political redemption. Indeed, a colleague who supports the resistance remarked that the only reason that Shi'is are in a position of empowerment today is because of Imam al-Sadr *and* Hizbullah.[2] According to him, both were necessary. And since Imam al-Sadr's disappearance, many supporters of the resistance have also experienced something of an absence. A scholar at one of Hizbullah's think-tanks pointed out how Imam al-Sadr started a social project that is not yet complete.[3] Another party supporter explained that while Shi'is are now in the position to finally realise his project, until now they have not been able to do so.[4] This may partly be due to the fact that there have sometimes been divisions among Imam al-Sadr's many followers. The Imam al-Sadr Foundation's ideas and practices have not always been in accordance with the politics of the Amal movement, and Hizbullah was born from the divisions within Amal. However, today these two political parties share a strong alliance in the government, and the foundation's relationship with Amal's leadership has recently improved.

Unfortunately, we may never know what really happened to Imam al-Sadr. Maybe he is still present among us, either waiting to be freed from a Libyan prison or soon to be revealed as the Hidden Imam. Or perhaps his larger project to empower Shi'is, while at the same time promoting coexistence in Lebanon, has become too lost in contemporary sectarian struggles, and his dead body is indeed buried in Sabha, a city 400 miles south of the Libyan capital, Tripoli. The only thing that we do know is that each of these explanations offers his followers something – all are meaningful in deeply personal ways. Together, they represent different ideas of religion, redemption, time and space, as well as faith and rationality, all of which are in some way interwoven into the contemporary social fabric of Lebanon's Shi'i communities today.

About the Imam al-Sadr Foundation

Because of the mystery surrounding Imam al-Sadr's sudden disappearance, there is an atemporal quality to his myth. In pictures, he will forever be a man of youth, and his life and work have now become part of the historicised religious narrative of Shi'is struggling against tyranny and injustice, providing a symbolic bridge between Imam Hussein, the Mahdi and the present day. This atemporal presence contrasts the worldly character of his institutional legacy in Lebanon, because he also awakened the Shi'is of southern Lebanon, in particular, and his work helped to lay the foundations of the resistance society that we see today. Also, unlike the vast network of charities associated with Hizbullah and al-Mabarrat Association, the Imam al-Sadr Foundation is quite distinct, both geographically and politically, as is described in more detail below. The foundation's main cultural compound in Sur, a coastal city in southern Lebanon, contains several buildings within a small but beautifully enclosed green space that is surrounded by a wall and located right next to the Mediterranean Sea. In contrast to the horizontal spatial restrictions, vertically the structures in the compound are open to the sky, many of them especially built to rely upon the sun for light. Indeed, the architecture was consciously designed to produce an environmentally friendly and open atmosphere.

While there are satellite health dispensaries throughout southern Lebanon, and a research centre based in Beirut, the cultural compound in Sur is the base of the foundation's activities and where most of my interviews took place. All my interviewees were employees of the foundation, and some of them even continued working while we were talking. This gave me the sense that they are constantly on the move, even though during the day many of them did not actually leave the foundation's physical premises. This sense of dynamism was verbally communicated as well, and in various ways. Many employees expressed a love for their work because each day is unique, suggesting that time passes in connected loops rather than a straight line. A young woman who helps develop the foundation's curriculum explained to me how the time passes, 'because it's like teach, assess or teach, implement or plan, implement and then give feedback and monitor and then we go back –

Figure 5.1 The mosque aside the Imam al-Sadr Foundation compound in Sur. Photo taken during fieldwork in Lebanon during summer 2010.

it's a cycle, we don't stop.'[5] An older woman in the Education Department told me how every day she comes in:

> with a new motive. It's not like the one the day before. Everything is new ... So, if we are doing something effective and it is positive for the society, this is why we are here. We live to give this. We are in this life to give something different, positive, new and effective.[6]

She even said that her job description was to constantly adapt and to learn new ways of thinking about the foundation's education programme. Another woman who works in special education explained that when working at other places she would usually tire after only one year, but at the foundation she is satisfied because they are 'always making something' new.[7]

Part of this 'always making something' new is self-reflexive, which was apparent when the employees discussed methods of evaluating the foundation's work. According to one of the managers of the Education Department, 'at the beginning of the year all the teachers will get plans, and at the end of the year they review these plans again,' asking themselves 'where are they now, where do they have to improve their performance?' She went on to say that there is 'a continuous assessment, a continuous learning … At the foundation we are a continuous learning organisation.'[8] This notion of progress, or development, may be quite similar to Western ideas, but it is also qualitatively different and always in flux. Indeed, as one of the curriculum developers further explained:

> What differentiates us from other schools is that we keep on progressing, in other words, all the time we're searching for new things, new strategies, new approaches and new stuff. The approach here is that everyone has to keep moving. You don't have more than annual plans, or even a long-term plan, let's say. You know, plans that are kept for three or four years? Well, every year we have a totally different new thing.[9]

According to the same employee, one of the main differences between the foundation and other charitable organisations working in Lebanon is this overwhelming focus on internal development. She told me how some of her friends criticise the foundation for not expanding its work to other places or programmes, saying to her,

> all of the time you are on the way, you're running, you're on the way … Just stop and do more things. Or, let's say, build another foundation rather than develop this one. But this is the approach here, this is the development.

More about what this notion of development means to the foundation will soon become apparent.

According to Mohammad Bassam, the foundation's head of research and development, Imam al-Sadr originally launched the foundation in 1962 because he wanted to empower the oppressed Shiʻi communities in Lebanon, who were economically and politically marginalised.[10] At the time, there were extreme disparities in wealth and access to services in Lebanon, especially between the urban and rural populations, and Imam al-Sadr was concerned that this was contributing to the unstable political environment throughout the country. Furthermore, migration to the cities produced even more social problems, because moving to the city highlighted existing inequalities, as Shiʻis mostly settled in the poorer areas. Also, leaving the southern part of Lebanon uninhabited was detrimental not only to agriculture but also to the Lebanese claim to the land, *sumud*, because the territory could be more easily seized by Israel or handed over to the Palestinian refugees who were forced to flee their lands in 1948 and again in 1967. The ultimate aim for Imam al-Sadr, according to Bassam, was keeping the Lebanese on their land while at the same time creating an environment for sustainable peace.

Bassam explained that the foundation has three main goals: participation, empowerment and ownership – all liberal concepts, but also shaped by faith, spirituality and what appears to be a remarkable commitment to all humans. In this way, the foundation is decentring secular liberalism by giving these concepts new values – embracing a universalism to aspire towards rather than one to enforce. Bassam described the foundation's notion of empowerment as the freedom or power to question, then to decide for oneself what kind of commitment to make. He said that this kind of outlook invites all participants into the political process by transforming the concept of ownership into being about one's own future as well as the future of the community. In fact, the foundation stresses the importance of engaging with the communities on the ground from the beginning of every project to its end. For example, some of the foundation's projects are designed to have an exit strategy, reaching a point where they can be handed over to the community to manage. Also, the foundation usually charges a nominal fee for its services, because the rationale is that if people are paying a small amount for something, then they feel more justified in making demands from these services (Hizbullah services are free for members while non-members pay a cost, and al-Mabarrat Association charges a more significant fee). Similar to the charities affiliated with Hizbullah and al-Mabarrat Association, the foundation's services are holistic. However, they are also less far reaching, because most of its work starts with the orphanage that houses the young girls: all programmes are developed according to the needs of these orphaned children.

The main sources of funding for the foundation are local contributions, government finances (each programme receives funds from different ministries), international aid agencies and remittances. According to Bassam, the Lebanese Diaspora community donates the greatest source of funds. Once or twice a year, the foundation hosts a banquet to raise money in the United States or Canada through its sister organisation in Dearborn, Michigan; however, recently some have expressed fear of contributing to the foundation because of the persecution of Muslim charities in the 'War on Terror'. Nevertheless, the foundation raises a lot of domestic support through annual *iftars*, meals that break the fast during Ramadan.

Bassam explained that the foundation tries to realise its social mission by working with three different sectors: members of the community, as partners and clients; the government, as a regulator, enforcer and forum for policy debates; and the international community, as major funders and managers of the development programmes. Theoretically, the foundation is open to all sects and its policy is not to ask the religious affiliation of beneficiaries, and as such they do not have any related statistics about their clients. However, Bassam admits that the vast majority of workers and beneficiaries are Shi'is, and he believes that some of the foundation's Islamic customs discourage Christians from participating. For example, he thinks that some women do not take part because of the *hijab* requirement. However, during my last visit to Lebanon in February 2017, he said that the foundation was engaging in a pilot project for Syrian refugees regardless of sect. To protect the Lebanese community, all grant proposals for the project stipulate that some of the funds must be allocated to local programmes.[11] As Dr Martha Mundy later noted, the Syrian presence in the country has created some frustration among the Lebanese poorer classes, because it brings competition for jobs and so much aid is designated for the refugees.[12] I heard similar frustrations expressed in Beirut.[13]

Description of the programmes offered

The main academic programme at the Imam al-Sadr Foundation is run by the Rihab al-Zahra' School, which 'focuses on the concepts of education for all and quality education'.[14] The school has three sections. The first section is the Kindergarten, working with both boys and girls between the ages of three and five from all socio-economic backgrounds. Established in 1988,

> its objective is to prepare children for the learning process through realising their potential and cultivation of their skills and abilities, so that at the completion of their full academic training they will be well prepared for society and will be able to contribute to its development and improvement.[15]

Kindergarten instruction is mainly in English, which is reflective of the Lebanese school system's preference for teaching primary education in either English or French rather than Arabic. The second section is for Elementary Education, established in 1981. This section works with the female students of the Rihab al-Zahra' orphanage, as well as other young female students in the community. The Elementary Education school 'aims to develop the personalities of the target girls on all the physical, emotional, mental, social and religious dimensions.'[16] And finally, the third section is for Special Education. Established in 1997, this section focuses on male and female students with various learning difficulties and physical disabilities, employing 'multiple techniques including occupational therapy, music therapy, psychological support, speech therapy and physical therapy' to help them overcome isolation.[17]

The foundation also runs adult educational activities at the cultural compound in Sur, as well as at their satellite branch in Beirut. For example, there is al-Afaq Development Institute, which includes three main programmes for female students: the Nursing School; Intensive Vocational Training, teaching girls and women technical specialties including hospitality, garden and flower arrangements, secretarial skills, health assistance, childcare assistance, hairdressing and make-up, photography, acupuncture and community participation; and the Social Work Branch, which trains women to become social workers or community activists to help extend the network of local development projects. According to the foundation, since being established in 2003, the Social Work Branch has rapidly expanded over the years, suggesting that it addresses a real need in the southern Lebanese communities and in society at large.[18]

Each of these educational programmes helps between 1–500 students. Another service is the Orphanage Care Programme, one of the longest running at the foundation. Established in 1962, the orphanage cares for girls who have lost one or both parents and other children who were born into difficult social and economic backgrounds in war-torn southern Lebanon. According to one of the managers at the Orphanage Care Programme:

One of the main visions is based on Imam al-Sadr's saying which is to remove the feeling that the person is an orphan from her heart. To be able to feel that she is a social being like any other being – a social being. Not to feel inferior to others and to be able to deliver to the community a person who is really equal to others and who does not feel inferior because of the fact she is an orphan.[19]

The orphanage usually provides care, consisting of comprehensive health and educational services, for between 300–400 girls, with the vast majority of them not actually living in the premises but at home with family members. The cultural compound usually houses between 30–40 orphans and is 'set up for the boarding girls to enjoy a safe, inclusive living environment where healthy food, transportation, clothing and laundry services, health facilities and other necessities are available to them.'[20] All the orphans have access to the foundation's three educational programmes, and the orphanage also provides funds to cover outside secondary and university courses. According to the foundation's literature, some of the graduates have later become employees of the foundation while others have celebrated their wedding ceremony at the foundation's premises among their fellow boarding girls.[21] When necessary, the foundation also assists the bride in establishing the family home.

The Health Programme is another important service offered by the foundation, and which provides a range of curative and preventive services, including general health awareness campaigns. The beneficiaries are mainly people of low income and the socially deprived – mostly those who are not covered by health insurance. The Health Programmes are carried out through eight different health dispensaries in the southern region, usually operating in locations that are strategic intersections for people to reach (Sidiquine, Jal al-Bahr, al-Shehabiya, Derdeghaya, Ankoun, Kfarhata, Aita al-Shaab and Deir Serian), as well as numerous mobile clinics that serve the remoter southern villages. In 2008, the Health Programme directly reached around 58,000 persons with services that included consultations, first aid, dentistry, laboratory tests, vaccination, drugs and physiotherapy.[22] The dispensary located at the cultural compound in Sur provides healthcare services to the foundation's students and staff members; it also organises visits to public schools in the region to treat local students.

In addition to the above, the foundation runs a series of social and rural development projects. This has included a programme for the Economic and Professional Empowerment of Female Farmers in the South, in cooperation with the Council for Development and Reconstruction and the World Bank. The initiative is focused on rural women in Aita al-Shaab and the surrounding villages and aims to improve working conditions in farming traditional crops, like tobacco, and introducing alternative crops that may be viable alternatives in future. Also in food, the foundation runs a Snack Supply to Public Schools initiative. This is a collaborative project with the International Orthodox Christian Charities and is financed by the United States Agency for International Development (USAID). The foundation supplies public schools in the villages close to the international borders in southern Lebanon with healthy snacks for the students, such as a bottle of milk or juice and a small cake.[23] And finally, the foundation has run a pilot project in cooperation with the World Health Organization to assess Reproductive Health in Aita al-Shaab and Rmeish, which includes a full survey of women between the ages of 15–44.

The foundation also runs several income generating programmes that raise funds for its services, while at the same time creating employment opportunities in the region. This includes Cafe Tyr, a small café on the Sur coastline (Tyre is the city's English name, Tyr the French) that opened in 2007 and serves hot beverages, fresh juice, ice cream and pastries made in the pastry section of the foundation's School Restaurant, the latter which operates as a training venue for students at the vocational school and provides an outlet for marketing food, sweets and dairy products to the local population. And there is Shawatina Restaurant, a large restaurant located at the side of the cultural compound (also along the coastline) that was launched in 2003 and produces Lebanese sweets and healthy natural food.[24] In addition to these three culinary enterprises, there is also The Milk Factory, which was constructed with the support of the International Fund for Agricultural Development in 2000, manufacturing a range of products, such as pasteurised milk, yogurt, labneh (strained yogurt) and butter.[25]

And finally, there is the affiliated Center of Imam Musa al-Sadr for Research and Studies in southern Beirut, a non-profit Lebanese institution founded in 1995 by a group of friends and researchers who were interested in contemporary intellectual issues. Today the centre helps to 'realise Imam Musa al-Sadr's dreams of attaining human integrity through spreading knowledge, activating people's roles in their community and enhancing rapprochement and dialogue with other religions.'[26] One of the centre's main focuses is collecting, documenting and collating information about the legacy of Imam al-Sadr to make it easily available for researchers and other interested parties. Recently, the centre has started to publish translations of Imam al-Sadr's work.[27] Another research interest of the centre is examining and sharing culture, for example, through the annual 'Common Terms' conference, a forum for clerics, lecturers, researchers and dignitaries to gather and exchange ideas on topics such as human rights, human development, religious dialogue, media representation, cultural identity and resistance.[28]

Similar to Hizbullah and al-Mabarrat Association, the foundation's facilities were also targeted during the 2006 war against Israel. According to a foundation publication, this included the destruction of their warehouse building in Beirut. There were also heavy damages to the Center of Imam Musa al-Sadr for Research and Studies in southern Beirut as well as to several of the health dispensaries across southern Lebanon.[29] The foundation's preliminary assessment of the cost of these physical damages totalled around US$300,000. In addition, the foundation evacuated all employees from the southern areas during the first days of the conflict and ceased operations for more than 45 days, suffering delays in the completion of services and contracts. Nevertheless, throughout the war, the foundation maintained constant communications with its network of friends and supporters, planning for the post-war period, and two health dispensaries (Ankoun and Kfarhata) were able to continue providing essential services.

Distancing from the resistance charities

Despite the Imam al-Sadr Foundation also being targeted by Israel, during my interviews many research participants distanced the foundation from the resistance charities. This happened in multiple ways, but perhaps the most subtle was when some employees expressed a clear conceptual distinction between religion and faith. For example, one of the employees in the Health Programme explained to me the difference:

> Faith is the spiritual dimension so you can feel it but you cannot touch it. And faith is present everywhere. This is my opinion of faith, so for me faith is different than religious behaviour. So, this is quite different; for instance, even non-believers can have faith in doing something, and vice versa, a believer cannot have faith. It depends on the impact and your way of doing it and how. And this is for me the spirit of faith.[30]

However, others were more confused over whether I was asking them about their ideas and expressions of faith, *iman* in Arabic, or religion, *diin.* This signified that views about religion and faith are somewhat contested, not only among Shi'is more generally but also within the foundation itself. The confusion is partially a linguistic one. All words in the Arabic language are derived from a three-letter root and the word faith, *iman*, comes from the root for 'to believe in' and 'to have faith in'. But words in Arabic usually have several different meanings and the noun form of *iman* can also mean 'true religion'. Furthermore, the root for *diin* means 'religion, faith and belief'. Thus, research participants initially thought that I wanted to know about which Islamic rules the foundation promotes, rather than what Islamic ideas and practices actually mean to them.

When I interviewed Rebab al-Sadr, the head of the foundation since Imam al-Sadr's disappearance, I asked her about the difference between faith and religion. The following day when I returned to the foundation, I was told that she had spent more time thinking about this question and had written the following explanation for me, translated from the Arabic:

> *Faith* is the internal emotional state where one will not be aware of the extent of its presence and persistence inside of the human except through external work in alignment with the understanding of rules set out in the intellectual framework that the human believes in. *Religion* is all that the human owes to or believes in. Thus, the word (religion) has become associated with the divine messages. Along with this meaning, religion is where God drew rules and set controls, then sending the apostles to preach by it. And the believer in a divine religion has to commit to all that came by the apostles of God's commands and prohibitions, all of which is a whole. There is no commitment to one legislative, moral, or legal side without the other. The commitment is rather to these larger subjects in their particularities and details. And the faithful believer is the one who holds to the particularities with all of their requirements without separation or fragmentation.[31]

Here, faith is clearly something that is internal even though it is only visible through a person's social expressions, whereas religion is the commitment to obey all of God's rules.

While most employees did not have adequate time to reflect upon their ideas of religion and faith, I suspect that their confusion was also related to politics, for two reasons. First, in English – the language of the majority of my interviews – the word religion is sometimes interchangeable with sect and the foundation seeks to overcome sectarianism and promote difference. Although it works mostly with Shi'is, employees frequently mentioned Christians and deliberately spoke about coexistence. Indeed, Nijad Charafeddine, one of the foundation's managers and the son of Rebab al-Sadr, told me how 'Imam al-Sadr believed that Lebanon is the community, or prototype, of the right Islamic–Christian dialogue, and even Eastern–Western dialogue.' He also explained how he personally thinks that:

> religion has many meanings and each was set to be in a different time. But this is God's will – we are all derived from one thing, from one source. And it's very, very obvious. So I, as a Muslim, I cannot be a Muslim if I am not a Christian. And I cannot be a Muslim and a Christian if I am not a Jew. No way.[32]

Second, many employees were also eager to differentiate themselves from the other Shi'i charities and institutions that are stricter in their interpretations of religious ideas and practices. As one of the curriculum developers told me:

> In some schools, they try to put religion into everything. For example, they say there is something in the Qur'an that tells us how to share equally. We don't do it in this way, by forcing things. Instead it comes naturally. We have things in the lessons of division or multiplication – things that show how life is more classified, because they go and find it in nature. They learn about God, for example, because we deal with the context. Like, if I'm giving numbers in billions, just to hint to it. I will say can you count and they will say no that is too much. They will find one hundred is too much. The million and the billion – you know that God made all of this. But we don't force things like other schools where everything is religion. They try to force it, and I don't think that's going to be more educational. So, we try to give things in their natural way. But we are a religious school even though some will say you're not like the other schools, you're not as religious as others because we don't force things. Yeah, we just let it go.[33]

She further explained how she herself comes from a strict religious family that goes back several generations, and even wears a conservative *chador*,[34] but while she was working on the religious curriculum her father, who is a *sheikh*, recommended that she just concentrate on developing the children's moral selves rather than making them memorise morality. This helped her to rethink tools of assessment as well:

> One of the most important things if you are working with a religious curriculum is the last part, the self-assessment or the motivation. At the end, what am I going to do? Okay, usually in the most religious, let's say the Islamic schools, they make a paper and pencil test, they memorise the parts from the Qur'an. But at the end what kind of person do you have? Maybe at the other schools they memorise more of the Qur'an and they look more religious, but let's say at the end the impact on students is just the paper and pencil test. Here we have more things for them.[35]

This kind of philosophy diverges somewhat from the other Shi'i charities in Lebanon, which embrace the public performance of religious rituals, ranging from prayer to fasting to participating in Ashura commemorations.[36] As Shaery-Eisenlohr (2008) notes, what defines a good citizen among many Shi'is in Lebanon is often directly linked to religiosity. And although the standards vary between the different parties, she finds that the leaders of Hizbullah, Amal and the followers of Ayatollah Fadlallah all connect being a good citizen to pious behaviours (Hizbullah's 'Order is part and parcel of faith' campaign, mentioned in Chapter 4, also supports this).

Religiosity may still be present in the case of the Imam al-Sadr Foundation, but it is more complicated. First, the foundation honours Islamic orthodoxy and religious holidays and I was told that it had recently refocused more attention on Islam and religion. The two managers of the Education Department explained to me that:

> In every area we are talking about, who said when we teach Arabic we are not teaching religion and ethics? Who said when we are teaching English, we are not teaching religion and ethics? Who said, and so on and so forth? Two, three years back when we saw that students were not giving that much importance to this subject, which is religion or Islamic studies, we made a new programme and we started with a column of things that if you are good in this subject, then it means you will improve in other subjects. And it has a relation with the other teachers and other subjects. It should be as a whole.[37]

Figure 5.2 Uncoloured copy of the Imam al-Sadr Foundation's religiously inspired student motivation chart. The students colour a green leaf if they pray on time, make an act of charity or do something kind; yellow to show that they do something bad; and a red apple for something extraordinary. Since the students love their trees to be green and fruitful, they learn to appreciate the good things that they have done. Document collected during fieldwork in Lebanon during summer 2010.

As a result, the foundation has reintegrated religion into the curricula. However, as already noted, this is not just a paper and pencil test, as the education managers added:

We [now] have special papers and texts that teach the Qur'an and Islamic studies. The elementary school has two sessions a week: one session for the Qur'an and one session for Islamic studies. But it's not limited to the two sessions that you teach them – the whole day, how the teachers work with the students and how much you are here with them. Yeah. It's a whole programme, all of the activities with the students. So, this is very important.[38]

While they went on to describe that Islamic rituals and holidays were important to the programme as well, especially Shi'i commemorations like Ashura, for them piety is more than just a public behaviour. As they further clarified:

> The faith is an act, so it is not just to read the Qur'an or to read the prayers. It should be through our doing – it is a way of life. We say that Islam is a way of life, not just a religion, and most of the *hadith*s are about that, which is Islam is a *diin al-'am*, or a public religion – how to behave around people, how to act and interact, how to be honest, how to suppress when you face, maybe some anxiety or something. How to do it, when to say it and when not. And how to show the righteous things at the right place and at the right moment.[39]

Therefore, correct religious behaviour relates to all aspects of one's life, not just good citizenship. But while all the women are required to wear the *hijab* and many employees talked about a strong sense of faith during the interviews, at times outward signs of religion were self-consciously checked in people's communications. In fact, within the foundation, liberalism often seemed to be the more appropriate standard to which people aspired, and this will become more evident as its activities are further analysed. Even in a promotional video for the foundation, a mother who does not cover her hair accompanies her children to the cultural compound, putting on a *hijab* matter of factly only as she enters the main office, as if making the point that this is merely a procedural formality rather than a required act of piety.[40] However, when the mother speaks to a foundation employee, asking for help for her and her children, she explains that her husband was martyred in the 2006 war, and his father during the 1982 Israeli invasion.[41] So even though this was indeed a more liberalised environment, where individual choices played a prominent role, it was not divorced from the resistance community.

And yet, at times, employees at the foundation deliberately distanced themselves from the resistance charities by calling to attention the foundation's limited geographical reach and its particular vision. As Charafeddine told me, 'We like to have our services and our work very near to our facilities, very near to our vision.' He also stressed that the foundation is a quality-oriented organisation.[42] So even though the foundation maintains a modest budget and a limited programme, he explained that what it offers is the best:

At many other foundations such as Muhammad Hussein Fadlallah or Hizbullah or Amal, they have big budgets, they're huge but maybe they need this for politics, or political issues, or for whatever issues, they need to go wide. They need to have followers from Bekaa and south and east and whatever. Maybe, but here at the foundation, we seek perfection. And when you want to perfect something, you have to go in-depth and not in-width. You cannot diversify – we say in Arabic, *mneshr*, or scatter all our work. No, you have to have roots and cultivate and always aggregate.[43]

Another employee of the Health Programme indirectly criticised the Lebanese system where political parties are also affiliated with charities. She complained that many people give to charity with an expectation of receiving something in return 'whether this giving back is something political, religious, or a social commitment.'[44] Of course, this criticism applies to humans everywhere, religiously minded or not.

Research participants often stressed their faith in empowerment, as both an individual and community goal. For example, the Orphanage Care Programme helps children to believe that they have something to give to others, and to see the problems in society in order to be able to solve them so that all can have a better social environment.[45] Other employees also discussed the relationship between faith and helping the community. As Charafeddine related:

From my own practices, from my view, faith is the motive and I think that commitment and faith, they are very close to each other. Now because you have faith in, whatever, in your work, in your God, in your religion, it will make you be committed to many things that you do. But I think here our faith is to build a community, to help build a healthy society. We believe in that and we are committed to achieving this goal.[46]

An employee in the Health Programme also explained to me that helping the community is one of the motivating factors for her own work at the foundation:

I think what attracted me to the foundation is that it works with the population, with the community, and with different projects, so it's to have something to give to people who are in need, and not just to work in a system in which everything is okay and there is no need. So, it's kind of a mission to be useful to people who are in need, and not wanting to be satisfied with being employed only for employment.[47]

Of course, serving the community is also a political act, because the foundation's values are integrated into its various programmes and services. While Mohammad Bassam recognises that politics and social services are always inseparable, he believes that the provision of social services should not be overly politicised.[48] However, claims to neutrality risk reproducing the violence of Western secular liberalism, as the foundation clearly has a political project to realise, a very particular kind of social transformation. The key guiding principle of the foundation today is not resistance against Israel, but the making of a sustainable, liberalised resistance community. Even so, research participants were somewhat ambivalent towards Western hegemonic ideas and practices, sometimes openly embracing Western standards, while at other times clearly privileging the values of the local community. Indeed, during our interviews, there seemed to be certain tensions between competing liberal, religious and communal values, tensions we will continue to encounter. So, overall, the political project of the foundation probably overlaps just as much with liberalism as it does with the resistance society in Lebanon, because it also challenges many of the ideas and practices of Western secularism, while modifying liberalism. In the following section, I tease out some of these tensions by examining how religious rationality is expressed in the ideas and practices of the foundation.

Religious rationality at the foundation

The Imam al-Sadr Foundation's approach to its work may not embody exactly the same ideas and practices of religion as the other Shi'i movements in Lebanon, but they do sometimes overlap. For example, the foundation has an official referral system to send people to al-Mabarrat Association when it is unable to provide the necessary services itself. More importantly, faith is always ever present. So, there are times when employees clearly reference shared religious obligations, and others when they deviate from normative conceptions of religion in sectarian Lebanon to focus more clearly on a personal or spiritual conception of faith. For example, an employee of the Health Programme described how faith and rationality play an important role in how the foundation conceives of and delivers its medical services:

I think that we treat health in a holistic approach. So, this means physical, mental, moral and spiritual. Even in the modern dimensions of the WHO (World Health Organization) and when giving meaning to health, spirituality has been a thing for ten years now in the concept and approach to health in general. Also, our understandings of faith, science, rationality and spirituality or religion are interactive. And when they are interactive it means that when I do something, like if I am a nurse or a physician and I want to cure, I will cure with the rational way, and also with the faith that I have to do something beyond the expectations, something beyond the physical, something because I have a commitment towards these people, towards humanity which is a part of God's Kingdom. And also, vice versa. It means human beings as being an image of God whether they have faith in God or not, we look at them as humans in general.[49]

She went on to explain that for her, faith and rationality work together in concert, where:

basic science is rationality. But I think there is always something that cannot be explained by physical means, which is beyond. And this is strong in us, in everyday life – the spirituality of human beings reflects itself upon the spirituality of life. And I think that the physical things are the basics and the rationality is the basics. But the halo, the heart, is the faith.[50]

Therefore, she thinks that both faith and rationality are necessary for human health and well-being, citing Imam Musa al-Sadr's understanding,

that science and faith are together and must be together – one cannot be without the other ... We are trying to reconstitute the two concepts. And so, everything that is done for the rational, or the good of the society, is accepted by God, and everything else which is against human well-being is not accepted by God or by faith.[51]

Here, society's determination of what is morally rational is God's will, rather than the other way around.

Charafeddine also challenged the more traditional reliance on 'God's will be done', when he spoke about managing the foundation's budget by criticising people's expectations of God. Instead, he preferred an approach that also relied upon instrumental rationality:

> In all religions, if you don't have enough of something God will send you more. We are more rational on this issue. At the foundation, the rationality of that is just to stop and to analyse what we are doing.[52]

Nevertheless, management decisions are also always constrained because the foundation is a charity and it upholds certain values and standards, quality being an important one. This results in contradictions that are difficult for employees to negotiate. While the foundation has auditors, a chief accountant and a financial manager who are always nagging about its finances, Charafeddine explains that, 'we are not creating these facilities and job opportunities just to make more money. We are spending money for God's sake.' Therefore, he believes that a more substantive kind of rationality is key:

> Here in the foundation, the whole facilities that we give, the whole services, many of them, I can say the majority, are in losses. But we are working to empower people. So, we have a couple of solutions. After you will know that, you will go and do a real analysis – a financial analysis – and either you will cut your expenses, not losing any of the quality aspect, or you will make more effort to bring more money. You don't have any other choice, because it's a charity, and the board and the CEO don't have dividends. So yes, you sometimes have to analyse what you are doing and the money issues, but you cannot conclude that this dispensary, this health centre, it's been in losses for a couple of months lately, so we will take the decision and stop it. No, you cannot do that.[53]

Because a certain kind of ethical rationality is necessary, Charafeddine also admitted that quantitative analyses were usually not the best approach for assessing the foundation's work. In fact, numbers and statistics were often ignored completely, because lost money is 'not a loss. It's always profit, because the impact is on the humanitarian side, the impact is there.'[54]

He suggested that the best way to assess the foundation is somewhere in between faith and numbers. This pragmatism is also evident in how the foundation approaches issues like gender equality. Enforcing particular standards from the outside are usually counterproductive, if not actively resisted, as an employee of the Health Programme remarked:

> If you want to try to empower women it is in relationship to building a social awareness for the new husband to a married woman and about how he is supposed to interact with his family in terms of gender. Because usually he will, living in a traditional and patriarchal society, deal with the woman and his role defined as being the chief of the family. And so, I think that this is also in relation with faith, and the understanding of faith, because what is gender? Sometimes when you only take gender and you give it a meaning that is coming from outside of these societies, it is refused. But when you take gender and you customise it to your own society then it is already integrated into the religious beliefs and how you understand these religious beliefs. And so here is when faith will empower social beliefs and health beliefs.[55]

Her approach is not unlike that of Mahmood (2005) and Deeb (2006), who both find that contemporary Muslim women in Egypt and Lebanon respectively are actively engaging in religious discourses and practices, thus transforming the role of women in modern society. These examples illustrate that religion can offer a progressive challenge to particular social norms without undermining conservative ethics. The foundation also uses religion to promote democratic values as well, connecting citizenship with love and sharing.[56] This was evident when one of the curriculum developers described the foundation's pedagogical approach to religious rationality:

> We are making also a peda-religious curriculum, which is not like it's religious, we're teaching religion as duties – as content. Yeah, it's more socially oriented and it has some scientific things like, we approach the idea of let's say God's existence by the five senses, through the five senses and let's say the blessings God gave us. That's our approach. And even religion here is not just religion, because it has these scientific backgrounds. It all merges together, for example, one of our religious lessons is about cooperation. So, it's not just about Islam, and who's the Prophet and about the book, let's say the Qur'an or something.

It's also about cooperation and how we should cooperate, and about cleanliness, the environment, abiding by the rules, and families – family life.[57]

She went on to describe in detail their lesson about cooperation, which is taught during the first year of religious classes. This lesson features a story about animals learning how to cooperate, and the foundation works with clerics and graphic designers to create interactive videos that incorporate songs and related activities for the children.

Along with the focus on gender equality, citizenship and democracy, the foundation also actively promotes environmentalism, again inspired by religious rationality. As Charafeddine explained:

I can tell you that this is the Imam al-Sadr Foundation point of view as a whole. We give because we know that when it will go around, it will benefit you as yourself. Not necessarily tomorrow, but whenever you give it will return back to you. For example, we have climate change. Everything we are now having – the disasters we are having is because of man and because of greed. So, this is actually what we did to ourselves. But if you do good, then it will return back to you, by time. So, I think this is the main philosophy. And it is not only for the sake of Islam, or for the sake of Allah, but also for the sake of the good.[58]

One recent programme the foundation has embarked upon is organic cultivation, which provides unpolluted fruits and vegetables for the foundation's food services and some for selling. The foundation also launched a solar water heating system in 2007 that was donated by the United Nations Development Programme and implemented through the Swedish International Development Agency (Charafeddine 2008). Another is a programme for schoolchildren to nurture their own plants. Each child names and looks after the plant, cultivating a respect for both nature and responsibility, a reflection of the foundation's commitment to building a healthy and sustainable society – one that is in harmony with nature.

Working towards a sustainable community requires that social workers and other staff reach out to parents and family members living in the wider community as part of the overall assessment process. For example, in the Health Programme one of the employees described how the foundation assesses and tracks the care of patients:

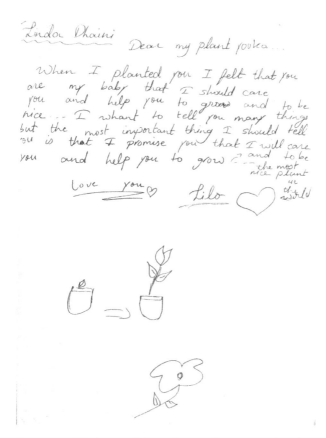

Figure 5.3 This is a sample letter that a student wrote to her plant expressing her love and commitment to watering it. Document collected during fieldwork in Lebanon during summer 2010.

We have some kinds of mechanisms, more formally, like for example all of our medical records and administrative files are from year one on the information system. So, we have the information system, we have monthly statistics dealing with a number of patients in the category of their age, their pathology, of the drugs, the running drugs, and the circulation of drugs. And so, this is the formal part. The informal part is in relation to the questionnaire of the satisfaction of patients. This is also measuring the quantitative part. The qualitative part is the interface between the people and the nurses. The nurses sometimes even go for home visits after hours, this is also mixed with faith. Even after the opening hours, they go to visit some of their patients, to have

Figure 5.4   Another sample letter that a student wrote to her plant expressing her love and commitment to watering it. Document collected during fieldwork in Lebanon during summer 2010.

communication with them and to interact socially with them to know if the treatment was efficient or not, and to ask how are they now? And this is an informal way by becoming sometimes a friend of these people. Or, if for example some patient does not come back to the foundation, they will ask some kin or some relatives where is he now? How is he doing?[59]

The foundation systematically evaluates its services using both formal and informal procedures and clearly defined standards. These are very rational systems that also include substantive qualitative measures, many of which are guided by ethical commitments. So, similar to the charities affiliated with Hizbullah and al-Mabarrat Association, the Imam al-Sadr Foundation is a modern, rational institution that incorporates faith as a value or guiding principle. The foundation also has designed a comprehensive programme of assessment of teachers:

> We have the 360-degree evaluation system from all the areas, so the teacher is assessed by the coordinator, her colleagues and her peers. And there is also a self-assessment, as well as the impact of the teacher's teaching on the student's learning. And we measure it by the percentage of development and the subset average of the class. The outcome here should be on the student's learning. It should be directly proportional to the student's learning. And we made a programme, we worked on the standards and criteria, where one is a low accomplishment, two it is made but with some mistakes, three is the average and four is it's done and developed. And for each number, we have assigned a statement, a projected statement. So, we have made a complete programme. It is digitised, so it's like we just put in the data and we have reports coming out.[60]

However, the standards and criteria involve much more than test scores. As the head of curriculum and his colleague both explained to me:

> We have 53 criteria. Each one of them you have to assign four grades. One – what does it mean? Two, three, four … The standards here are related to job commitment. For example, we have the uniform, we have sharing in public activities, coordination, planning and organisation, and self-assessment and impact. We have the percentile for the success rate of students, the class average, and we have the progress average, and we have the students' expectations about the subject, whether the students realise the importance of the subject that they're learning. The students' interaction to the session, the students listening to each other, the students' care of the performance, the students are motivated internally to do the work on time … This is what we were talking about.[61]

This is a complex system of teacher evaluation that requires an incredible amount of time and resources to manage. But as one of the managers of the Education Department reasoned, the foundation cannot just rely on student test scores, because if you only count that then 'here the teachers at the foundation would be all failures because our students come from the fringes and the underprivileged areas' of southern Lebanon.[62] The foundation's teachers also comprehensively assess the students as well:

> We assess student performance in three P elements – the process, the progress, and the performance. The performance is based on an authentic assessment – we ask students to make their own project related to their own life, and they relate their knowledge, skills and understanding to their real-life context to make a project, an authentic project, which they then present orally or written. This is the performance. The progress, we assess students by using the portfolio as the main tool in the domain of progress. We have the journals where they have to write about … here we have those articles in the broadsheets and they approach the concept, mathematical concepts, nation-wide maps … we care about both the process and progress. In fact, we are up to date with the ASCD, the [US-based] Association for Supervision and Curriculum Development.[63]

So, similar to Hizbullah and al-Mabarrat Association, the Imam al-Sadr Foundation recognises the importance of international standards in the management and evaluation of its institutions. However, in reality, the foundation's curriculum is actually a mix of various influences: the foundation starts with the Lebanese curriculum and then adds to it from different resources like the American, Belgian and Moroccan curriculum. Indeed, the foundation often adopts a highly pragmatic approach to creating programmes that benefit the community. Of course, pragmatism can also mean unwelcome compromise. A critique of the Imam al-Sadr Foundation, Hizbullah and al-Mabarrat Association follows.

6

The Problem of Resistance and Power

shit is complicated
— Suheir Hammad, 'First Writing Since'

'An open sectarian wound'

There are several important critiques of the Islamic resistance movement that I seek to address in this chapter, but I first need to provide some context about recent developments across the Middle East, namely, the rise of a new sectarianism. As Salloukh *et al.* (2015: 2) argue, the 2003 US-led invasion of Iraq and subsequent collapse of the Baathist state, followed by the militarisation of the Arab uprisings, set alight previously dormant sectarian, tribal, religious and ethnic affiliations across the Arab world. According to Haddad, Shiʻis, once only accused of ethnic Otherness, 'are now being cast as outside the Muslim community itself. Exclusion on doctrinal grounds was a mostly Saudi exception in the framing of Shiʻism. It is now increasingly becoming the regional rule' (2013). While earlier discourses were demeaning, Haddad suggests that there is a qualitative difference between calling Shiʻis foreigners and dismissing their religion altogether, using the Arabic word *rafidha* – meaning 'those who reject or refuse', relating to Shiʻis' belief that Imam Ali was the successor to the Prophet Mohammad (rather than the first three Caliphs, Abu Bakr, Umar and Uthman). This paradigm shift means that many Sunnis now think that Shiʻis ought to be excluded from not only the Arab state, but also the Muslim community, because Shiʻis are 'beyond redemption until they renounce their beliefs' (Haddad 2013). The Middle East journalist Patrick Cockburn has argued that simply being identified today as a Shiʻi or an Alawi (a subsect of Shiʻism) in Sunni rebel-held parts of Iraq and Syria 'has become as dangerous as being a Jew was in Nazi-controlled parts of Europe in 1940' (2014).

When I returned to Lebanon in 2017 to update my fieldwork, I did not expect to find so many supporters of the resistance approvingly resigned to Hizbullah's role in Syria and the new sectarianism is central to understanding why. Rosen (2010) provides an exhaustive account of what the International Crisis Group (ICG 2017: 11) calls the 'open sectarian wound' that emerged after the fall of Saddam Hussein's regime in Iraq. Rosen explains in detail the excruciatingly violent sectarian acts of Shi'i militias in Iraq; however, he also travels across the region to speak with disaffected Sunnis, who express extreme bigotry and hatred towards Shi'is. Many Salafi-Jihadi leaders blamed Iraqi Shi'is for supporting the Americans, feeding into sectarian hatreds of all Shi'is. Of course, the opposite argument is now at play in Syria, with Shi'is blaming Sunnis for siding with imperialist allies. One Jordanian man told Rosen that: 'The infidel sects are one, if they are Jews or Shi'is,' justifying this view by misquoting the thirteenth-century scholar loved by Salafis, Ibn Taymiyyah, for saying that Shi'is were actually 'worse than Jews or Christians' (2010: Kindle edn). Others expressed similar views.

Extremist anti-Shi'i bigotry has been commonplace in modern Saudi Arabia, which exports its biases through publishing activities and funding mosques and *madrasas*. According to Zabad (2017: 158), anti-Shi'i hatred played an essential role for Mohammad ibn Abd al-Wahhab in founding Wahhabism. He explains that Shi'is in Saudi Arabia today have no political representation, their religious practices are closely monitored by the religious police and they are not represented in the country's highest religious authority (Zabad 2017). In recent decades, the oppression has also worsened. Twenty-two senior Saudi clerics signed a statement (Know them and Beware of them) in 2008 that excommunicated Shi'is. Meanwhile, popular and pro-government Sunni clerics have regularly advocated anti-Shi'i violence (Zabad 2017: 160). One Lebanese Shi'i looked helpless when explaining to me that everybody was sleeping while Saudi Arabia was developing schools across the Muslim world teaching this hateful type of Wahhabism, asking: 'What did we expect would be the outcome?'[1]

A common statement that Rosen heard from Salafi-Jihadis, and which I myself was told by some Arab Muslim supporters of the Muslim Brotherhood, is that Shi'is hate Sunnis. Although I only had limited access to research participants, I did spend almost two and a half years conducting fieldwork in Lebanon and three months in Tehran. During this time, I did not meet any Shi'i who could substantiate this claim, only that there was distrust and fear. Rosen (2010: Kindle edn) suggests that as far back as 2003, Iraqi Shi'is 'were terrified of a phantom Wahhabi threat,' harking back to Saudi Arabia's founding history when Wahhabis attacked Shi'i shrines, adding that: 'Now Shi'is feared Wahhabis would poison the food distributed to pilgrims. Soon many Shi'is would view all Sunnis as Wahhabis.' Sadly, almost 15 years later, this may now be true across the Middle East, but fear is not the same as hatred.

Another theme in Rosen's interviews with Salafi-Jihadists is Syria; many believed that the Americans were planning to attack Syria, something the US government did at one point anticipate (Borger, White, MacAskill and Watt 2003). One man who worked with Abu Musab al-Zarqawi, the founder of the Islamic State in Iraq (ISIS), claimed that:

> The US wants to get inside the capital of Islam, which is Sham [Damascus]. This entrance will be through Syria. Syria will be the slaughterhouse of Americans and their supporters, so they are welcome to get inside Syria and be butchered.
>
> (Rosen 2010: Kindle edn)

Salafi-Jahadis soon started to infiltrate the Palestinians' camps in northern Lebanon, notably Nahr al-Bared, bringing this extremist Sunni ideology onto Lebanese soil. It may have already been there, but the power vacuum created by the assassination of Prime Minister Rafik Hariri in 2005 left an increasingly marginalised Sunni population vulnerable to extremism and violence. Part of the problem is the growing impoverishment of Sunnis in northern Lebanon (OCHA 2016); another is the lack of Sunni political leadership. While many initially had put their hopes in Rafik's son, Saad Hariri, who served as prime minister from 2009 until 2011, and again since 2016, he continues to face political and financial trouble (Speetjens 2016).

Rosen (2010: Kindle edn) describes how in early 2007, dozens of Arab 'foreigners' – mostly Lebanese, Saudis, Yemenis, Syrians and Iraqis – mysteriously started appearing in highly securitised Palestinian camps in Lebanon, ostensibly through infiltrating Fatah al-Intifada, an anti-occupation Palestinian party. The foreigners soon broke away into a militant group they called Fatah al-Islam. Four Syrians from this new group were accused of a bus bombing in Lebanon that killed three people in February 2007 (Al Jazeera 2007). In early summer 2007, several members of Fatah al-Islam overtook the Nahr al-Bared offices of Fatah al-Intifada. The Lebanese Armed Forces responded swiftly and with brutality, ultimately destroying pretty much the entire camp and

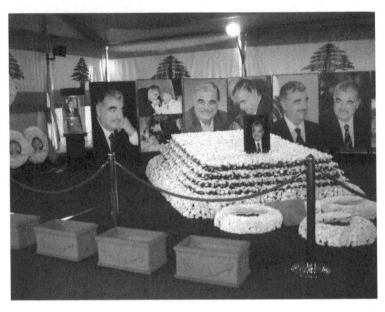

Figure 6.1 The temporary memorial for assassinated Prime Minister Rafik Hariri in Martyr's Square in downtown Beirut. Photograph taken during in Beirut during summer 2009.

leaving a wasteland that remained an uninhabitable war zone for many years to come.[2] The fighting lasted for three months and claimed the lives of 158 members of the Lebanese Armed Forces (Dakroub 2007). It also reignited the civil–international war cleavage between the Lebanese and the Palestinians, with the former blaming the latter for harbouring extremists (ICG 2012). Throughout my fieldwork, I witnessed first-hand the hostility that many Lebanese still feel for Palestinians.[3]

In the case of the Lebanese response to Nahr al-Bared, the animosity was based on nationality, not sect (even if the Fatah al-Islam extremists were not Palestinian and were possibly motivated by sectarian hatred). This mostly stems from the suffering that the Lebanese have endured since Israel's expulsion of Palestinians in 1948 and again in 1967, the ramifications of which have destabilised their country. Since, then, however, other cleavages have emerged across the Middle East, namely, the Sunni–Shi'i schism, intensified by the US-led invasion and occupation of Iraq. After the Syrian withdrawal from Lebanon in 2005, the Sunni establishment in Lebanon openly embraced Salafists, giving them more legitimacy (Daragahi 2008). The northern areas have witnessed the most violence in recent years, with Alawis and Sunnis regularly fighting in Tripoli (Strickland 2015); Salafi-Jihadis from Syria breaching the boarders in Arsal in 2014; and Lebanese extremists waging a three-day war in Tripoli against the Lebanese Armed Forces in the same year (Reuters 2014c). Two years later, Sunnis in Tripoli rejected Hariri's alliance with the billionaire Najib Miqati in municipal elections (New Arab 2016), opting instead for a list backed by the 'hawkish' former justice minister Ashraf Rifi (Reuters 2016), who fiercely opposes Hizbullah and has been accused of sympathising with Salafi-Jihadi groups (Asharq Al-Awsat 2014). My point in providing this context is that when politics is ruled more by 'the enemy of my enemy is my friend', and identities are multi-faceted, 'an open sectarian wound' is a bloody mess. Writing about the fallout from the attacks in New York on 11 September 2001, the Palestin-ian-American poet Suheir Hammad perfectly sums up this predicament: 'shit is complicated'.

Conceptualising resistance and intersectionality

The same holds true for conceptualising resistance. As Kafka (2016) illustrates in his parable, 'Before the Law', resistance is always met by counter-resistance. Therefore, knowing what constitutes resistance first requires some understanding of what is being resisted. For example, Caygill points out that while a crowd standing may not appear to be resistant, standing may be 'the reciprocal of the police charge: to defy or take a stand assumes a capacity to resist, which is the outcome of previous stands within previous scenarios of opposed forces' (2013: 3). Similarly, when I speak about a resistance subjectivity, I am not referring to a physical or military readiness but a counter-hegemonic state of mind that centres its values around faith, Islam and a commitment to the margins. However, as Caygill also adds, our social interactions are never static, but fluid and dynamic: 'There is never a moment of pure resistance, but always a reciprocal play of resistances that form clusters or sequences of resistance and counter-resistance responding to each other in surrendering or seizing initiative' (2013: 5). Thus, any resistance subjectivity will manifest itself differently depending on the context. In his powerful meditation on the history of resistance as an idea and practice, Caygill is ultimately asking us to think about its social, political and human consequences.

Importantly, Caygill stresses that the 'unification of practices of resistance into a concept and institution of *the* Resistance, while tactically necessary in certain contexts, risks emptying resistance of its very capacity to resist' (2013: 6). In other words, although some consistency of ideas and practices are required to sustain any resistance movement, defining resistance as any one particular formation not only limits its flexibility in responding to new developments, but also exposes it to co-optation by other competing power blocs. But aside from this one affirmation, Caygill shows that ideas and practices of resistance have historically been dynamic. For Clausewitz, war is always about the capacity to resist (Caygill 2013: 16); and the goal of any pure war of resistance is to maintain this potential (2013: 27). Nietzsche's conception of resistance is solely linked to revenge (2013: 36), but Marx's texts offer both vengeance and the possibility of another world (2013: 37). Lenin also embraced this creative aspect of resistance, arguing 'that "trade union consciousness" is a reactive *ressentiment* resistance – it says no to particular injustices while affirming the institutional structure of capitalism; it does not say yes in the name of something new' (Caygill 2013: 46).

Building on the work of the Italian Marxist Antonio Gramsci, the Frankfurt School incorporated culture into the existing resistance framework, introducing 'aesthetic resistance, messianic/prophetic resistance, even the resistance of the concept – in short, a universe of resistances no longer tied to the discourses of consciousness and force' (Caygill 2013: 51). From the subaltern perspective of unfreedom, Levinas offered the tentative notion of a resistant subjectivity (Caygill 2013: 95), which Fanon further developed by describing a zone of non-being where the colonist makes history and the colonised is immobilised:

> Colonialism is not satisfied with snaring the people in its net or of draining the colonised brain of any form or substance. With a kind of perverted logic, it turns its attention to the past of the colonised people and distorts it, disfigures it and destroys it. This effort to demean history prior to colonisation today takes on a dialectical significance.
>
> (Fanon 2004: 149)

However, Caygill points out that from within this kind of resistant subjectivity it is difficult to realise the creative aspect of resistance, what he calls 'an affirmative, inventive resistance that does not just react to an intolerable predicament but transforms itself and its condition through the work of resistance, the actualising of its capacity to resist' (2013: 98–99). He further adds that, 'The resistant subject does not discover possibility and freedom, but their own necessity to resist' (Caygill 2013: 103).

Many unanswered questions emerge from these various understandings of resistance. If resistance is always met by counter-resistance, how do we resist overlapping oppressions that come from different locations? To complicate matters ever further, we all have a plurality of identities from which to resist (sect, race, class, gender, sexuality etc.) and these identities are often fluid; some may be intersecting (white male privilege), while others are more contradictory (wealthy but racially marginalised). Since resistance is a form of *jihad* in Islam, we can also think about the negotiations that pious Muslims confront regarding the complimentary or contradictory demands of the inward and outward struggles. As that one Hizbullah party supporter told me, faith and a certain kind of relationship with God means that you could love your enemies if they are being oppressed and challenge your brother even when he is being the oppressor. However, oppression is never that clear cut, always coming in multiple layers. All of us are guilty of oppression, against both humans and nature. Does that necessarily mean that we are all oppressors to be resisted? Or only occasionally so? What kind of oppression justifies resistance? Scott (2016) also asks what happens when a resistance identity triggers itself, thus reproducing its own resistance?

Discussions of intersectionality further articulate the problem. Leslie McCall (2005: 1771) describes intersectionality as 'the relationships among multiple dimensions and modalities of social relations and subject formations.' Kimberle Crenshaw (1989 and 1991) first popularised the term within the American academy, but Jennifer Nash (2008: 3) points out that black feminist scholarship had long supported the notion that identity is formed by the interrelated forces of race, gender, class and sexuality. Working from within the legal tradition, Crenshaw explains that her own objective is:

> to illustrate that many of the experiences black women face are not subsumed within the traditional boundaries of race or gender discrimination as these boundaries are currently understood, and that the intersection of racism and sexism factors into black women's lives in ways that cannot be captured wholly by looking at the race or gender dimensions of those experiences separately.
>
> (Crenshaw 1991: 1224)

Nevertheless, while the idea of intersectionality powerfully highlights the violence of identity categories in the law, Nash points out that: 'it has left activists struggling with balancing the efficiency of working "as women" or "as blacks" with the necessary attention to variation and diversity within "women" and "blacks"' (2008: 4). Her point is that the concept of intersectionality may unintentionally reify racial and gender categories that are the tools of an oppressive hegemony. She goes on to clarify that: 'Intersectionality's investment in "particularity" is evident in its investment in using black women's experience to problematise the rigid distinction between race and gender while maintaining a fundamental faith in both categories as meaningful, legible and coherent' (Nash 2011: 6).

The risk here is to alienate the wholeness of oppressed individuals. Also writing from the position as an African-American female lawyer, Wing explains that:

> We, as black women, can no longer afford to think of ourselves or let the law think of us as merely the sum of separate parts. The actuality of our layered experience is multiplicative. Multiply each of my parts together, one x one x one x one, and you have one indivisible being.
>
> (Wing 1990: 194)

Writing earlier, Patricia Williams anticipates this concern by conceptualising oppression 'as a capital moral offense', or something akin to what she calls 'spirit-murder' (1987: 129). This poetic framing elevates the potential devastation that racism and other forms of bigotry and social oppression wreak upon the human psyche: 'We need to see it as a cultural cancer; we need to open our eyes to the spiritual genocide it is wreaking on blacks, whites, and the abandoned and abused of all races and ages' (Williams 1987: 155). This framing resonates well with that of the Islamic resistance movement, which has built a conceptual framework capable of recognising cultural cancer and spiritual genocide, whereas Western secular modernity cannot. It is in this sense, above and beyond any other, that I argue the movement *is* decolonial.

But then where does this leave us in conceptualising resistance in everyday lives? We can argue that any resistance movement that is based on identity politics – including a subjectivity distinctly Islamic – is bound to alienate some, as we will see below. Nash argues that the love offered by African-American womanists like Alice Walker, June Jordan and Audre Lorde can act:

as a doing, a call for a labour of the self, an appeal for transcending
the self, a strategy for remaking the public sphere, a plea to unleash
the radical imagination and a critique of the state's blindness to the
violence it inflicts and enables.

(Nash 2011: 19)

For his part, Caygill is drawn to the efforts of the Zapatistas, a revolutionary leftist political movement based in Chiapas, Mexico: 'Their
enmity is to power itself, and their friendship is with and of resistance'
(2013: 187). While I am drawn to both selfless conceptions of love and
resistance, it is also wrong for me to centre a discussion of these aspirations in any one location. Is it possible for Shi'is in Lebanon to focus
on the struggle against oppression from a position that transcends the
self, in friendship, when the structures that oppress them are global?
Whatever answer any one person offers to this question, we must still
ask: what are the consequences of mobilising resistance according to
sectarian identity politics?

The limits of a sectarianism resistance

As noted above, the US-led invasion of Iraq continues to impact the
Middle East and beyond, having created 'an open sectarian wound'.
However, as Weiss (2010) notes, sectarianism is complex, involving institutions, politics and identities as much or even more than historicity.
According to Fanar Haddad (2013), some Shi'is in the Middle East today
have even embraced their religious Otherness, ultimately exacerbat-
ing this sectarian schism. Interviews in the field during February 2017
suggest that the civil–international war in Syria has only worsened this
problem. According to one Shi'i scholar, the Shi'i narratives of resistance
have gone deeper, embodying not only Imam Hussein and Sayyida
Zeinab, but all the figures of Ahl al-Bayt, or family of the Prophet
Muhammad. He explained that you can now hear this in their mourning
rituals. Even before the Arab uprisings, the resistance project's reliance
on sectarian figures as role models was problematic. Hussein and Zeinab
both suffered at the hands of Sunnis during the Battle of Karbala at a
time when the Muslim community was experiencing a cleavage, whereas
other Muslim women tend to look to the Prophet Muhammad's daughter
Fatima as a model, who is important to both Sunnis and Shi'is. Indeed,
the Iranian revolutionary thinker Ali Shari'ati even published a book of

lectures suggesting that Fatima is an Islamic role model.[4] Perhaps her importance to all Muslims, and not just Shi'is, is one of the reasons why Ayatollah Fadlallah also preferred to emphasise Fatima over Zeinab as an activist model for pious Muslim women. Similar to Grand Ayatollah Baqir al-Sadr in Iraq, who deliberately drew attention to Imam Ali, the Prophet's cousin and son-in-law, the goal was to choose an historical figure that could better unite the Sunnis and Shi'is.

There are other sectarian dimensions of the Islamic resistance movement. One typical criticism I heard from Hizbullah's opponents was that its sectarian provision of social services contributes to the weakening of the state. Shi'i and non-Shi'i members of one Beirut-based NGO, which identifies itself as 'secular and liberal', offered this critique during a meeting.[5] They expressed frustration that Shi'is were unwilling to participate in their own organisation's development programmes and blamed Hizbullah for creating a climate of fear. With the restrictions that I faced as an American researcher, unfortunately it was not possible for me to determine whether the resistance charities do, in fact, hold a monopoly on the provision of social services. Another NGO based in Saida, which is not affiliated with any religious sect and delivers various types of social services, did acknowledge to me that it could be possible for some organisations to face hostility from religious charities; however, they also stressed that their own work has become trusted and they recounted how they collaborated with Hizbullah to carry out the massive relief effort in response to the 2006 war against Israel.[6] They also told me that their organisation rarely receives any money from the Lebanese government because they work across sectarian lines; thus, it is not in any sectarian ministry's interests to help them. Explaining further, they recalled how back in 1958, an era that predates Hizbullah, the Archbishop of the Christian church created a successful social movement to assist disadvantaged Christians, but when trying to extend the network to the Muslim community the government opposed the movement's efforts.

Several Lebanese academics I met with also suggested that the Lebanese state prefers to support sectarian organisations, merely following the logic of the sectarian state. For example, Bassel Salloukh, a professor of political science at the Lebanese American University, questioned whether the state even wants to be a unified secular power.[7] When I asked the members of the Beirut-based organisation if the Lebanese state actively supports sectarianism, they too replied yes. However, if this were indeed the case, then blaming only Hizbullah for sectarianism would seem unjust. When I asked Dr Ali Fayyad about this topic, he told me that:

> We have a sectarian state here, and all the sects here are in alliance with somebody outside, on the relational level. What about the relationship between the Sunni and Saudi Arabia, what about the relationship between some Christians and Europe and France, and then what about our relations with Iran? I think this is the problem with the political regime in this country. And because our state is fragile and the state has failed, we need to substitute. We need to help people in solving their problems. For these reasons, we have to build hospitals, we have to establish Jihad al-Binaa institution, we have to establish the charities. But look, this is a transitional era. We need to shift to build a real state in this country. A non-sectarian state based on the concept of citizenship. No differences between the sects, I am talking at the political level. We don't mind to have social sectarianism. This is the freedom of the people. They have to believe in God or be secularists or be Marxists, these are their rights. But if we want to talk about the political system, about the state, this state must be neutral, not politicised, to be representative of the whole of Lebanese communities. And to be a real democratic state.[8]

Ironically, I was told that the fallout of the Syrian civil–international war has forced the resistance charities to become more open to dispel fears and meet the needs of refugees; a Lebanese Sunni colleague has cousins who send their children to Hizbullah schools.[9]

It is important to stress that the Imam al-Sadr Foundation is well regarded by many Lebanese, irrespective of sectarian affiliation. Indeed, many of my research contacts, including Christians, Sunni and Druze, spoke highly of the foundation's work. Furthermore, the foundation's emphasis on empowering women is notable and its chairperson, Rebab al-Sadr, is seen both as a role model for pious women and a strong promoter of women's rights. As she explains, 'when it comes to women's rights, God has given us our rights clearly in the Holy Qur'an, from an Islamic religious point of view our rights are given and it does equal men's rights and in some instances it is more.'[10] The vast majority of the foundation's employees are women, which was reflective in the composition of my research participants. As an employee in the Health Programme explained to me:

I think that the foundation is a great example of women's leadership and empowerment in the society. And this model, this example encourages more people, and projects itself more in the communities we are working with. For example, in our medical social centres, we have contractual doctors, but every centre is managed not by a doctor, but by an infirmary nurse.[11]

When I interviewed one of the female managers of the Orphanage Programme, she told me that she learned about the foundation as a young girl, and this inspired her to go into social work. Unfortunately, I was not granted similar access to the charities affiliated with Hizbullah and al-Mabarrat Association and thus cannot make a comparable assessment on their approach to gender, although I was told by a former employee of the latter that it also employs many women and invests in their professional training.[12]

Flanigan and Abdel-Samad (2009: 67–68) raise the possibility that Hizbullah could use social services to recruit sectarian militants, which is another common criticism of the resistance charities in Lebanon. The authors cite the existence of the Mahdi Scouts programme and how children march in Ashura parades wearing army fatigues. I attended one Hizbullah commemoration for the martyred leaders of the resistance, and one young child even had his face painted in camouflage.[13] The adult holding him raised him above his head proudly and international photographers swarmed to capture the image on film. However, it is important to recognise that children everywhere are often subject to problematic adult politics,[14] and boy scouts in the United States and elsewhere also wear military style uniforms and march in cadres in public ceremonies.[15] Indeed, it is not unusual for states and political movements to start preparing segments of the population to police and/ or protect their communities from a very young age. Hizbullah, after all, does police the streets, protect its communities and defend Lebanon in the same way as other armed forces. The militarisation of everyday lives can be critiqued on various levels, but in the case of Lebanon, it is not at all unusual for other sectarian parties to behave in similarly militant and sectarian ways.[16]

Other Lebanese are critical of the Islamic resistance movement simply because of its religious identity, mistrusting its recent pluralist turn. The party's revised manifesto, released in 2009, attempts to play down the Islamic goals of the party, instead focusing on its nationalist goals, stressing 'a unified Lebanon for all Lebanese alike' (Nasrallah 2009). I was in the Bekaa Valley shortly after the 2009 parliamentary elections and saw campaign banners for Hizbullah featuring the following three phrases, each one crossed out: 'Your Lebanon', 'Our Lebanon', and 'Their Lebanon'. Then, underneath in large green letters, was 'Lebanon' without any possessive markers.[17] During my discussions with party members, many also expressed a preference for living in a multicultural society. As Dr Fayyad explained,

> because we have diversity and we have pluralism, I think this will enrich our society, make it more beautiful, make it more creative. But this is on condition of us being successful in our coexistence here ... We need to be a positive diversity and not a fighting diversity.[18]

I also met many supporters of Hizbullah who are not Shi'is (including many communist atheists). Those who are non-religious still draw strength from the party's military resistance against Israel and its cultural

Figure 6.2   An election banner for Hizbullah in Baalbek, in the Bekaa Valley, which features the following three phrases, each one crossed out: 'Your Lebanon', 'Our Lebanon', and 'Their Lebanon'. Then, underneath in large green letters is the word 'Lebanon' without any possessive markers. Photograph taken during fieldwork in summer 2009.

resistance against imperialism, giving supporters a sense of beautiful pride. A 2012 article published by *al-Akhbar English* newspaper relates the story of one devoted supporter of Hizbullah who is a Christian Lebanese woman. Her love for Sayyid Hassan Nasrallah is so intense that she places a portrait of him with green and red background on top of her Christmas tree instead of a star (Merhi 2012). Zurayk also explains how the party's enemies are fearful of Hizbullah's ability to make all Arabs feel more empowered:

> the resistance had provided a revolutionary model of opposition to the dominant world order, a model that defied the long-established notion that the Arabs are a defeated nation. We understood that the resistance had been sentenced to death precisely because of that: Because it made the Arab people see ourselves differently, because it dispelled the clichéd image of the Arab as a vanquished people, and because it undermined the myth of the invincible Israeli–US alliance. In brief, the resistance gave us courage, self-respect, and hope.
>
> (Zurayk 2010: Kindle edn)

Over the years, Hizbullah has adjusted its ideas and practices, attempting to create an identity as a national resistance movement. Nevertheless, the party's military involvement in Syria has undoubtedly set these goals back years or even decades, and perhaps irreversibly. As the ICG reports, some Hizbullah members lump 'all Syrian rebels together as *takfiris* [people of the book who commit apostasy] and call its Lebanese and Syrian political opponents Israeli or Western agents, while saying its fight is non-sectarian' (2017: 4–5). Of course, reports that Israel has been collaborating with Syrian rebels for years do not help to de-escalate the use of such stigmatising rhetoric (Jones 2017).

The struggle for Syria

I was in Lebanon in December 2010 when a demoralised Tunisian street vendor named Mohamed Bouazizi doused himself in gasoline in protest over what he perceived as his abject degradation. The subsequent Tunisian uprising surprised many, even the Middle East journalists whom I was staying with in Beirut. Like so many people around the world, I was inspired by the events unfolding in Egypt, Yemen, Bahrain, Libya and Syria, where mass popular protests overwhelmed many urban centres. There were even a few anti-sectarian marches in Lebanon, one of which I attended in Beirut.[19] However, this movement soon fractured. On the one hand, Salloukh et al. (2015: 60) argue that NGO activists participating in the popular protests did so 'as individuals rather than as representatives of their own associations,' thus limiting the movement's organisational backbone. On the other, some protesters reportedly criticised the Amal movement after it officially encouraged its members to attend the marches, accusing it of hijacking the initiative (Wood 2011).

The struggle for Syria would prove the bloodiest and most divisive for the region. Robin Yassin-Kassab and Leila al-Shami (2016) provide a powerful account of the regime's inhumane violence against democracy activists both before and after the Syrian uprising began. There is no question about the brutality of the government under Bashar al-Assad; however, it is difficult to believe that the uprising could ever withstand becoming sectarian, despite the authors protestations, when taking into consideration the extremism that Nir Rosen (2010) experienced in the country and Thomas Pierret's (2013) work on the increasing religiosity of the Syrian population, despite its internal fragmentation, not to mention the conservativism of rural Syrians forced to migrate to the cities because of years of drought.[20] Many Syrian protestors undoubtedly wanted freedom for both themselves and their neighbours, but others were already precariously drawn into the messy sectarian regional conflict.

After the US-led invasion, among the Arab countries, Syria was the most welcoming to Iraqi refugees (also to the Lebanese during the 2006 war with Israel). In 2007, the United Nations estimated that around 1.2 million Iraqi refugees were living in Syria (Al-Miqdad 2008). According to Rosen, screeners from the UN 'reported seeing numerous victims of torture, detention, rape and kidnapping among newly arrived Iraqis. Most had family members who had been killed, and many were intellectuals' (2010: Kindle edn). Rosen also met with Salafi-Jihadists sheltering in Syria. This means that stories of sectarian horrors flowed into the country, while Salafi-Jihadist fighters flowed out. A Western diplomat told Rosen that: 'The Syrian government is very capable of managing those issues, but sectarianism was at its peak in the region, and Syria, which was once a major exporter of fighters to Iraq, may face its own blowback' (2010: Kindle edn). One political insider told me that the Iranians had also warned Bashar al-Assad that the Salafi-Jihadis freely crossing the borders would become a real problem.[21] The Syrian regime's viciousness against its own and its decision to shelter Iraqi extremists undoubtedly worsened the conflict significantly.

However, the regime is only one highly flawed actor in an incredibly messy conflict plagued by outside interference. The Syrian conflict is a human tragedy. Those Syrians who were bravely asking for a more democratic state in 2011 were soon overwhelmed by the new sectarian hatred of Others and were caught off guard by the negative implications of welcoming Arab and Western support for their cause. Of course, nothing justifies the brutality of the regime's initial response to their protests, but regional and international involvement has certainly made matters worse. Thus, Yassin-Kassab and al-Shami (2016: Kindle edn) are being disingenuous when claiming that, 'Nobody supported the revolutionaries.' While their support may have been ineffective, the American and British governments provided considerable financial and political assistance, with Western mainstream media largely propagating the opposition's demands. The Gulf states and Turkey also provided financial, political and logistical support. Indeed, the hegemonic narrative of the conflict remains one dominated by 'Syrian revolutionaries', despite the horrific situation for those living not only in Syria, but also in neighbouring Iraq and Lebanon. This has only played into the hands of those framing the conflict as an existential fight to defend the so-called resistance axis.

In hindsight, the collective euphoria over the Arab uprisings was probably short-sighted. Street protests may be inspiring to many, but they are not necessarily representative of societies. Furthermore, mass street mobilisations can also be used to justify terror, as in Egypt under the military regime of Abdel Fattah al-Sisi shows. Lila Abu-Lughod points out that: 'If the systems of power are multiple, then resisting at one level may catch people up at other levels' (1990: 53). When resisting one authority (e.g. the state), we may be unwittingly subordinating ourselves to another (e.g. interests that are imperialist, nationalist, capitalist or sectarian). Debord argued that modern neoliberal life is nothing but a collection of spectacles, where 'everything that was directly lived has receded into a representation' (1994: 1). In this way, mass street mobilisations become commodified into representing progressive democracy, but without delivering justice or equality.

Years later, the result of these uprisings has mostly been chaos, conflict and repression. Ironically enough, Lebanon is probably the most stable of those countries that experienced popular protest movements.[22]

Yemen, Libya and Syria are all experiencing civil–international wars, while Egypt and Bahrain are more authoritarian than ever. Despite the promising transfer of power in Tunisia, in 2015, the country suffered from Salafi-Jihadi attacks in the cities of Tunis (BBC 2015b) and Sousse (Elgot 2015); and Tunisian nationals were reportedly responsible for similar attacks in the European cities of Berlin and Nice (Macdonald and Waggoner 2017). In spring 2017, disaffected youths in the southern region of Tunisia shut down a major oil pumping station in protest of local poverty and unemployment, claiming that this was the country's 'second revolution' (Gall 2017).

Furthermore, Tunisia's crackdown on Salafism merely pushed the extremists further east (Al Jazeera 2014). Tunisia is thought to have exported the highest number of foreign fighters to Iraq and Syria – by February 2017, an estimated 7,000 Tunisians had joined ISIS. This comprises a significant proportion of its foreign fighters; in 2016, the United Nations estimated that they numbered approximately 30,000, in total, across Iraq and Syria (Kroet 2016). However, it is impossible to know exactly how many ISIS fighters there are, either foreign or national – estimated numbers range from 40,000 to 200,000. Berger and Morgan (2015: 7–12) identified 46,000 'overt ISIS supporter accounts' on Twitter during 2015, with the largest cluster of location-enabled accounts (28 per cent) found in Iraq and Syria, followed by Saudi Arabia (27 per cent). Meanwhile, the British government estimated in 2015 that there were about 20,000 Syrian fighters among the Western-backed Free Syrian Army, in addition to 45,000 'other moderate' opposition fighters (Lister 2015). Taking into consideration these varying estimations, Iraq and Syria are clearly suffering messy civil–international wars that are difficult to make sense of. In both countries, the governments and opposition are committing atrocities, causing massive bloodshed and displacement.

Over the course of my main stretch of fieldwork, I became increasingly alarmed by Hizbullah's overt support for the Syrian government while it was brutally attacking opposition activists; after all, resistance is about fighting oppression, not one's neighbours. After the tragic loss of life during the Palestinian Nakba commemorations in May 2011,[23] there was a ceremony in July of that year at the Mar Elias camp in Beirut for the 14 Palestinians from Lebanon and Syria who were martyred.[24] Both party and religious leaders gave speeches; and mostly Palestinian and Lebanese flags were waved. However, flags of the Syrian Socialist National Party (SSNP), a secular party closely aligned with Hizbullah and the Syrian government, were also present. And at the end of the event, there was a procession of youths carrying Syrian flags along with pictures of Syrian President Bashar al-Assad. As 2011 progressed into 2012, I observed that political participation in Hizbullah's solidarity events for Palestine was gradually reduced to the SSNP and Palestinian groups like Islamic Jihad and the Popular Front for the Liberation of Palestine General Command, both of which have remained loyal to the Syrian regime throughout recent years.

To my dismay, this level of partisanship was not uncommon. The regionalisation of the Syrian conflict also destroyed a vibrant global activist movement for Palestine launched in 2010 and led by diaspora Palestinians alongside an international committee, of which I was a member. On the one side, there were those who supported the Muslim Brotherhood, Hamas and the opposition in Syria; and on the other, those more ideologically aligned with Hizbullah, Iran and the Syrian regime.[25] The political fallout in March 2012 was ugly and speaks to recent developments across the Middle East. After the US-led coalition toppled the regime of Saddam Hussein in 2003, Iraqi Shi'is adopted a decidedly majoritarian attitude towards governing, marginalising Iraqi Sunnis. The Muslim Brotherhood in Egypt embraced a similarly arrogant interpretation of governing after the fall of Hosni Mubarak in 2011, ultimately giving the army a seemingly popular mandate to topple the democratically elected government of Mohammad Morsi in July 2013. The global movement for Palestine was no different: after the fallout, Shi'is were excluded from leadership roles, which were instead allocated to Muslim Brotherhood sympathisers regardless of desire or merit. I witnessed some particularly ugly rhetoric against Shi'is coming from the movement's leadership. And in June 2013, a group of Pakistani Shi'is, who were dedicated activists for Palestine, were not allowed to participate in the global movement's annual celebrations in the Gaza Strip.[26]

All of this demonstrates that shit really is complicated. And not just in the Middle East, but everywhere. The Western secular liberal project, with its affiliated anthropologies of logic and rationality, does not reflect realities anywhere (Crehan 2002).[27] And yet, this framework continues to bias Western-based scholars doing research in non-Western contexts. Despite most foreign analyses, the majority of Lebanese Shi'is, even non-believers on the left, now appear to be relatively supportive of Hizbullah's military involvement in Syria.[28] This is not to say that the party has not lost support; it certainly has.[29] A former leader of Hizbullah,

Sheikh Subhi al-Tufayli, has been an outspoken critic of its intervention.[30] One critical Shi'i told me that the party has lost some legitimacy: 'First, it was the occupation, okay. But now Syria? What next? What is to be resisted? And then what next?'[31] At the same time, one Shi'i political insider explained that Shi'is feel the existential threat very deeply, especially after a car bombing in Dahiyeh that injured around 53 in July 2013 and a suicide attack the next month that killed at least 25 (ICG 2017: 11). Another Shi'i scholar argued that Hizbullah's role in Syria has been positive because if the pro-Salafi strand could establish control, this would be the death of the resistance.[32] One Shi'i journalist was even more candid: 'ISIS is only a one and a half hour drive away from Dahiyeh, and so of course Hizbullah had to go there to fight.' He added that if they had not gone, ISIS would now be in control of Dahiyeh.[33]

When I had left the field back in 2012, the public mood was less defiant. But the growing sectarianism, the emergence of ISIS, al-Qaeda and the bombings inside of Lebanon have all had an impact. While Lebanon's left initially faced internal attacks for supporting the Syrian uprising (Cassel 2011b), the leftist international debate marginalised Lebanese voices. When pushed on the possibility that the Syrian regime was, in fact, using chemical weapons against civilians, one Hizbullah member expressed frustration that they were always seen to be the guilty party, even without evidence. A Shi'i writer and activist also pointed out that anti-Iraq war protesters were never accused of being pro-Saddam Hussein, as is the case with those against foreign intervention in Syria. Meanwhile, when supporters of the Syrian opposition are asked which groups do you support, he complained that they never answer and instead always go back to being against Bashar al-Assad.[34] The reality is a lot more complicated. The latest iteration of al-Qaeda in Syria, Tahrir al-Sham, is now possibly the most powerful armed opposition group in Syria (Lister 2017). Another major militia, Ahrar al-Sham, part of the Islamist/Salafist rebel spectrum, refused to unite with Tahrir al-Sham, but the two have fought together before and share extremist views. According to Steinberg:

> the Ahrar leadership uses the negative term 'Nazarenes' (*nasrani*) – which is popular among Salafists – to describe Christians, rather than the usual Arabic *masihi*. Alawites and Shiites are dismissed as *nusairi* and *rafida* … Ahrar regards the fight against Asad and the Syrian Alawites as a 'holy war' against the expansion of Shi'i Islam and

Tehran's supposed plan to create a Shi'i state extending from Palestine through Lebanon, Syria and Iraq to Iran.

(Steinberg 2016: 2)

He adds that Ahrar al-Sham's fighters have committed brutality against minority civilians, refused to condemn ISIS and continue to have sympathies with al-Qaeda (Steinberg 2016: 2).

So, while almost everybody I spoke to in February 2017 expressed some degree of support for the initial protests in Syria and/or antipathy towards Bashar al-Assad, even Hizbullah party members, they argue that groups like ISIS, al-Qaeda, Tahrir al-Sham and Ahrar al-Sham, through support from Turkey and the Gulf states, hijacked the Syrian uprising. Meanwhile, reports suggest that many Syrian refugees in Lebanon willingly voted for Bashar al-Assad (AP 2014; and Atassi 2014). Interestingly, despite Hizbullah's military involvement, all three Shi'i movements have programmes supporting Syrian refugees in Lebanon, regardless of their sectarian affiliation.[35] Dr Martha Mundy, a professor emeritus at the London School of Economics who is currently living in southern Lebanon, explained that Hizbullah's policy has been to support the refugees, for example, by giving them medical treatment. Of course, the party is careful and keeps a watchful eye over the refugees, but it also provides generous aid.[36] The ICG (2017: 10) fully corroborates this account.

In the early stages of the Syrian conflict, Hizbullah kept its military involvement a secret, with a senior Hizbullah official telling the ICG in 2012:

we know that our decision [to intervene] would turn some people against us. However, we don't take decisions based on how popular they are, but on a clear vision and consistent principles. When we stood against the [US] occupation in Iraq, Iraqi Shi'is opposed us. Yes, popular support is important, but not at any cost.

(ICG 2017: 2–3)

However, the party would soon publicly justify sending its military forces into Syria to protect the Sayyida Zeinab shrine in Damascus. The shrine has an important political and religious significance for Shi'is, something that Salafi-Jihadis condemn as unIslamic (hence their tendency to attack shrines). And as Szanto (2013: 81) points out, the Sayyida Zeinab shrine is normally under the authority of the Supreme Leader of Iran, Ali Khamenei, with Hizbullah providing daily management.

My last visit to Lebanon in February 2017 helped me to understand Hizbullah's involvement in Syria more as a loving stranger,[37] because research participants articulated a completely decentred narrative that unexpectedly resonated with my humanness. Sharmine Narwani, an independent American-Iranian journalist living in Beirut with her family, explained that today's struggle is about self-determination and looking for indigenous solutions to contemporary local problems. She too expressed frustration that the conflict in Syria has been so polarising within the international left, denying people in the region any voice to contextualise their positions. Until now, I myself have largely refrained from saying anything publicly about Syria, mostly out of fear, despite participating in the first meeting of a civil society initiative organised by anti-imperialist colleagues in Europe that brought together Syrians from all sides of the conflict willing to engage in non-official talks at Schlaining Castle, south of Vienna.[38] But it is one thing for me as an American to self-censor on this conflict; for those directly experiencing the conflict to feel silenced is not right.

Narwani explained that human security, not human rights, is currently the major organising principle in the Middle East. The Islamic resistance movement knows the region, the people and that the fight is existential. As another journalist also pointed out, it was Hizbullah's intervention that stopped the wave of attacks which hit Beirut in 2013. Hassan Sakr, head of foreign affairs for the SSNP, told me that his party has always called for more freedom and democracy in Syria, but is currently fighting alongside Hizbullah in Syria to protect diversity in the Middle East, citing the sectarian aims of the Salafi-Jihadists.[39] Narwani even referenced developments in international law, known as the right to protect, to justify Hizbullah's intervention. And why not? Yes, anti-war activists will protest this framework with good reason, but when this 'universal right' has been brutally claimed by some for political purposes, why should others not try to reclaim the concept? Narwani stressed that efficiency is Hizbullah's primary characteristic; the party abides by international law but without worrying about what Western powers think. However, the resistance is engaged in an existential struggle, thus they are still in a reactive mode, fighting for their survival. But as a Shi'i writer and activist added, Hizbullah is confident, flexible and dynamic, which continuously influences their strategies socially, politically and militarily.

Figure 6.3 A musical performance to commemorate the Syrian Socialist Nationalist Party's martyrs in the civil–international war in Syria. Photograph taken in Beirut during winter 2017.

The limits of a liberal resistance

Although many outside observers argue that Hizbullah's involvement in Syria will be its downfall, critical Shi'is are more concerned about the party compromising its values and principles by participating in corrupt political and economic systems. Some scholars have framed Hizbullah's political pragmatism positively (Saad-Ghorayeb 2002; Hamzeh 2004; Harb and Leenders 2005; Harik 2005; Alagha 2006; and Norton 2014); but others have critiqued the party for ideologically going too far towards the West (Abisaab 2006; and Marei 2016). While Lebanese politics has witnessed turbulence in recent decades, Hizbullah's political power has grown, and yet neoliberalism has remained unchallenged and political corruption continues. In 2009, the Lebanese investor Salah Ezzedine was charged with fraud after his billion-dollar pyramid scheme collapsed. Many Lebanese Shi'is had trusted him with their life savings because of his connections to Hizbullah members, and the party was forced to set up 'a "crisis network" to assess each investor's losses' (Worth 2009). Furthermore, the situation for Palestinian refugees in Lebanon remains as hopeless as ever: they are still denied basic civil rights such as owning property, employment and freedom of movement.[40]

All three Shi'i movements tend to converge in relation to their economic policy, because, to varying degrees, all their charities promote liberal economic ideas and practices that are related to empowerment, capacity building and self-sufficiency, even though their work is also mediated by faith, religious rationality and the community. So, in a sense, these charities have merely re-mystified today's liberal economic norms.[41] This is a process of economic reform rather than revolution, even if the reforms challenge neoliberalism similar to other social democratic trends. Activists refer to this kind of counter-movement as 'non-reformist reforms', which Hahnel explains are 'reforms that improve people's lives while undermining the material, social, or ideological underpinnings of the capitalist system' (2005). When I raised the issue of economic policy with Dr Ali Fayyad, he said:

> If you would like to analyse the theoretical background of [Hizbullah's] economic approach, I think you will find it close to the social democratic government and parties. And we defended the Keynesian state – the worker's state. I mean that we are not against the liberal economic system, but we are strongly against neoliberalism. We are caring about the poor people in the remote countries and we have to safeguard the social guarantees with the necessary systems, institutions, procedures and policies. The neoliberal policy says it is not necessary for the state to help the poor people. The state must just work in legislation and the market will organise itself, but this is not true. We are not ready to accept that. The state must work to balance the markets and to distribute the interest of economics.

Thus, once again, we see a pragmatic willingness to work within the dominant framework – a capitalist market economy governed by liberalism – despite the strong anti-capitalist discourse of Hizbullah's political manifesto. Perhaps this is partly because economics is subordinate to the political goals of the resistance charities. As Dr Fayyad further explained:

> Here in Lebanon, the Shi'i charities are parts of our battery against the occupation and the external challenges. Because our society, or Hizbullah and the Amal movement, and all the Shi'i movements, they

believe we need a strong society to win our war against the occupation. From this point of view, there is a revolutionary dimension to these charities. There is a resistant dimension to these charities. We don't mind for the poor people to be rich, but this is not the cause of these charities.

On the other hand, the Imam al-Sadr Foundation's cause is a more enchanted conception of liberalism. In other words, the wider political project of the foundation diverges from that of the resistance charities affiliated with Hizbullah and al-Mabarrat Association, and hence the deliberate distancing, even though there is a considerable overlap in their embrace of faith, religion and the liberal market economy.

We can understand this better by thinking of Gramsci's notion of 'common sense'. Economic liberalism is one set of ideas among many in Lebanon that competing blocs can transform by articulating them in particular ways. Thus, while the foundation is employing the same liberal economic framework as the resistance charities, referencing the same ideas, it does so to realise a very different political goal. The resistance charities see economic empowerment as a means to strengthen the resistance, whereas for the foundation, enchanted liberal development is the end. The foundation is promoting a liberalised version of the resistance society in Lebanon not to better resist, but to empower people as individuals in a reformed capitalist system. However, combining these sometimes-contradictory goals – openly working within the global liberal economic system while also resisting against its local social contradictions – ultimately creates certain tensions in the foundation's work.

One contradiction is that while the Imam al-Sadr Foundation partners with neoliberal international aid organisations, it refuses to engage in exploitative capitalist practices locally. This means that the foundation will not consider raising local revenue through profitable ventures that contradict its particular vision, even if this would deliver more financial resources to expand its services. As Nijad Charafeddine, head of the Income Generating Programme told me, although others keep raising the prospect 'to create or to build gas stations, actually I'm always against this, because it's not in our culture.'[42] Al-Mabarrat Association owns a petrol station in Beirut that raises a considerable amount of money to support its vast charitable network. Assaha Village also operates 'franchise' hotels in Sudan and the United Kingdom, and restaurants and event spaces in Iraq, Kuwait, Qatar, Sudan and the United

Kingdom.[43] But although the Imam al-Sadr Foundation is resisting the exploitative capitalist practices embraced by the resistance community within Lebanon, it is uncritically embracing the exploitative neoliberal ideas of the international aid community, which as we shall see below, could potentially bleed into its own practices.

The dangers of capitalism and neoliberalism

The last line of critique I want to address centres on all three Shi'i movements' quiet embrace of capitalism and/or neoliberalism. As noted above, Al-Mabarrat Association owns capital in the form of a petrol station. I was told that it is the most successful petrol station in Lebanon because people were sick of elites and corruption and felt they could trust its prices and services.[44] However, can there ever be ethical petrol in today's world? Daher (2016) responds to a similar line of questioning, critiquing the political economy of Hizbullah more generally as both capitalist and neoliberal. But while Daher raises several valuable critiques of the party's approach to Lebanon's political economy, he occasionally relies on questionable sources that are pro-Israel, Islamophobic or anti-Hizbullah to support his argument.[45] Another problem is that he speaks in depth of the party's charities without recognising this to be an alternative model to neoliberal capitalism. Furthermore, he frequently does not contextualise the environment in which Hizbullah's policies prove controversial. For example, he calls out party officials' decision to support the privatisation of Lebanon's electricity supply (Daher 2016: 57–58), without explaining that electricity has been rationed in Lebanon for many years. Currently, most Lebanese experience only 10–12 hours of electricity each day.[46] So, while the decision to privatise electricity is indeed in line with neoliberal capitalism, the status quo in Lebanon is untenable for human dignity. Furthermore, what alternatives exist in a society where the politics of sectarianism make state-owned resources inefficient?

The question of what possible alternatives could exist plagues anti-imperialists more generally, including the Islamic resistance movement in Lebanon. According to one Shi'i journalist and party supporter, while Sayyid Hassan does set the perfect example for living a non-materialistic life, Lebanese society, including the Shi'is, is still not ready for this kind of asceticism.[47] In order to get there, he thinks that Lebanese society first needs some kind of 'mental revolution' away from favouring materialism, for example, their extreme attachment to clothes, mobile phones and cars, to prioritising faith.[48] He laughingly recounted a story about how when he was thinking of buying a car, one of his close relatives who is very pious told him to buy an American-made Jeep, because the trend in Lebanon was to buy Jeeps, and not cars. That said, the same journalist does believe that Shi'i ideas and practices are currently responding to this need for a 'mental revolution' by offering an alternative social project, one which develops more community oriented and critical thinkers, although there are still more changes that first must happen before this project can be truly realised.

Other potential supporters of the resistance project are questioning whether the movement has become too entrenched in the capitalist system. Deeb and Harb find that some Shi'a of the vanguard generation – those who chose to publicly embrace their religion when Shi'i was an identity of inferiority – 'find both the wealth in the newfound community and the consumption practices of youths disturbing' (2013: 59). As one young Shi'i Marxist explained to me, before the assassination of former Prime Minister Rafik Hariri in 2005, the political alliance between the Sunnis and Shi'is meant that Hizbullah was permitted to keep its arms in exchange for agreeing to Sunni dominance over the economy. Therefore, the party was barely enmeshed in the domestic capitalist system, instead receiving money from Iran, remittances from emigrants and subsidies from the government. However, the situation has now changed and the areas that are strongholds of the resistance are now becoming capitalist.[49]

Today in Beirut's southern suburbs and in the south, there are numerous Western corporations. In the south, banners of Imam al-Sadr and Ayatollah Khomeini compete with advertisements for American companies like Kentucky Fried Chicken, with slogans like 'finger lickin' good' printed in English, selling an Americanised version of what fast food is. Some believe that the party allowed for these businesses to open in Shi'i-dominated areas so that Shi'is would not have to travel elsewhere to consume such products, thus keeping the community more tightly knit. However, the young Marxist told me that he does not support Hizbullah because the party focuses too much on armed struggle rather than coming up with new economic frameworks based on Islamic or traditional principles that value the society and the people. Dr Fayyad also suggested that this was a weak point for Islamic movements everywhere, because 'they are not concerned enough about the economic issues.'[50] Perhaps the newly emerging sphere of Islamic entertainment is attempting to do this, with places like Assaha Village. However, Harb (2006: 11) also asks whether this kind of pious entertainment is 'losing its moral authority and legitimacy by accepting the market logic of consumption?' The building of a luxury spa in recent years at Assaha in southern Beirut is one example of this type of concern.

Still, the discourse that Hizbullah employs remains strongly anti-capitalist and spirituality could potentially shape future conceptions of commodities. Research participants I engaged with are highly critical of neoliberalism; and Hizbullah's 2009 political manifesto speaks against 'savage capitalist forces' (Nasrallah 2009). According to Alleik, the general director of Jihad al-Binaa, the party ultimately aimed to confront neoliberalism, because:

> Such policies concentrate economic wealth and consolidate political power within a small fraction of the population at the expense of the great majority. They impoverish the poor and enrich the wealthy. Poverty will affect hundreds of thousands of households. Our strategies aim to create new outlets for local production and dignified job opportunities. Our ultimate objective is to safeguard the dignity of the working class. Our work brings economic autonomy to people, which directly translates into political autonomy. Local politics in Lebanon are a mask for profiteering and personal interests: the country's politicians and leaders are essentially businessmen and businesswomen who are not genuinely concerned with the public good. They want the population to engage in the endless pursuit of dollars and cents, to wake up, to labour, to go to the bar, to sleep then wake up again like automatons and modern slaves. One is forbidden from having control over one's economic destiny, political identity and the freedom to choose.
>
> (Atalla and Alleik 2008)

Alleik expresses a desire for Shi'is to become economically and politically independent. However, many Lebanese continue to discriminate against Shi'is, considering them second-class citizens. This means that discouraging Shi'is from embracing the dominant materialist trends in Lebanon, where consumerism is linked to self-worth, will be even more difficult when money can buy an economic status that is otherwise denied to them. Another problem is that local consumption in Lebanon is largely sustained through remittances from lucrative businesses in

Africa, North America and Latin America. This helps Shiʻis to finance the building of large houses, even mansions, throughout southern Lebanon, sending a powerful message to Israel that the supporters of the resistance are thriving and not retreating. However, the exploitation that is needed to sustain this lifestyle, and which is counter to the ideology of the resistance, is not visible from Lebanon.

Meanwhile, the Imam al-Sadr Foundation faces another set of tensions: those arising from an increasing engagement with neoliberal international partners. These tensions are evident in its 2004 publication called *The Arabic Glossary of Development Terms*, sponsored by the World Bank and the United Nations Economic and Social Commission for Western Asia. The publication is divided into various sections, consisting of but not limited to community development, environment, gender, human development and empowerment, human rights, international conventions, microfinance, management, and public finance and economy. The glossary is quite comprehensive and many of the terms that are defined are in line with the neoliberal ideology, which places the regulatory responsibility on the individual or private sector rather than the state. A small selection of these terms includes: comparative risk analysis, cluster evaluation, demand assessment, deliverables, free trade zone, good governance, human capital, incentive, institutional development, intellectual copyright, market failure, performance indicator, risk assessment, stakeholders analysis, strategic framework and transparency. However, the publication also defines other important terms that challenge or nuance the neoliberal project, such as: collective rights, commodification, fordism, gender studies, labour relations, Orientalism, participatory research, semiotics, subaltern, and third way, as well as key Islamic economic concepts. Thus, while the neoliberal terminology dominates this publication, the inclusion of these latter terms still leaves open the possibility for creating an altered interpretation of the dominant neoliberal framework.

Similar tensions are evident elsewhere. In 2011, the Imam al-Sadr Foundation was the recipient of pro-bono work by Booz & Company,[51] a massive US-based firm that provides global management consulting.[52] The company, working through Lebanon's Central Bank, provided recommendations for the foundation as a Corporate Social Responsibility service; however, it completely disregarded the role of religion or faith, ultimately secularising the foundation by excluding any reference at all to its Islamic character, and instead directing it even closer towards neoliberalism. For example, the strategic objectives include focusing on an 'innovative service portfolio targeted' to women by both expanding and reconfiguring the services currently offered; establishing visibility through 'strong brand recognition'; and seeking peer recognition as 'a pioneer, innovative, high-impact, and thought leader (awards, professional recognition, peer benchmarking, etc.)'. Other recommendations include a formal rationalisation of the foundation by creating a hierarchy of specialists under a chief executive officer and separating the income generating programmes as a distinct commercial organisation; empowering the board of directors to oversee 'cooperate governance' as well as planning and management; and focusing more attention on performance-based outcomes, for example, the employment prospects of beneficiaries. The 'execution roadmap' for achieving these recommendations includes a five-year strategic plan for the foundation and three-year plans for the various 'business units' the consultancy had designated.

Although the foundation did not solicit these recommendations, I was told that it has taken most of them seriously, implementing a new human resources department to better the management practices at the foundation. These changes will undoubtedly appeal to its existing funders like the World Bank and USAID.[53] However, the foundation's insistence on incorporating faith into its ideas and practices, its keen interest in sustainable development, which applies equally to people, planet and profit (Charafeddine 2008), and its history of participatory practices also suggest that any fundamental changes to its operations would probably need to be acceptable not only to its funders, but also to the people on the ground, as well as the foundation's employees.

Conclusion

Since Orientalist narratives continue to frame the Islamic resistance movement in Lebanon, it is not often critically engaged with it on its own terms. In this book, I have attempted to understand the movement from within, while also acknowledging that even loving strangers sometimes fail to understand. Nevertheless, I hope that this approach brings us closer to knowing each other. While we all face similar struggles in today's world – we are limited by fear, uncertainty, isolation, illness and death – imperialist dynamics continue to influence our knowledge of ourselves and others. Furthermore, Shi'is in Lebanon still face discrimination both domestically and abroad, despite becoming quite powerful politically and economically. Like the rest of us, Lebanese Shi'is also suffer from their own human failings, and the Islamic resistance movement is no exception. Reflecting on my many years of research, and perhaps influenced by the time I have recently spent working and living in post-apartheid South Africa, I feel even more of a stranger in Lebanon, even though I now also better understand some of the struggles facing the Islamic resistance movement.

Hopefully, in this book I have been able to at least achieve the following: to communicate, in new ways, how Islamic movements in Lebanon are entangling faith and rationality in their ideas and practices of charity in an effort to create a resistance society to empower their communities; to highlight how these movements are building on the work of revolutionary religious activists in the mid-twentieth century who incorporated Marxist ideas into religious ideologies to craft theologies of liberation; and to illustrate how a shared faith creates a commitment between humans, where religious rationality shapes the guiding principles of these movements in their negotiation with secular liberalism, all the while challenging Orientalism, imperialism and some aspects of secularism, and selectively embracing liberalism.

Critically stepping back to review this radical social project, how can we characterise the Islamic resistance movement? What can we learn from adopting a decolonial approach to understanding it and other theologies of liberation? How can we assess revolutionary movements within any historical moment when the world is messy and full of inter-secting layers of injustice and the contradicting struggles against them? How can we know which struggles to prioritise when the act of choosing necessarily excludes other struggles?

The first two questions are easier for me to answer, and so this is where I will begin. Critically reflecting, I think the Islamic resistance movement is a flawed emancipatory project based on Islamic liberation theology and the marginalised socio-political context of Lebanese Shi'is. As discussed in Chapter 6, the movement can be critiqued for being too sectarian and for prioritising political and economic power over maintaining its resistance ideology. However, unlike the African National Congress in South Africa and the Palestine Liberation Organi-zation, the Islamic resistance movement does have a coherent decolonial ideology. The movement's strong challenge to Western secular liberalism is apparent when deconstructing its conceptual framework and social realities, which are primarily centred around faith, religious rationality and a resistance subjectivity.

While the Islamic resistance movement may be inconsistent in its attempts to apply this decolonial ideology in a complex, unequal and yet interconnected world, there is enough coherence and consistency within this conceptual framework and its practical realisation to make it sensible in a human world that will always be incoherent and inconsist-ent, but which can also make enough sense to prevail. Only by adopting a decolonial approach to the Islamic resistance movement, where faith and love are openly embraced in the process of our human efforts to understand others and construct knowledge, do religious rationality and loving strangers become revolutionary agents that widen decolonial horizons, expanding the possibilities for realising a more just world. This approach also allows for a less politicised evaluation of the differ-ences between the competing Shi'i movements in Lebanon, illustrating that decoloniality can take on many forms. While the Imam al-Sadr Foundation may distance itself from the resistance charities, it shares similar decolonial aspirations.

That said, ideology must always be measured against political realities. The Islamic resistance movement still has a lot of uncom-fortable inconsistencies to account for. For example, Hizbullah and the Syrian regime are allies in the struggle against Zionist expansion. But looking at recent history, critics correctly point out that the Syrian regime's anti-Israel stance is mostly rhetorical, with a ceasefire holding in the occupied Golan Heights since 1974 (Yassin-Kassab and al-Shami 2016). On the other hand, Hizbullah waged armed resistance to remove Israel's occupation from southern Lebanon; but Lebanese also suffered from Israeli aggression in 2006, with some blaming Hizbullah. At the same time, the Syrian government grants Palestinian refugees almost the same rights as Syrian citizens, even though they are denied citizenship, whereas the Lebanese government denies Palestinian refugees not only citizenship but also the most basic of civil rights. The situation for Palestinians living in Lebanon has not significantly changed since 2011 when Hizbullah joined the government coalition (UNHCR 2016). How can a resistance party participate in a government that forces Palestinians to live in such degrading conditions?

At the time of writing, sectarian struggles continue to destabilise the region. Nevertheless, new divisions and alliances continue to emerge, with a major cleavage now rocking the Sunni Arab world: in June 2017, Saudi Arabia and the neighbouring Gulf monarchies decided to blockade Qatar, demanding that the small peninsula nation, also governed by a monarchy, cut off ties with Iran, the Muslim Brotherhood in Egypt and Hamas in the Gaza Strip, sparking a diplomatic crisis (Wintour 2017). This spiteful policy only appears to be pushing Qatar and Turkey closer to Iran (Jafari 2017). But whatever the result of these recent policies, the dangers of sectarianism today are very real. In the present-day context of the conflicts in Syria, Iraq and Yemen, where Sunnis and Shi'is are caught up in a violent confrontation fuelled by regional and international players, a sectarian critique of the resistance project in Lebanon is perhaps most relevant. Frantz Fanon was remarkably sceptical towards the Islamic character of revolutionary struggles. In his correspondence with Ali Shari'ati, Fanon wrote:

I respect your view that in the Third World (and if you don't mind, I would prefer to say in the Near and Middle East), Islam, more than any other social and ideological force, has had an anti-colonialist capacity and an anti-Western nature ... I, for one, fear that the fact of revitalising the spirit of sectarianism and religion may result in a setback for a nation that is engaged in the process of becoming, of distancing itself from its future and immobilising it in its past.

(quoted in Hudis 2015: Kindle edn)

However, is it even possible to ignore the spiritual importance of faith and religion when trying to imagine a new Fanonian humanism – one which does not repeat the violence of Western secular modernity? Are sectarian political movements inherently exclusivist, or can they appeal across religious boundaries? Because the irony of a strictly sectarian theology of liberation is that if there truly is a God, she *must prefer none and love us all equally*. But if so, is it possible for there to be a decolonial theology of liberation in today's world?

By drawing parallels between the projects of Christian, Islamic and other theologies of liberation, we can create a stronger critical framework to imagine decolonial possibilities. In every case, we can ask from which position are these movements starting, and to where are they going? Analysing the transformation of Malcolm X's political thought, in particular, provides important insights. Although best known for his work in raising the black consciousness of African-Americans, towards the end of his life Malcolm X started gravitating more towards a more anti-capitalist framework for human emancipation – an unfinished project (Ramadan 2013). For example, when Malcolm X (2007: 44) visited the Middle East and Africa in 1959, he told his biographer that he 'was trying to internationalise our problem', adding that he wanted:

> to make the Africans think, feel their *kinship* with us Afro-Americans. I made them *think* about it, that they are our blood brothers, and we all come from the same foreparents. That's why the Africans loved me, the same way the Asians loved me because I was religious.
>
> (Malcolm X 2007: 44)

The day Malcolm was assassinated, he also spoke about the importance of unity among those who have been historically oppressed. Only minutes before his assassination, Malcolm X reportedly told his assistant:

> I'm going to ease some of this tension [in the African American community] by telling the black man not to fight himself – that's all a part of the White man's manoeuvre, to keep us fighting among ourselves, against each other.
>
> (Malcolm X 2007: 71)

Malcolm's efforts to unify African-Americans and move towards Third Worldism during the final years of his life show how he turned away from personal enhancement and moved towards humanity. As Clasby explained: 'Malcolm had abandoned power for spirit, force for leadership which drew others to it and engendered love. In the mirror of Malcolm's concern, the oppressed could see themselves as valuable' (1988: 182). Continuing this political struggle facing certain death, some have even likened him to Imam Hussein (Morrow 2012).

In his biography of Malcolm X, Marable (2011) picked up on this theme of transformation, what he called reinvention.[1] As he summarised:

Malcolm's journey of reinvention was in many ways centred on his lifelong quest to discern the meaning and substance of faith … Malcolm came to adopt true Islam's universalism, and its belief that all could find Allah's grace regardless of race. Islam was also the spiritual platform from which he constructed a politics of Third World revolution.

(Marable 2011: 12)

Unlike the integrationist story told in Malcolm X's autobiography, however, Marable is more nuanced. As he detailed, Malcolm X's journey was full of contradictions, including a willingness to speak with the Ku Klux Klan and an abusive attitude towards women. Furthermore, not all Muslims are colour blind. And while Malcolm admitted that his 'racial philosophy' was altered after all he had seen during his 1964 Hajj pilgrimage, where he encountered 'thousands of people of different races and colours who treated [him] as a human being' (Marable 2011: 319), and thus started to embrace a unified black struggle for civil rights in the Unites States, he also continued to remain deeply sceptical of white power and increasingly critiqued racial exploitation under capitalism. As Malcolm X remarked towards the end of his life: 'It's impossible for a white person to believe in capitalism and not believe in racism' (Marable 2011: 336). At the same time, however, he 'continued to emphasise the development of black-owned businesses in black communities' (Marable 2011: 337).

In my view, Malcolm X's questions and suspicion were and are necessary – the hermeneutic circle depends on having both. Further-more, Malcolm X's mission went beyond seeking political rights for African-Americans; it was a much greater political project, a quest to decolonise minds. Malcolm X observed that: 'Separation is not the goal of the African-American, nor is integration the goal. They are merely methods to his real end – respect as a human being' (Marable 2011: 319). Both methods have social consequences, but only the latter is decolonial. Since the end goal – respecting all humans – has not been fully realised under Western secular liberalism, including its accompanying notions of multiculturalism and tolerance, exclusivist emancipatory movements may still be necessary in the struggle for humanity. As Clasby notes, 'the goal of liberation is the creation of a new level of consciousness capable of synthesising opposites and of transforming the existing order' (1988: 178). This ultimately is a mutually transformative process, as Taylor (1994) calls for. Because challenging the coloniality of being is required for human freedom, as Fanon argued:

> By appealing, therefore, to our humanity – to our feelings of dignity, love, and charity – it would be easy to prove and have acknowledged that the black man is equal to the white man. But that is not our purpose. What we are striving for is to liberate the black man from the arsenal of complexes that germinated in a colonial situation.
>
> (cited in Hudis 2015: Kindle edn)

In other words, until the 'universalistic' pretentions of Western secular modernity are properly unsettled by a new hegemony, 'the arsenal of complexes' will continue to reproduce themselves. Decolonial challenges will not involve a linear programme of 'development', but much like the Hajj pilgrim in Mecca, the 'traveller must find the hidden, circular paths that lead back to the shrine at the centre of the world' (Clasby 1988: 180).

Writing during the time of apartheid in South Africa, Steve Biko also made a compelling argument for exclusivist emancipatory movements, explaining why black South African students had to create a separate political group 'to formulate their own thinking unpolluted by the ideas emanating from a group with lots at stake in the *status quo*' (2004: 11). But even so, the oppressed must still contend with the global economic system, on their own terms. Marable explained that Marcus Garvey, who was both a pro-capitalist and black nationalist, 'used pageantry to great effect in building the culture of his movement. Exalted titles and colourful uniforms created a sense of historical import and seriousness, and gave poor African-Americans a sense of pride and excitement' (2011: 19). In this way, Garvey was a black political nationalist by means of promoting the integration of African-Americans into the capitalist system. While Malcolm X grew increasingly critical of the role that the African-

American bourgeoisie played in the systematic exploitation of the urban poor, his economic message was more contradictory, similar to that of the Islamic resistance movement in Lebanon. Furthermore, Hizbullah has also willingly integrated into Lebanon's corrupt sectarian state. This brings us back to the dilemma of the decolonial moment: are there any radical possibilities through engaging with neoliberal capitalism today?

This is an important line of questioning, but not one that I am willing to directly answer because of my white-centred privilege. I raise these questions for all of us to consider, and for each human to answer on her own terms. My contribution is only to describe what I have come to understand about the Islamic resistance movement and to critically assess the contradictions of its negotiation with economic and political power, hoping to bridge the wide chasm between Marxist idealism and everyday lives in post-colonial societies.

What I can say is that while the charities affiliated with Hizbullah, al-Mabarrat Association and the Imam al-Sadr Foundation have economically empowered Lebanese Shi'is, their struggle against capitalism has been compromised, because all are willingly engaging with the Western liberal economic project, reproducing its norms. This is anything but a breaking away from the global capitalist system – these charities have internalised the economic model of a centre and periphery, where some own capital while others do not, even though their goal may be to narrow the distance between the two. That said, there is disagreement among Lebanese Shi'is over what role economic liberalism should play in society. For Hizbullah and al-Mabarrat Association, the struggle against capitalism is subordinate to political goals, and so economic empowerment is merely a means to realise a community more capable of resistance. For the Imam al-Sadr Foundation, economic liberalism is the goal. The foundation seeks to empower individuals to take control of their own lives. This is an example of how Gramsci's notion of common sense works in today's world, where competing blocs can frame the same ideas in their own unique ways to achieve very different political projects.

Ultimately, Shi'is need to compromise in their political struggle because Lebanon is a multi-confessional society; thus, this is a question of self-preservation. Marable's (2011: 344–347) account of Malcolm X's life also shows that, at times, he also had to occasionally play the game: in one example, Malcolm X pretends to still believe in the Nation of Islam in front of the courts to secure ownership of his family's home. So, obviously, these kinds of compromises and contradictions are very human. My fear is that we have come to believe that both are deviations from decoloniality, forgetting what Schütz (1944) and Bauman (1991) observed in their profiles of the stranger, or what Ward (2012: 128) notes in her work on Chinese medicine: that contradictions are inherent when engaging with 'the Other'. The contradictions within Western secular liberalism are easily apparent to anybody who bothers to look for them – despite our supposed disenchantment, new myths have replaced the old, leaving us more enchanted than ever towards a system of oppression and violence.

As discussed in Chapter 6, the concepts of resistance and revolution are extremely complicated to unpack in modern lives. There are many layers of oppression in today's world that require just as many layers of resistance. However, these struggles do not always coalesce, as the theories of intersectionality tend to ignore, and in fact, many are at odds with one another, for instance, the struggles for equality and the recognition of difference (Fraser 1997).[2] Therefore, contradictory compromises are always going to be necessary. But why have these revolutionary movements willingly become complicit in the capitalist system of inequality? Perhaps one reason why they are willing to engage in only a slightly altered system of capitalism is because of the residue of colonialism and Orientalism. The Western discourse of the Orient and Orientals as backwards and 'underdeveloped' has been repeated so often that it is now internalised. As Fanon argued, 'You hate yourself for who you are in order to obtain the love that you aspire to receive' (Hudis 2015: Kindle edn). Here, the easiest way to respond to this hatred is for the countries in the Global South to become more 'developed', thus proving the West wrong. However, there is also the possibility that the seductiveness of capitalism is far stronger than any of us will concede.

Either way, the secular liberal framework is not being completely rejected by these anti-imperialist movements, merely modified – or locally enchanted – to empower non-Western cultures that value faith, religion and community. Of course, there is also a chance that if the Islamic resistance movement compromises too much in its struggle for political and economic liberation, this will reproduce systems that continue to marginalise Shiʻis, because of the intersecting forces that have historically oppressed them. So, while my research shows the many ways that the charities affiliated with Hizbullah, al-Mabarrat Association and the Imam al-Sadr Foundation are empowering Shiʻi communities, my field experiences also illustrate that Shiʻis are still discriminated against based on ideas of nationalism, class and sectarianism. My own response to this is to ask even more loudly: 'When will the responsibility shift from those demanding humanity to those denying it?' Because if, as Fanon argued, 'it is a struggle to acquire hatred, which has to be dragged into being' (cited in Hudis 2015: Kindle edn), how much emancipation can any hated group ever truly achieve when those who are hateful refuse to struggle against their own hatred?

Putting that idealism aside and recalling Sayyid's (2014a: 2) notion that, 'People become without history not because they lack a past but because, paradoxically, they cannot narrate themselves into the future,' I will end by saying that the Islamic resistance movement is clearly attempting to narrate its own future, however humanly flawed this attempt may be, and that has made its supporters deeply proud. The struggle for liberation continues …

Notes

1. Speaking from the location of South Africa, Sabelo Ndlovu-Gatsheni contends that:

   Decoloniality is born out of a realisation that ours is an asymmetrical world order that is sustained not only by colonial matrices of power but also by pedagogies and epistemologies of equilibrium that continue to produce alienated Africans who are socialised into hating the Africa that produced them, and liking the Europe and America that rejects them.

   (Ndlovu-Gatsheni 2013)

2. As I note later in the Preface, the legacy and presence of English language words related to Islam and the Islamicate are impacted by colonialism and imperialism, but Hizbullah refers to itself as the Islamic resistance movement (in Arabic *al-muqawama al-islamiya*).

3. Western colonists misused the idea of discovery to justify the conquest of native lands and peoples, as if these lands and peoples had not existed before being seen by Western eyes.

4. The charities and organisations affiliated with Hizbullah that the US Treasury Department lists as 'Specially Designated Nationals', or SDNs, include: the Martyr's Foundation, assisting those wounded in wars as well as the families of martyrs; the Emdad Committee, assisting children, mainly orphans and the poor; Jihad al-Binaa, building social and humanitarian infrastructure; Waad Rebuild, managing the massive reconstruction efforts after the 2006 war against Israel; al-Nour Broadcasting, the party's radio station; and finally, al-Manar, the party's television channel. The United States designated Ayatollah Fadlallah, the founder of al-Mabarrat Association, as a terrorist because of his political support for the resistance.

5. Observations in the field in Lebanon February 2017; and 'Lebanon Population', Country Meters, n.d., http://countrymeters.info/en/Lebanon. Accessed 19 June 2017.

6. Several journalists and scholars have reported that under the George W. Bush Administration, the US was arming and supporting Sunni extremist groups throughout the Middle East to counter the perceived threat from Hizbullah, Syria and Iran. See Hersh (2007); AbuKhalil (2008); and Daragahi and Rafei (2008).

1. Introduction

1. 'The Moment of Truth: The Kairos Documents' was written in 1985 by mostly black South African theologians and called on the world church to

recognise the vicious policies of the apartheid state in South Africa. http://ujamaa.ukzn.ac.za/Libraries/manuals/The_Kairos_Documents.sflb.ashx. Accessed 4 April 2017.

2. 'Homepage', Kairos Palestine: A Moment of Truth, n.d., www.kairospalestine.ps/. Accessed 4 April 2017.

3. Ironically, the field of neuroscience is increasingly debunking the notion that conscious rational deliberation is even possible. See Burton 2016.

4. Chapter 6 will recognise and unpack some of the critiques of intersectionality.

5. Workshop at the University of Johannesburg during spring semester 2016.

6. Asad (2003a: 168) says that medieval Spain disrupts this narrative because its Muslim identity is temporally and geographically disconnected from Europe.

7. Asad (2003a: 107) points to the example of torture, which Enlightenment critics like Voltaire and Beccaria deemed unacceptable because it is both inefficient and immoral. His point is that questions of efficiency weighed into a debate about an unquestionably immoral act. And although torture was condemned by the UN General Assembly in 1948, many countries have continued the practice to obtain information during times of war. The film *The Battle of Algiers*, directed by Gillo Pontecorvo (1966), provides some insight into why the French adopted this practice in Algeria. In the film, Colonel Mathieu, the French paratrooper commander, explains to his military officers that,

> the reason for this work is information. And interrogation becomes a method when conducted in a manner so as always to obtain a result, or rather an answer. In practice, demonstrating a false humanitarianism only leads to the ridiculous and to impotence. I am certain all units will act accordingly.

To this day, scholars study and debate the 'effectiveness' of torture.

8. Take, for example, Adam Smith's (2003: 572) argument that individuals freely engaging in economic activity would collectively be guided by 'an invisible hand', or the force that is thought to promote the most efficient and mutually beneficial outcomes in a liberal economic market system. Of course, trade is dependent on particular conditions and must be carefully managed; and, even then, it only works imperfectly.

9. The equation 2 + 2 = 4 is an example of the former, and 'I see a tree' is an example of the latter.

10. This helps to explain the difficulty many Western Christians have experienced in justifying the rationality of their religious beliefs since the introduction of evolutionary theory. While I was in the field, I happened to read a report about a science textbook used in Christian schools in Louisiana that cited the existence of the Loch Ness Monster as proof that evolutionary theory is wrong. According to a representative of Accelerated Christian Education, which designed the school's curriculum, 'true science will never contradict the Bible because God created both the universe and scripture. If

a scientific theory contradicts the Bible, then the theory is wrong and must be discarded' (see RT 2012).

11. Weber argued that the rationalisation process is universal, although by no means unilinear, and the way it is realised is qualitatively different depending upon the society (see Kalberg 1980).

12. Koch takes the following quotations directly from Weber.

13. Kalberg (1980) uses slightly different categorisations for the first two types of Weberian rationality, calling them theoretical and practical, respectively.

14. The rational logic of the bureaucratic state is based on a system where a hierarchy of experts, known as technocrats, carry out public policy according to certain rules and regulations. The rational logic of the capitalist market economy is based on a system where consumers seek to maximise utility and businesses measure costs quantitatively. Those who believe in efficiency, discipline, precision and dependability may find that their substantive rationality becomes a means of realising formal rationality (Kalberg 1980: 1162).

15. For a beautiful retelling of the historical battle, see Aslan (2005).

16. Lecture by Nelson Maldonado-Torres at the University of Johannesburg on 22 March 2016.

2. The rise of religious activism in Lebanon and beyond

1. Saudi Arabia frequently oppresses Saudi Shi'is living in the oil rich eastern part of the country (see, e.g. BBC News 2011; Al Jazeera 2011; Matthiesen 2012; and Reuters 2014a). The Kingdom also sent its military forces to support the Sunni royal family controlling Bahrain in a violent crackdown in 2011 against peaceful Shi'i demonstrators (Hawley 2011). Even before Saudi Arabia's recent military offensive in Yemen, its military had often used extreme force to quell uprisings among Yemeni Shi'i populations living close to the northern borders with the Kingdom (Press Association 2010). And in recent years, the so-called Islamic State in Iraq and Syria has also posed a threat to Shi'is throughout the region. In 2015, ISIS fighters killed five Saudi Shi'is during Ashura commemorations, following a series of bomb attacks against Shi'i mosques that killed dozens more (BBC 2015a).

2. For example, in Iraq and Syria, cases discussed in Chapter 6.

3. This is a trend that empowers those marginalised by US and Israeli hegemony, but is also paradoxically being used to oppress anybody challenging the authority of the resistance axis.

4. According to Kamali (1998), Iran's clerical establishment was financially independent during the Safavid Empire, giving it political autonomy until the nineteenth century.

5. The scholar above the *mujtahid* is the *marja' al-taqlid,* or source of emulation.

6. This does not in any way infer that culture has lost its spiritual dimension. See Szanto (2013).

7. As Mobarez (1972: 22) reports, the Confederation of Iranian Students published a book in 1972 detailing some of the human rights atrocities that occurred during the 1950s and 1960s under SAVAK. A selection of newspaper headlines from the world press at the time included: 'More Death Sentences in Persia'; 'Death Penalties for Communists'; 'More Doomed by Iranian Army'; 'Trial of Iranian Students'; and 'The Tehran Trial: One Accused Denounces the Tortures Inflicted upon Him'.

8. In a lecture for the course 'The Iranian Revolution in Comparative Perspective' on 1 May 2006 at the City University of New York, Professor Ervand Abrahamian explained that, at the time, there were two classes of peasants in Iran. One class had been granted the right to cultivate land and the other had not.

9. Ali Shari'ati, 'Islamology: The Basic Design for a School of Thought and Action', n.d., www.shariati.com/kotob.html. Accessed 11 July 2017.

10. *Ibid.*

11. Ali Shari'ati, 'Red Shi'ism: The Religion of Martyrdom and Black Shi'ism: The Religion of Mourning', n.d., www.shariati.com/kotob.html. Accessed 11 July 2017.

12. Another noted Iranian scholar who combined religion and Marxism was Ayatollah Mahmood Taleqani, who wrote a popular book about Islam and collective ownership (Taleqani 2003 [1985]). Other Iranian clerics, like Ayatollah Ruhollah Khomeini and Ayatollah Morteza Motahari, were influenced by these works and, like other Shi'i activists across the region, they deliberately framed Islam as a better alternative to Marxism.

13. Observations during fieldwork in Tehran during summer 2008.

14. According to Keddie (2003: 225), the article questioned Khomeini's past and suggested that he had received large sums of money from the English to oppose the Shah.

15. For example, the people directly elect the president, but s/he must be confirmed by the *faqih*, or Supreme Leader. The latter serves a lifetime appointment and is elected by the Assembly of Experts, a body that comprises clerical members who are directly elected by the people. The parliament, or *majles*, is also directly elected by the people and must confirm the president and the Council of Guardians. The latter examines the Islamic character of laws passed by the Parliament. The Supreme Leader appoints six of the Council of Guardians and the Judiciary chooses the other six.

16. Interview with Fereshteh Bazargan during fieldwork in Tehran on 15 July 2008.

17. Conversation with a volunteer for Hizbullah during fieldwork in Lebanon in summer 2011.

18. Privileging the objective value alone is what Marx (1867) criticises as fetishism under capitalism.

19. While Ayatollah Fadlallah expressed ideological solidarity with the party before he left Iraq for Lebanon in 1966, he was never an official member. For more information, see Chapter 4.

20. Observations during fieldwork in Lebanon in summer 2011.

21. Weiss (2010: 40) goes on to explain that the origins of the world are probably '*mata waliyyan li-'Ali*', or, 'he died as a friend of (Imam) 'Ali (bin Abi Talib)'.

22. Interview with Mohammad Bassam, head of Research and Assessment for the Imam Sadr Foundation, during fieldwork in Lebanon on 10 August 2009.

23. Even the Arabic word for clerics, *ulama*, refers to scientists as well as learned people.

24. Imam al-Sadr, 'Introduction' to the Arabic edition of *Natural Sciences in the Holy Qur'an* by Youssef Mruweh, n.d. Translation into English provided by Louay H. Charafeddine of the Imam Sadr Foundation during fieldwork in Beirut on 17 June 2010.

25. Observations during fieldwork in Lebanon on 20 September 2011.

26. Amal developed into a sectarian militia during the civil–international war and eventually a secular but sectarian political party post-war.

27. Conversation with a volunteer for Hizbullah during fieldwork in Lebanon in summer 2011.

28. Observations during fieldwork in Lebanon in summer 2011.

29. This story was repeated to me several times during my field research in Lebanon.

30. Conversation with Sheikh Yaacoub's niece during fieldwork in Beirut on 7 August 2009.

31. Meeting with Imam al-Sadr's daughter Maliha during fieldwork in Tehran on 24 May 2010.

32. Conversation with the head of translation at Ayatollah Fadlallah's office during fieldwork in Lebanon in autumn 2011.

33. Observations during fieldwork in Lebanon in summer 2011.

3. Deconstructing terrorism and resistance

1. Regarding Christian liberation theology, McGovern quotes a US advertisement from 1988 that warns of 'the harmful influence of the so-called "theology of liberation" which proposed to install Communism in the name of Christianity and which has been the seedbed of more terrorists in the region than any outright Marxist parties' (1989: ix).

2. 'Resource Center', US Department of the Treasury, n.d., www.treasury.gov/resource-center/sanctions/SDN-List/Pages/default.aspx. Accessed 11 July 2017.

3. The US Department of the Treasury (2007) listed the Martyr's Foundation after the 2006 war with Israel, saying that: 'senior Martyrs Foundation officials were directly involved in Hizbullah operations against Israel during the July–August 2006 conflict', but without providing any evidence of the said officials targeting civilians.

4. Observations during fieldwork in Beirut on 31 May 2010.

5. The Holy Land Foundation helped to raise funds for people misplaced by natural and man-made disasters, focusing primarily on Palestinian refugees living in the Occupied Territories and neighbouring countries, but

also helping American victims of tornadoes and floods. Federal prosecutors accused the Holy Land Foundation of providing financial assistance to individuals and organisations linked to Hamas, claiming this constituted support of terrorism because the money that was sent to religious community groups to build hospitals and feed the poor relieved Hamas of the burden (Marusek 2017a).

6. The actions of US peacekeepers were biased towards the Christian militias. In response, the Islamic resistance movement conducted reprisal attacks on the US embassy and marine barracks (Greenway 1983).

7. Solidere is French for Société Libanaise pour le Développement et la Reconstruction de Beyrouth, or in English, Lebanese Company for the Development and Reconstruction of Beirut Central District.

8. At an urban conference at the American University of Beirut (AUB) in spring 2011, a panel discussed Solidere's reconstruction of the capital city after the civil–international war in comparison with the more recent work of Waad Rebuild, an organisation affiliated with Hizbullah that reconstructed southern Beirut after the July 2006 war with Israel. The audience asked pointed questions to the panel about the lack of public participation in Solidere's decision-making, despite it being a quasi-governmental and cooperative organisation. They also criticised the gentrification and exclusion that has resulted from the company's work. According to the Solidere representative, only 30 per cent of downtown's original buildings were restored, meaning that the majority of the city's historical buildings were torn down and rebuilt. Few in the audience seemed to have benefitted from the Solidere reconstruction, and many applauded after the first critical question was posed. As one gentleman succinctly summed up, 'One project (Waad Rebuild) brought the people back, and the other (Solidere) sent them away.' Audience discussion during the 'City Debates 2011: Contemporary Urbanism in the Arab World' conference held at the Architecture Lecture Hall, American University of Beirut on 12–13 May 2011.

9. For example, Solidere opened the Beirut Souks in 2012, replacing the city's historical shopping centre with an outdoor luxury mall that is home to elite designer shops beyond the economic reach of most Lebanese (Hamilton 2012).

10. Israel's involvement in the Lebanese civil–international war was widely criticised by the Israelis themselves. For two recent films that are critical of the military invasion from an Israeli perspective, see *Lebanon* (2010) by director Samuel Maoz and *Waltz with Bashir* (2008) by director Ari Folman.

11. David Hirst witnessed some of the humiliations of this occupation, saying that when Israeli forces left the international airport in Beirut, the Americans had to 'remove the stinking mounds of excrement that, as in so many other places in the country, adorned just about everything, floors, elevators, chairs, desks and drawers' (2010: 171). Hirst (2010: 143) reports that the Israelis subjected hospitals, houses, churches and mosques to a similar fate.

12. For a popular critique, see the film *Under the Bombs* (2007) directed by Philippe Aractingi.
13. Observations during fieldwork in Lebanon in winter 2010.
14. Observations during fieldwork in Lebanon in summer 2009.
15. This came on the heels of Hizbullah and Lebanese security services uncovering a large series of Israeli spy rings between 2008 and 2010 (Economist 2010).
16. An official Hizbullah communiqué sent to me by email from the international relations department on 9 December 2011.
17. Observations during fieldwork in Lebanon on 22 March 2011.
18. These activities included doing interviews with anti-imperialist television stations like Press TV, RT and al-Manar; attending weekly meetings over the course of several months in the Palestinian refugee camps; and participating in rallies and demonstrations, all of which helped me to build trust with the Islamic resistance movement.
19. While this kind of investigative or tabloid style journalism is common in the West, it was then unusual in Lebanon.
20. Observations during fieldwork in Lebanon in May 2011.

4. Lebanon's resistance charities

1. The following history is recounted in a 1993 newspaper interview with Sayyid Hassan Nasrallah that was later translated into English and republished in Noe (2007: 116–143).
2. A break away movement called the Islamic Movement Amal was created in 1982 after Amal's new leader Nabih Berri formed an alliance with a group that included the leader of a right-wing Christian militia.
3. Observation during fieldwork in Beirut on 8 May 2012.
4. Interview with Zahra during fieldwork in Beirut on 8 August 2009.
5. Interview with Sonia during fieldwork in Beirut on 27 July 2009.
6. Observations during fieldwork in Beirut in 2011.
7. Observations during fieldwork in Lebanon on 8 May 2012.
8. Some leading Islamic thinkers, including Sayyid Qutb and Ayatollah Khomeini, also tended towards adopting an 'us' versus 'them' dichotomy in their writing.
9. Field observation in Beirut on 22 May 2010.
10. Field observation in Beirut on 6 December 2011.
11. Ayatollah Khomeini established the Imam Khomeini Relief Foundation in 1979 to promote the following objectives:

> developing useful and national network of communication and support in order to carry out deep, permanent, efficient and effective tasks for the deprived class of the society by respecting the comprehensive and demanded principles; and having a major role as the powerful arm of the Islamic Republic of Iran in strengthening social support and balance,

assisting government in carrying out social programmes, services and supports.

The foundation states that it encourages civic engagement and emphasises the dignity of the family. For more information, see www.emdad.ir.

12. 'Islamic Charity Emdad Committee', United Nations Development Programme Lebanon, n.d., http://portal.undp.org.lb/ngo/NGOSearchAc. cfm?Acronym=ICEC. Accessed 12 July 2017.

13. Islamic Charity Emdad Committee, n.d., www.alemdad.net/. Accessed 12 July 2017.

14. 'Domains of Service', Islamic Charity Emdad Committee, n.d., www. alemdad.net/article.php?id=264&cid=134. Accessed 12 July 2017.

15. *Ibid.*

16. Observation during fieldwork in Beirut in May 2012.

17. Observation during fieldwork in Beirut in August 2009.

18. 'Foundation for the Wounded', n.d., www.aljarha.net/. Accessed 12 July 2017.

19. A similar foundation was first created in the Islamic Republic of Iran back in 1980 to assist those affected by the devastating war with Iraq. The Martyr's Foundation in Iran offers the following services to the families of martyrs: priority in admission to all educational institutions, from primary school to university; priority in obtaining basic economic needs; priority in obtaining employment; exemption in fares on all state-owned city transport, and the payment of half the fare of all intercity transport; medical insurance and special drug care; hospitalisation and treatment for the disabled and wounded. There is a housing unit that provides housing to clients, and even a marriage unit to facilitate the marriage of war widows and veterans. The latter unit doles out cash grants and organises loans. See 'Bonyad-e Sahid', *Encyclopedia Iranica*, n.d., www.iranicaonline.org/articles/bonyad-e-sahid. Accessed 12 July 2017.

20. 'Martyr's Foundation', n.d., www.alshahid.org/. Accessed 12 July 2017.

21. I know two activists who were in Lebanon participating in solidarity activities for Palestine, one European and the other American, who received medical treatment free of charge here in Lebanon, provided by Hizbullah. Their political orientation probably played a role in the decision to serve them without charge.

22. From 'In Defiance of the Israeli Aggression, Charity will Persevere: A Report on the Institutions of al-Mabarrat Association Destroyed or Damaged in the Last War on Lebanon (July 2006).' I also received preparatory notes made for this publication containing more detailed information about the charitable programmes and the destruction resulting from the war. Documents collected during fieldwork in Lebanon in summer 2010.

23. Meeting with the press office of al-Mabarrat Association during fieldwork in Beirut on 21 January 2010.

24. Documents collected during fieldwork in Lebanon in summer 2010.

25. Meeting with the press office of al-Mabarrat Association during fieldwork in Beirut on 21 January 2010.
26. Documents collected during fieldwork in Lebanon in summer 2010.
27. *Ibid.*
28. Meeting with the press office of al-Mabarrat Association during fieldwork in Beirut on 21 January 2010. Bahman Hospital has no connection to Iran, and was named after Abd al-Hussein Bahman, a philanthropist living in Kuwait, who donated money to the Association to build the hospital, among other facilities. See Böttcher (2002).
29. 'About', Bahman Hospital Facebook, n.d., www.facebook.com/pg/Bahman.International.Hospital/about/. Accessed 12 July 2017.
30. Documents collected during fieldwork in Lebanon in summer 2010.
31. Observations during fieldwork in Beirut on 21 January 2010.
32. Apparently, the cost of an al-Mabarrat Association secondary school in Beirut can run several thousand dollars per student annually. Observations during fieldwork in Beirut on 25 February 2012.
33. Throughout my fieldwork, I visited Assaha often to attend various events and meetings, and over time I noticed that in the restaurant the managers started visiting each table to ensure that everything is okay and asking for a personal assessment of the dining experience, which, at that time, was an unusual practice in Lebanon and hardly necessary to gain a competitive edge in a market Assaha already holds a monopoly over. The restaurant then communicates with customers who have provided written feedback through text messages, wishing them blessings during Islamic holidays. These kinds of qualitative measures are also common in many of the Imam al-Sadr Foundation's various projects, as Chapter 5 details.
34. This story is also explained on the restaurant menus. Observations during fieldwork in Beirut throughout 2011–2012.
35. Interestingly, this was the catchphrase of reformist Iranian President Mohammad Khatami (1997–2005).
36. Documents collected during fieldwork in Lebanon in summer 2010.
37. *Ibid.*
38. The speech delivered by the Hizbullah Secretary-General Sayyid Hassan Nasrallah on the Resistance and Liberation Day on 25 May 2011. Translation provided by the media department of Hizbullah.
39. Interview with Dr Ali Fayyad during fieldwork in Beirut in June 2012.
40. *Ibid.*
41. *Ibid.*
42. *Ibid.*
43. Observations during fieldwork in Beirut on 7 July 2011.
44. Interview with Dr Ali Fayyad during fieldwork in Beirut in June 2012.
45. Observations during fieldwork in Beirut on 20 September 2011.
46. Interview with Dr Ali Fayyad during fieldwork in Beirut in June 2012.
47. Much of the literature focuses on computers and scientific libraries, as well as special technologies to assist the blind and deaf. Documents collected during fieldwork in Lebanon in summer 2010.

48. 'The Administrative Board', Bahman Hospital, n.d., www.bahmanhospital. com/bahman-hospital/word-by-the-administrative-board/. Accessed 12 July 2017.
49. Documents collected during fieldwork in Lebanon in summer 2010.
50. Observations during fieldwork in Beirut on 3 February 2012.
51. Observations during fieldwork in Lebanon on 9 August 2011.

5. The Imam al-Sadr Foundation

1. Interview with Rebab al-Sadr, President of the Imam al-Sadr Foundation, during fieldwork in Lebanon in July 2010.
2. Observations during fieldwork in Beirut on 7 July 2011.
3. Observations during fieldwork April 2012.
4. Observations during fieldwork in Beirut in July 2011.
5. Interview with an employee of the Education Department at the Imam al-Sadr Foundation in July 2010.
6. *Ibid.*
7. *Ibid.*
8. Interview with the managers of the Education Department at the Imam al-Sadr Foundation in July 2010.
9. Interview with an employee of the Education Department at the Imam al-Sadr Foundation in July 2010.
10. The following section is based on an interview with Mohammad Bassam, head of research and development for the Imam al-Sadr Foundation in Sur on 10 August 2009.
11. Interview with Mohammad Bassam in Sur on 15 February 2017.
12. Interview with Dr Martha Mundy in Lebanon on 28 February 2017.
13. Observations in the field in Lebanon during February 2017.
14. 'Education', Imam al-Sadr Foundation, n.d., http://imamsadrfoundation. org/programs/education/. Accessed 4 July 2017.
15. Documents collected during fieldwork in Lebanon during summer 2010.
16. 'Elementary School', Imam al-Sadr Foundation, n.d., http://imamsadr foundation.org/programs/education/elementary-school/14/2/1/. Accessed 4 July 2017.
17. 'Special Education Department', Imam al-Sadr Foundation, n.d., http:// imamsadrfoundation.org/programs/education/special-education-department/14/1/1/. Accessed 4 July 2017.
18. Documents collected during fieldwork in Lebanon during summer 2010.
19. Interview with the managers of the Orphanage Care Programme at the Imam al-Sadr Foundation in Sur in July 2010.
20. Documents collected during fieldwork in Beirut in summer 2010.
21. *Ibid.*
22. *Together: Towards a Brighter Future*, booklet published by Imam al-Sadr Foundation in 2009.
23. Documents collected during fieldwork in Beirut in summer 2010.

24. On two occasions, I participated in Hizbullah organised delegations to southern Lebanon and both times we dined at Shawatina Restaurant. Observations during fieldwork in Lebanon 2010–2011.
25. Documents collected during fieldwork in Beirut in summer 2010.
26. *Together: Towards a Brighter Future*, booklet published by Imam al-Sadr Foundation in 2009.
27. Currently, French translations are available to order at the Arabic website of the Center of Imam Musa al-Sadr for Research and Studies, n.d., http://imamsadr.net/Home/index.php. Accessed 12 July 2017.
28. Documents collected during fieldwork in Lebanon in summer 2010.
29. *Ibid.*
30. Interview with the head of nursing at the Imam al-Sadr Foundation in Sur in July 2010.
31. Document collected during fieldwork in Lebanon during summer 2010 and translated with the generous help of Khaldoun Abou Assi, a Lebanese researcher, friend and colleague.
32. Interview with Nijad Charafeddine head of the Income Generating Programme at the Imam al-Sadr Foundation in Sur in July 2010.
33. Interview with an employee of the Education Department at the Imam al-Sadr Foundation in July 2010.
34. The *chador* is a full length Islamic covering for women, usually in black, that is held under the chin by hand or fastener and is worn by some Lebanese Shi'is. Many women also wear the *chador* to enter mosques and shrines.
35. Interview with an employee of the Education Department at the Imam al-Sadr Foundation in July 2010.
36. Observations during fieldwork in Lebanon 2009–2012.
37. Interview with managers of the Education Department at Imam al-Sadr Foundation in Sur in July 2010.
38. *Ibid.*
39. *Ibid.*
40. I was not asked to wear a *hijab* at the foundation. Neither was I required to wear one at al-Mabarrat Association's offices or Hizbullah events. In fact, it was only necessary when meeting with religious leaders or entering mosques.
41. Imam al-Sadr Foundation documentary released in 2009.
42. See Charafeddine (2008).
43. Interview with Nijad Charafeddine head of the Income Generating Programme at the Imam al-Sadr Foundation in Sur in July 2010.
44. Interview with the head of nursing at the Imam al-Sadr Foundation in Sur in July 2010.
45. Interview with the managers of the Orphanage Care Programme at the Imam al-Sadr Foundation in Sur in July 2010.
46. Interview with Nijad Charafeddine head of the Income Generating Programme at the Imam al-Sadr Foundation in Sur in July 2010.
47. Interview with the head of nursing at the Imam al-Sadr Foundation in Sur in July 2010.

48. Interview with Mohammad Bassam, head of research and development for the Imam al-Sadr Foundation in Sur on 10 August 2009.
49. Interview with the head of nursing at the Imam al-Sadr Foundation in Sur in July 2010.
50. *Ibid.*
51. *Ibid.*
52. Interview with Nijad Charafeddine head of the Income Generating Programme at the Imam al-Sadr Foundation in Sur in July 2010.
53. *Ibid.*
54. *Ibid.*
55. Interview with a manager of nursing at the Imam al-Sadr Foundation in Sur in July 2010.
56. Interview with managers of the Education Department at Imam al-Sadr Foundation in Sur in July 2010.
57. Interview with an employee of the Education Department at the Imam al-Sadr Foundation in July 2010.
58. Interview with Nijad Charafeddine head of the Income Generating Programme at the Imam al-Sadr Foundation in Sur in July 2010.
59. Interview with the head of nursing at the Imam al-Sadr Foundation in Sur in July 2010.
60. Interview with an employee of the Education Department at the Imam al-Sadr Foundation in July 2010.
61. Interview with a manager of the Education Department and his employee at the Imam al-Sadr Foundation in July 2010.
62. Interview with managers of the Education Department at Imam al-Sadr Foundation in Sur in July 2010.
63. Interview with a manager of the Education Department and his employee at the Imam al-Sadr Foundation in July 2010.

6. The problem of resistance and power

1. Observations during fieldwork in Lebanon during February 2017.
2. Observations during fieldwork in Lebanon in autumn 2012.
3. In one example, I wore a T-shirt to my Arabic lesson at the Lebanese American University, which stated the 'right to return' in Arabic. The ensuing distress that this caused was both unexpected and unintended. Observations during fieldwork in Lebanon in summer 2010.
4. Ali Shariati, *Fatima is Fatima,* n.d., www.al-islam.org/fatima-is-fatima-dr-ali-shariati. Accessed 22 June 2017.
5. Observations during fieldwork in Beirut in August 2009.
6. Observations during fieldwork in Lebanon on 25 July 2009.
7. Observations during fieldwork in Beirut on 20 July 2009.
8. Interview with Dr Ali Fayyad during fieldwork in Beirut in June 2012.
9. Observations during fieldwork in Lebanon in February 2017.
10. Interview with Rebab al-Sadr by *Middle East News and World Report,* 11 December 2002.

11. Interview with the head of nursing at the Imam al-Sadr Foundation in Sur in July 2010.
12. Observations during fieldwork in Beirut in February 2017.
13. Observations during fieldwork in Beirut in February 2012.
14. As illustrated by the photographs of Egyptian children placing army boots on top of their heads, meant to express support for the Egyptian army during the 2013 state commemoration of the revolution in Egypt (Daragahi 2014).
15. Another way that the Mahdi Scouts are similar to the American boy scouts is that both organisations formulate policies according to particular religious agendas. In the US, this created controversy over the boy scouts' policy to exclude gays. Interestingly, the organisation does not overtly focus on the religious motivation for this policy, instead claiming that this reflects its beliefs and perspectives (Eckholm 2012). The chief executive did recently nod to theology, but reverted to a discourse of rights to justify the policy, arguing that: 'the vast majority of the parents of youth we serve value their right to address issues of same-sex orientation within their family, with spiritual advisors and at the appropriate time and in the right setting.' Indeed, the boy scouts' spokesperson 'would not comment on whether the decision was influenced by the Catholic and Mormon churches,' and some believe that the decision has more to do with the organisation's financial sponsorship than a belief in religious values (Hennessy-Fiske 2012). In 2015, the organisation relaxed the ban partially by accepting gay leaders (Leopold 2015).
16. I was repeatedly told that all political factions in Lebanon have secret militias and weapons caches. Furthermore, the Sunni Future movement also maintains a sectarian boy scouts programme (Lynch 2011).
17. Observations during fieldwork in Lebanon in summer 2009.
18. Interview with Dr Ali Fayyad during fieldwork in Beirut in June 2012.
19. Observations during fieldwork in Lebanon in spring 2011.
20. Yassin-Kassab and al-Shami (2016) do recognise the conservative culture of Syrian society. During my last visit to Lebanon, aid workers explained their difficulties in servicing Syrian women due to gender restrictions, and young women complained about increased harassment from young Syrian men who did not understand urban culture.
21. Observations during fieldwork in Beirut in February 2017.
22. Indeed, Beirut has been the focus of several recent international articles promoting the city as a vibrant tourist destination (Balls 2017; and Marino 2017).
23. I attended the peaceful demonstration in Maroun al-Ras in southern Lebanon, on the border with Israel, witnessing first-hand the panic, injury and death that resulted from Israeli soldiers shooting at unarmed Palestinians. Similar bloody demonstrations took place in Syria. See Cassel (2011a).
24. Observations during fieldwork in Lebanon in July 2011.
25. Many of the international activists supporting this movement also unwittingly played a divisive role, including myself.

26. I was an organiser for the movement and personally attended the Gaza demonstrations.

27. For example, even near the end of his term, over half of Republicans believed that former US President Barack Obama was a Muslim 'deep down' (Taylor 2016).

28. According to a 2015 survey held by Hayya Bina, an organisation that is outspoken in its opposition to Hizbullah, 78.7 per cent of Lebanese Shi'is supported the intervention (quoted in ICG 2017: 3).

29. An indication of Hizbullah's recognition of its difficulties is evident in its decision to bury martyrs killed in Syria in Imad Mughniyeh's shrine in Dahiyeh. Mughniyeh was a celebrated military leader and so this is a special honour.

30. See Al Arabiya (2013a and 2013b); and Groisman (2016).

31. Observations doing fieldwork in southern Lebanon during February 2017.

32. Observations doing fieldwork in Beirut during February 2017.

33. *Ibid.*

34. *Ibid.*

35. Accessing precise information, however, proved too sensitive.

36. Observations doing fieldwork in Lebanon during February 2017.

37. All subsequent interviews in this section happened during fieldwork in Lebanon during February 2017.

38. See International Peace Initiative for Syria, n.d., www.peaceinsyria.org/. Accessed 22 June 2017.

39. The SSNP's involvement challenges the sectarian narrative of the conflict as it is an open party. Dozens of SSNP fighters have lost their lives. Interview with Hassan Sakr and observations during fieldwork in Beirut in February–March 2017.

40. There are several factors that help to explain why Lebanon has not granted Palestinians civil rights and citizenship. Legally there is the principle of reciprocity: since Palestinians do not have a state to respond in kind, they cannot be granted any rights in Lebanon (Yassine 2010: 3). Lebanese also believe that as a collective Palestinians are lower class. Indeed, as Simon Haddad points out, 'Palestinians are classified as special case category foreigners, along with Sri Lankans, Thais, Filipinos, Kurds and Syrians, who together constitute Lebanon's imported working class' (2004: 248). And then, of course, there is the precarious sectarian balance in the country. A study by Haddad (2004: 248) finds that most Christians and Shi'is have negative opinions of Palestinian resettlement in Lebanon, whereas most Sunnis do not.

41. This is nothing new, and it is not only religious movements that have been re-mystifying liberalism. In the mid-twentieth century, artists crafted surrealism and abstract expressionism as an attempt to re-introduce myth into their everyday lives because the rational world had let them down. These artists were looking to shake up the formal social systems of bureaucracy and capitalism. The art critic Robert Hughes even describes the German painter Max Ernst's work as being 'akin to an act of terrorism'.

See 'The Threshold of Liberty' from *The Shock of the New* documentary television series by Robert Hughes produced by the BBC in association with Time-Life Films and RM Productions in 1980.

42. Interview with Nijad Charafeddine head of the Income Generating Programme at the Imam al-Sadr Foundation in Sur in July 2010.

43. Assaha Village website, n.d., www.assahavillage.com/home/2/-1/Lebanon. Accessed 12 July 2017.

44. Observations during fieldwork in Lebanon in February 2017.

45. This resonates with Daher's (2016: 2) contention that Hizbullah is a fundamentalist Islamist group; he quotes the Sunni Muslim Brotherhood official to qualify this claim. Daher cites Matthew Levitt, the American 'terrorism expert', whose research has been widely criticised by journalists and scholars (Cronin, Marusek and Miller 2016), as well as the Middle East Media Research Institute, known as MEMRI, an American–Israeli organisation that provides free English language translations of Arabic, Persian, Urdu, Pashto and Turkish media reports. The journalist Brian Whitaker has criticised MEMRI for posing 'as a research institute when it's basically a propaganda operation' (Guardian 2003). Daher also frequently cites *Now News* (previously *Now Lebanon*) and *Ya Liban*, Lebanese media that are highly critical of Hizbullah and the 8 March movement more generally.

46. Between 2009 and 2014, Bouri and El Assad (2016) estimate that the total losses of power cuts to the Lebanese economy reached US$23.23 billion. For doubts on reforming the system, see Habib (2017).

47. Observations during fieldwork in Beirut on 7 July 2011.

48. Interestingly, the journalist believes a social revolution will happen in Lebanon because of immigrants returning who were not subject to the Lebanese social pressures as children.

49. Observations during fieldwork in Beirut on 8 August 2009.

50. Interview with Dr Ali Fayyad during fieldwork in Beirut in June 2012.

51. Ironically, R. James Woolsey is a Vice-President of Booz & Company – he's the former director of the CIA and an advisor to a number of Islamophobic organisations, such as MEMRI, Henry Jackson Society, Foundation for the Defense of Democracies and NGO Monitor.

52. This information is based on the Booz & Company Powerpoint presentation made for an Imam al-Sadr Foundation workshop on 29 January 2011, collected during fieldwork in Beirut in summer 2012.

53. 'Current Projects', Imam al-Sadr Foundation, n.d., www.imamsadrfoundation.org/projects/. Accessed 12 July 2017.

Conclusion

1. Marable's focus on the contradictions of Malcolm X's life caused considerable controversy. On the 2013 anniversary of his assassination, I attended a commemorative event where his daughters were in attendance and there was a heated debate when Marable's biography was mentioned. Observations in New York City at the Shabazz Center on 21 February 2013.

2. Fraser (1997: 14) argues that there are generally two kinds of injustice today. One is socio-economic injustice, which is best addressed by some form of redistribution promoting group de-differentiation. There is also what she calls cultural or symbolic injustice, which is rooted in discursive practices. Examples of the latter include cultural domination, non-recognition and disrespect. This type of injustice requires social change that leads to recognition, which conversely promotes group differentiation. Fraser suggests that recognition could involve revaluing the identity of those suffering injustice, valorising the diversity of the society at large, or the 'transformation of societal patterns of representation, interpretation, and communication in ways that would change everybody's sense of self' (1997: 15). For his part, MacIntyre (2007) also argues that contemporary conceptions of justice are incommensurable because the libertarian focuses on procedural justice and the social liberal on redistributive justice.

References

Abisaab, Rula Jurdi (2006) 'The Cleric as Organic Intellectual', in H.E. Chehabi (ed.), *Distant Relations: Iran and Lebanon in the Last 500 Years*. New York: I.B. Tauris, 231–258.

Abrahamian, Ervand (1982) 'Ali Shari'ati: Ideologue of the Iranian Revolution'. *MERIP Middle East Report* 102 (January): 24–28.

Abrahamian, Ervand (2008) *A History of Modern Iran*. New York: Cambridge University Press.

AbuKhalil, As'ad (2008) '81 Dead in Lebanon as Hezbollah Clashes with US-Backed Pro-Government Forces'. *Democracy Now*, 12 May.

Abu-Lughod, Lila (1990) 'The Romance of Resistance: Tracing Transformations of Power Through Bedouin Women'. *American Ethnologist* 17(1): 41–55.

Agar, Michael H. (1996) *The Professional Stranger*. London: Academic Press.

Al-Ahed News (2009) '"Order is Part & Parcel of Faith" Campaign Hurls Toward Implementation'. *Al-Ahed News*, 19 November.

Ajami, Fouad (1986) *The Vanished Imam: Musa al-Sadr and the Shia of Lebanon*. Ithaca, NY: Cornell University Press.

Ajami, Fouad (2013a) 'Hezbollah Fighters Killed in Syria will "Go to Hell," Says Former Leader'. *Al Arabiya*, 26 February.

Ajami, Fouad (2013b) 'Hezbollah Provoking the World, Ex-Militia Chief Says'. *Al Arabiya*, 8 June.

Alagha, Joseph Elie (2006) *The Shifts in Hizbullah's Ideology: Religious Ideology, Political Ideology and Political Program*. Leiden: Amsterdam University Press.

Al-e Ahmad, Jalal (1997) *Weststruckness*. Costa Mesa, CA: Mazda Publishers.

Algar, Hamid (1980) *Religion and State in Iran, 1785–1906: The Role of the Ulama in the Qajar Period*. Berkeley, CA: University of California Press.

Al–Hajal, Khalil (2009) 'Sadr Foundation: Raising Hope from Despair'. Imam al-Sadr Foundation, 6 March.

Al Jazeera (2007) 'Lebanon: Syrians Admit Bus Bombing'. *Al Jazeera*, 14 March.

Al Jazeera (2009) 'I Knew Khomeini'. *Al Jazeera*, January.

Al Jazeera (2011) 'Saudi Security Forces "Fire on Protesters"'. *Al Jazeera*, 22 November.

Al Jazeera (2012) 'The Imam and the Colonel'. *Al Jazeera*, 24 July.

Al Jazeera (2014) 'Tunisia to Close Down Salafist-Run Mosques'. *Al Jazeera*, 20 July.

Al-Manar (2005) 'The Hidden Imam'. *Al–Manar*.

Al-Manar (2011) 'CIA used Awkar Embassy to Spy on Hezbollah'. *Al–Manar*, November 12.

Al-Miqdad, Faisal (2008) 'Iraqi Refugees in Syria'. *Forced Migration Review: IRAQ Special Issue* 19: 18–19.

AP (2014) 'Syrians in Lebanon Battle Crowds to Vote for Bashar al-Assad'. *The Guardian*, 28 May.

Araki, Mohsen (2003) 'A Short Biography of Martyr Ayatollah al-Sadr', in Muhammad Baqir al-Sadr, *Principles of Islamic Jurisprudence According to Shi'i Law*, trans. Arif Abdul Hussain and Hamid Algar. North Haledon, NJ: Islamic Publications International, 11–23.

Arjomand, Said Amir (1988) *The Turban for the Crown: The Islamic Revolution in Iran*. New York: Oxford University Press.

Arnove, Robert and Pinede, Nadine (2007) 'Revisiting the "Big Three" Foundations'. *Critical Sociology* 33: 389–425.

Arquilla, John and Ronfeldt, David (eds) (2001) *Networks and Netwars: The Future of Terror, Crime and Militancy*. Arlington: RAND Corporation.

Arthur, C.J. (1970) 'Introduction' in Karl Marx and Frederick Engels, *The German Ideology*. New York: International Publishers, 4–34.

Asad, Talal (2003a) *Formations of the Secular: Christianity, Islam, Modernity*. Stanford, CA: University of California Press.

Asad, Talal (2003b) *Genealogies of Religion: Discipline and Reasons of Power in Christianity and Islam*. Baltimore, MD: Johns Hopkins University Press.

Asad, Talal (2014) 'Lebanese Minister Calls for ISIS Flag Burners to Face Trial'. *Asharq Al-Awsat*, 31 August.

Aslan, Reza (2005) *No god but God*. New York: Random House.

Atalla, Imad and Alleik, Kassem (2008) 'Guilty by Association: Jihad al-Bina's Reconstruction Terrorism'. *Publio: Culture at the Boiling Point*, No. 3.

Atassi, Basma (2014) 'Huge Turnout for Syrian Vote in Lebanon'. *Al Jazeera*, 28 May.

Bakhash, Shaul (1984) *The Reign of the Ayatollahs: Iran and the Islamic Revolution*. New York: Basic Books.

Balls, Katy (2017) 'The Bright Lights of Beirut'. *The Spectator*, 2 May.

Baqir al-Sadr, Muhammad (1990) *A Discussion Concerning the Mahdi*, trans. Mujahid Husayn. Beirut: Dar al Ta'aruflil–Matbu'at. https://goaloflife.files.wordpress.com/2011/08/shaheed–muhammad–baqir–as–sadr–a–discussion–concerning–the–mahdi.pdf. Accessed 2 July 2017.

Baqir al-Sadr, Muhammad (2003) *Principles of Islamic Jurisprudence According to Shi'i Law*, trans. Arif Abdul Hussain and Hamid Algar. North Haledon, NJ: Islamic Publications International.

Barnard, Anne (2012). 'Loyalty to Syrian President Could Isolate Hezbollah'. *New York Times*, 5 April.

Barthes, Roland (1978) *A Lover's Discourse*. New York: Farrar, Straus and Giroux.

Bathish, Hani M. (2007) 'Orphans, Disabled Still Bear Brunt of Israeli Attacks on Al-Mabarrat Charity'. *The Daily* Star, 17 February.

Bauman, Zygmunt (1976) *Socialism: The Active Utopia*. Crows Nest, NSW: George Allen & Unwin.

Bauman, Zygmunt (1990) 'Modernity and Ambivalence', in Mike Featherstone (ed.), *Global Culture: Nationalism, Globalization and Modernity*. London: Sage Publications, 143–169.

Bauman, Zygmunt (1991) *Modernity and Ambivalence*. Cambridge: Polity Press.

BBC News (2006a) 'Middle East Crisis: Facts and Figures'. *BBC News*, 31 August.

BBC News (2006b) 'Million Bomblets' in South Lebanon'. *BBC News*, 26 September.

BBC News (2011) 'Saudi Arabia Rejects Amnesty Repression Claims'. *BBC News*, 1 December.

BBC News (2015a) 'Saudi Arabia Shia Attack: Five Killed at Ashura Event'. *BBC News*, 17 October.

BBC News (2015b) 'Tunis Attack: Gunmen Kill Tourists in Museum Rampage'. *BBC News*, 18 March.

Behdad, Sohrab (2005) Revolutionary Surge and Quiet Demise of Islamic Economics in Iran'. Paper presented to *Centre for Near Eastern Studies*, University of Los Angeles, CA.

Belaon, Adam (2014) *Muslim Charities: A Suspect Sector*. London: Claystone.

Bellah, Robert N. (1999) 'Max Weber and World Denying-Love: A Look at the Historical Sociology of Religion'. *Journal of the American Academy of Religion* 67(2): 277–304.

Bender, Courtney and Taves, Ann (eds) (2012) *What Matters?: Ethnographies of Value in a Not So Secular Age*. New York: Columbia University Press.

Benjamin, Walter (1978) 'Paris, Capital of the Nineteenth Century,' in Peter Demetz (ed.), *Reflections: Essays, Aphorisms, Autobiographical Writings*. New York: Schocken, 147–162.

Berger, J.M. and Morgan, Jonathon (2015) 'The ISIS Twitter Census: Defining and Describing the Population of ISIS Supporters on Twitter'. The Brookings Project on US Relations with the Islamic World, Analysis Paper Number 20, March. www.brookings.edu/wp-content/uploads/2016/06/isis_twitter_census_berger_morgan.pdf. Accessed on 10 June 2017.

Biko, Steve (2004) *I Write What I like*. Johannesburg: Picador Africa.

Blanford, Nicholas (2011) 'As Gaddafi Teeters, will the Mystery of Lebanon's Missing Imam be Solved?'. *Time*, 25 February.

Bobbio, Norberto (1988) 'Gramsci and the Concept of Civil Society', in J. Keane (ed.), *Civil Society and the State: New European Perspectives*. London: Verso, 73–99.

Boff, Leonardo and Boff, Clodovis (1987) *A Concise History of Liberation Theology*. Maryknoll, NY: Orbis Books. www.landreform.org/boff2.htm. Accessed 11 July 2017.

Bompani, Barbara and Frahm–Arp, Maria (eds) (2010) *Development and Politics from Below: Exploring Religious Spaces in the African State*. New York: Palgrave Macmillan.

Borger, Julian and White, Michael, MacAskill, Ewen and Watt, Nicholas (2003) 'Bush Vetoes Syria War Plan'. *The Guardian*, 15 April.

Böttcher, Annabelle (2002) 'The Ayatollah's Dollars: Financing Islamic Networks'. *Neue Zürcher Zeitung*, 18 October.

Bouri, Elie and El Assad, Joseph (2016) 'The Lebanese Electricity Woes: An Estimation of the Economical Costs of Power Interruptions'. *Energies* 9(583): 1–12.

Brown, Wendy (2006) *Regulating Aversion: Tolerance in the Age of Identity and Empire*. Princeton, NJ: Princeton University Press.

Brown, Wendy (2009) 'Is Critique Secular?: Blasphemy, Injury and Free Speech'. *The Townsend Papers in the Humanities*, No. 2.

Burton, Robert A. (2016) 'A Life of Meaning (Reason Not Required)'. *New York Times*, 5 September.

Cahill, Caitlin (2007) 'The Personal is Political: Developing New Subjectivities Through Participatory Action Research'. *Gender, Place & Culture* 14(3): 267–292.

Calvino, Italo. 2010. *Invisible Cities*, trans. William Weaver. London: Vintage Books.

Cambanis, Thanassis (2010) *A Privilege to Die*. New York: Free Press.

Cammet, Melani (2014) *Compassionate Communalism, Welfare and Sectarianism in Lebanon*. Ithaca, NY: Cornell University Press.

Cassel, Matthew (2011a) 'Palestinians in Lebanon, at the Lonely End of the Arab Uprisings'. *The Guardian*, 16 May.

Cassel, Matthew (2011b) 'Lebanon's Left Splits over Syria'. *Al Jazeera*, 26 June.

Caygill, Howard (2013) *On Resistance: A Philosophy of Defiance*. London: Bloomsbury.

Charafeddine, Raed H. (2008) 'Quality: The Roadmap to Sustainability'. Paper presented at the *2nd Annual Quality Conference Congress Middle East: Creating Architecture of Quality & Excellence in the Middle East* in Dubai, UAE, 6–9 April.

Chehabi, H.E. (ed.) (2006) *Distant Relations: Iran and Lebanon in the Last 500 Years*. New York: I.B. Tauris.

Chehabi, H.E and Tafreshi, Majid (2006) 'Musa al-Sadr and Iran,' in H.E. (ed.), Chehabi *Distant Relations: Iran and Lebanon in the Last 500 Years*. New York: I.B. Tauris, 137–161.

Chittick, William C. (2011) 'Divine and Human Love in Islam,' in Jeff Levin and Stephen G. Post (eds), *Divine Love: Perspectives from the World's Traditions*. West Conshohocken, PA: Templeton Press, 163–200.

Clasby, Nancy Tenfelde (1988) 'Malcolm X and Liberation Theology'. *CrossCurrents* 38 (2): 173–184.

CNN (2006) 'Bush: "Hezbollah suffered a defeat"'. CNN, 14 August.

Cochrane, Paul (2011) 'Book Review: The Road to Fatima Gate'. *Executive Magazine*, 5 October.

Cockburn, Patrick (2014) 'Iraq Crisis: How Saudi Arabia helped ISIS Take Over the North of the Country'. *Independent*, 12 July.

Cottle, Michelle (2017) 'Are the New Megadonors Distorting American Society?' *New York Times*, 28 April.

Crehan, Kate (2002) *Gramsci, Anthropology and Culture*. Berkeley, CA: University of California Press.

Crenshaw, Kimberle (1989) 'Demarginalizing the Intersection of Race and Sex: A Black Feminist Critique of Antidiscrimination Doctrine, Feminist Theory and Antiracist Politics'. *University of Chicago Legal Forum* 140(1): 139–167.

Crenshaw, Kimberle (1991) 'Mapping the Margins: Intersectionality, Identity Politics and Violence Against Women of Color'. *Stanford Law Review* 43(6): 1241–1299.

Cronin, David, Marusek, Sarah and Miller, David (2016) *The Israel Lobby and the European Union*. London: Public Interest Investigations.

Crooke, Alastair (2009) *Resistance: The Essence of the Islamist Revolution*. London: Pluto Press.

Daher, Joseph (2011a) 'Beirut Set to Host Second Meeting on Cluster Munitions'. *The Daily Star*, 10 September.

Daher, Joseph (2011b) 'Hezbollah MP: CIA Officers Meet Lebanese Agents in Public'. *The Daily Star*, 13 December.

Daher, Joseph (2016) *Hezbollah: The Political Economy of the Party of God*. London: Pluto Press.

Dakroub, Hussein (2007) 'Three-Month Battle Ends as Army Takes Over Refugee Camp'. *The Guardian*, 3 September.

Daly, Lew (2009) *God's Economy: Faith-Based Initiatives and the Caring State*. Chicago, IL: University of Chicago Press.

Daragahi, Borzou (2008) 'An Unlikely Political Mix in Lebanon'. *Los Angeles Times*, 17 November.

Daragahi, Borzou (2014) 'Jingoistic Nationalism Replaces Revolution in Egypt'. *The Financial Times*, 28 January.

Daragahi, Borzou and Rafei, Raed (2008) 'Private Force No Match for Hezbollah'. *The Los Angeles Times*, 12 May.

Davies, Gail and Dwyer, Claire (2007) 'Qualitative Methods: Are You Enchanted or Are You Alienated?'. *Progress in Human Geography* 31(2): 257–266.

Debord, Guy (1994). *The Society of the Spectacle*, trans. Donald Nicholson-Smith. New York: Zone Books.

Deeb, Lara (2006) *An Enchanted Modern: Gender and Public Piety in Shi'i Lebanon*. Princeton, NJ: Princeton University Press.

Deeb, Lara (2009) 'Emulating and/or Embodying the Ideal: The Gendering of Temporal Frameworks and Islamic Role Models in Shi'i Lebanon'. *American Ethnologist* 36(2): 242–257.

Deeb, Lara and Harb, Mona (2013) *Leisurely Islam: Negotiating Geography and Morality in Shi'ite South Beirut*. Princeton, NJ: Princeton University Press.

Dehghan, Saeed Kamali (2011) 'Lebanon and Iran Urge Libyan Rebels to Probe 33-Year-Old Mystery'. *The Guardian*, 24 August.

Delmar-Morgan, Alex and Oborne, Peter (2014) 'Why is the Muslim Charity Interpal Being Blacklisted as a Terrorist Organisation?'. *The Telegraph*, 26 November.

Dick, Marlin (2011) 'A Year After his Death, Fadlallah's Legacy Alive'. *The Daily Star*, 4 July.

Dreher, Sabine and Smith, Peter J. (eds) (2016) *Religious Activism in the Global Economy*. London: Rowman & Littlefield.

Eagleton, Terry (2009) *Reason, Faith and Revolution: Reflections on the God Debate*. New Haven, CT: Yale University Press.

Eckholm, Erik (2010) 'Israeli Spies in Lebanon: Not Such a Success'. *The Economist*, 25 February.

Eckholm, Erik (2012) 'Boy Scouts to Continue Excluding Gay People'. *New York Times*, 17 July.

Egan, Paul (2007) 'Feds Tie Dearborn Charity to Terror'. *The Detroit News*, 25 July.

Elgot, Jessica (2015) 'Deadly Attack on Tunisia Tourist Hotel in Sousse Resort'. *The Guardian*, 26 June.

El-Hussein, Rola (2008) 'Resistance, Jihad, and Martyrdom in Contemporary Lebanese Shi'a Discourse'. *Middle East Journal* 62(3): 399–414.

Enayat, Hamid (2011) *Modern Islamic Political Thought*. New York: ACLS Humanities.

Entekhabifard, Camelia (2011) 'Another of Qaddafi's Crimes?'. *Al-Arabiya*, 14 April.

Esack, Farid (2002) *Qur'an Liberation and Pluralism: An Islamic Perspective of Interreligious Solidarity Against Oppression*. Oxford: Oneworld Publications.

Esack, Farid (2004) 'An Islamic View of the South African Situation,' in Jerald D. Gort, Hendrik M. Vroom, Henry Jansen (eds), *Religion, Conflict and Reconciliation: Multifaith Ideals and Realities*. Amsterdam: Rodopi, 290–297.

Fadlallah, Muhammad Hussein (2011) *Islam and the Logic of Force*. Beirut: Dar-Almalak.

Fanon, Frantz (2004) *The Wretched of the Earth*. New York: Grove Press.

Fanon, Frantz (2008) *Black Skin, White Masks*. London: Pluto Press.

Farrell, Michael B. (2007) 'Saudi Arabia Casts Wary Eye on its Shiites'. *The Christian Science Monitor*, 18 January.

Fawaz, Leila (1984) 'The City and the Mountain: Beirut's Political Radius in the Nineteenth Century as Revealed in the Crisis of 1860'. *International Journal of Middle East Studies* 16(4): 489–495.

Fawaz, Mona (2000) 'Agency and Ideology in the Service Provision of Islamic Organizations in the Southern Suburb of Beirut, Lebanon'. Paper presented at a conference on NGO and Governance in Arab Countries, 29–31 March.

Fayyad, Ali (2010) 'Anti-Imperialist Camp: Interview with Ali Fayyad, MP of Hezbollah, Lebanon'. Conducted by the Sumud delegation in Beirut, 6 August.

Fisk, Robert (2001) *Pity the Nation: The Abduction of Lebanon*. New York: Nation Books.

Fisk, Robert (2014) 'Pluralism was Once the Hallmark of the Arab World, so the Exodus of Christians from the Middle East is Painful to One Islamic Scholar'. *The Independent*, 23 February.

Flanigan, Shawn Teresa and Abdel-Samad, Mounah (2009) Hezbollah's Social Jihad: Nonprofits as Resistance Organisations'. *Middle East Policy Council* 16(2): 122–137.

Foroohar, Kambiz (2006) 'Hezbollah, with $100 Bills, Struggles to Repair Lebanon Damage'. *Bloomberg News*, 28 September.

Fraser, Nancy (1997) *Justice Interruptus*. New York: Routledge.

Freire, Paolo (2005) *Pedagogy of the Oppressed*, trans. Myra Bergman Ramos. New York: Continuum.

Gall, Carlotta (2017) 'Young and Unemployed, Tunisians Agitate for a "Second Revolution"'. *New York Times*, 27 May.

Gebauer, Matthias (2006) 'Armed Militants Helping Lebanon Rebuild'. *Der Spiegel*, 19 April.

Germino, Dante (1990) *Antonio Gramsci: Architect of a New Politics*. Baton Rouge, LA: Lousiana State University Press.

Goizueta, Roberto S. (2004) 'Gustavo Gutiérrez', in Peter Scott and William T. Cavanaugh (eds), *The Blackwell Companion to Political Theology*. Malden, MA: Blackwell Publishing, 288–301.

Gouldner, Alvin W. (1970) *The Coming Crisis of Western Sociology*. New York: Avon Books.

Graham, Robert (1980) *Iran: The Illusion of Power*. New York: St. Martin's Press.

Grahlfs, F. Lincoln (2009) 'More Catalyst Than Cause', in M. Morgan (ed.), *The Impact of 9/11 on Politics and War: The Day That Changed Everything?* New York: Palgrave Macmillan, 189–196.

Gramsci, Antonio (2005) *Selections from the Prison Notebooks*. New York: International Publishers.

Greenway, H.D.S. (1983) 'Keeping the Peace in Lebanon and the US Presence'. *Boston Globe*, 24 October.

Gregory, Derek (2004) *The Colonial Present*. Cambridge: Blackwell Publishers.

Groisman, Maayan (2016) '"Hezbollah has Become a Small Faction Serving the Russian Bear", Group's Founder Says'. *The Jerusalem Post*, 21 February.

Grosfoguel, Ramón (2003) 'Email Debate: Yigal Carmon and Brian Whitaker'. *The Guardian*, 23 January.

Grosfoguel, Ramón (2007) 'The Epistemic Decolonial Turn'. *Cultural Studies* 21(2–3): 211–223.

Gutiérrez, Gustavo (1995a) 'Doing Theology'. Drummond Lectures delivered at Stirling University, Scotland, 8 March. www.alastairmcintosh.com/general/1995-gustavo-gutierrez-audio.htm. Accessed 2 July 2017.

Gutiérrez, Gustavo (1995b) 'Announcing the Gospel'. Drummond Lectures delivered at Stirling University, Scotland, 9 March. www.alastairmcintosh.com/general/1995-gustavo-gutierrez-audio.htm. Accessed 11 July 2017.

Gutiérrez, Gustavo (1996) *Gustavo Gutiérrez: Essential Writings*, James B. Nickoloff (ed.). New York: Orbis Books.

Gutiérrez, Gustavo (1997) 'Renewing the Option for the Poor', in David Bastone, Eduardo Mendiata, Lois Ann Lorentzen and Dwight N. Hopkins (eds), *Liberation Theologies, Postmodernity and the Americas*. New York: Routledge, 69–82.

Gutiérrez, Gustavo (2003) *A Theology of Liberation*. New York: Orbis Books.

Haaretz (2008) 'Survey: Nasrallah is the Most Admired Leader In the Arab World'. *Haaretz*, 16 April.

Habermas, Jurgen (1970) *Toward a Rational Society*. Boston, MA: Beacon.

Habib, Osama (2017) 'Lebanon's Summer Electricity Ambitions met with Scepticism'. *The Daily Star*, 30 March.

Haddad, Fanar (2013) 'The Language of Anti-Shiism'. *Foreign Policy*, 9 August.

Haddad, Simon (2004) 'The Origins of Popular Opposition to Palestinian Reset-tlement in Lebanon'. *International Migration Review* 38(2): 470–492.

Haddad, Yvonne (2005) 'Muhammad Abduh: Pioneer of Islam Reform', in Ali Rahnema (ed.), *Pioneers of Islamic Revival*. London: Zed Books, 30–63.

Hage, Ghassan (2009) 'Hating Israel in the Field: On Ethnography and Political Emotions'. *Anthropological Theory* 9(1): 59–79.

Hahnel, Robin (2005) 'Fighting for Reforms Without Becoming Reformist'. Paper presented at the National Conference on Organized Resistance held at the American University and Southern Maryland Greens in Washington, DC, 4–6 February.

Hall, Stuart (1992) 'The West and the Rest: Discourse and Power', in Stuart Hall and Bram Gieben (eds), *Formations of Modernity*, London: Polity Press, 275–329.

Halliday, Fred (1978) 'Iran: The Economic Contradictions'. *Middle East Report* 69: 12–20.

Hamilton, Douglas (2012) 'Beirut: All Gucci and No Gigabytes'. *Reuters*, 27 July.

Hamzeh, Ahmad Nizar (2004) *In the Path of Hizbullah*. Syracuse, NY: Syracuse University Press.

Hamzeh, Ahmad Nizar (2007) 'Hizballah: Islamic Charity in Lebanon', in Jon B. Alterman, and Karin von Hippel (eds), *Understanding Islamic Charities*. Washington, DC: Center for Strategic and International Studies, 137–146.

Haney, Lynne (2002) 'Negotiating Power and Expertise in the Field', in Tim May (ed.), *Qualitative Research in Action*. Thousand Oaks, CA: Sage Publications, 287–299.

Hankela, Elina (2017) '"There is a Reason": A Call to Re-Consider the Relation-ship Between Charity and Social Justice'. *Exchange* 46(1): 46–71.

Harb, Mona (2006) 'Pious Entertainment in Beirut: Al-Saha Traditional Village'. *ISIM Review* 17: 10–11.

Harb, Mona and Leenders, Reinoud (2005) 'Know Thy Enemy: Hizbullah, "Terrorism" and the Politics of Perception'. *Third World Quarterly* 26(1): 173–197.

Harik, Judith Palmer (2005) *Hezbollah: The Changing Face of Terrorism*. New York: I.B. Tauris.

Hartmann, Martin and Honneth, Axel (2005) 'Paradoxes of Capitalism'. *Constellations* 15(1): 42–58.

Hawley, Caroline (2011) 'Gulf States Send Forces to Bahrain Following Protests'. *BBC News*, 14 March.

Hendry, Joy and Fitznor, Laara (eds) (2012) *Anthropologists, Indigenous Scholars and the Research Endeavour: Seeking Bridges Towards Mutual Respect*. New York: Routledge.

Hennessy-Fiske, Molly (2012) 'Boy Scout Ban on Gays to Continue'. *Los Angeles Times*, 18 July.

Herndl Carl G. and Bauer, Danny A. (2003) 'Speaking Matters: Liberation Theology, Rhetorical Performance, and Social Action'. *College Composition and Communication* 54(4): 558–585.

Hersh, Seymour M. (2007) 'The Redirection'. *The New Yorker*, 5 March.

Hilal, Khashan and Moussawi, Ibrahim (2007) 'Hizbullah's Jihad Concept'. *Journal of Religion and Society* 9: 1–55.

Hinkelammart, Franz J. (1997) 'Liberation Theology in the Economic and Social Context of Latin America: Economy and Theology, or the Irrationality of the Rationalised', in David Bastone, Eduardo Mendiata, Lois Ann Lorentzen and Dwight N. Hopkins (eds), *Liberation Theologies, Postmodernity and the Americas*. New York: Routledge, 25–52.

Hirst, David (2010) *Beware of Small States: Lebanon, Battleground of the Middle East*. New York: Nation Books.

Hodgson, Marshall G.S. (2009) *The Venture of Islam: Conscience and History in a World Civilisation*. Chicago, IL: University of Chicago Press.

Hoffman, Bruce (1992) 'Current Research on Terrorism and Low-Intensity Conflict'. *Studies in Conflict and Terrorism* 15: 25–37.

Hosenball, Mark (2011) 'Hezbollah, Iran Uncover CIA Informants'. *Reuters*, 21 November.

Hourani, Albert (2006) 'From Jabal 'Amil to Persia', in H.E. Chehabi (ed.), *Distant Relations: Iran and Lebanon in the Last 500 Years*. New York: I.B. Tauris, 51–61.

Hudis, Peter (2015) *Frantz Fanon: Philosopher of the Barricades*. London: Pluto Press.

Huntington, Samuel P. (1993) 'The Clash of Civilizations?'. *Foreign Affairs* (Summer): 22–49.

Hussain, Ali J. (2005) 'The Mourning of History and the History of Mourning: The Evolution of Ritual Commemoration of the Battle of Karbala'. *Comparative Studies of South Asia, Africa and the Middle East* 25(1): 78–88.

ICG (International Crisis Group) (2005) 'The Shiite Question in Saudi Arabia'. *Middle East Report*, No. 45, 19 September.

ICG (International Crisis Group) (2012) 'Lebanon's Palestinian Dilemma: The Struggle Over Nahr al-Bared'. *Middle East Report*, No. 117, 1 March.

ICG (International Crisis Group) (2017) 'Hizbollah's Syria Conundrum'. *Middle East Report*, No. 175, 14 March.

Imam al-Sadr, Musa (1975) 'Lebanon's Wealth Lies in its Citizens'. Lecture delivered to Kabbouchiyeh Church in Beirut, Lebanon on February. Translation into English provided by Louay H. Charafeddine on 17 June 2010.

Jackson, Richard (2007) 'Constructing Enemies: "Islamic Terrorism" in Political and Academic Discourse'. *Government and Opposition* 42(3): 394–426.

Jackson, Timothy P. (2009) *The Priority of Love: Christian Charity and Social Justice*. Princeton, NJ: Princeton University Press.

Jacobs, Alan (2001) *A Theology of Reading: The Hermeneutics of Love*. Boulder, CO: Westview Press.

Jafari, Saeid (2017) 'Saudi-Led Qatar Blockade Brings Iran, Turkey Together'. *Al Monitor*, 3 July.

Jones, Rory (2017) 'Israel gives Secret Aid to Syrian Rebels'. *Wall Street Journal*, 18 June.

Joseph, Suad (1997) 'The Public/Private: The Imagined Boundary in the Imagined Nation/State/Community'. *Feminist Review* 57: 73–92.

Kafka, Franz (2016) *The Trial*. Lindenhurst, NY: Tribeca Books.

Kalberg, Stephen (1980) 'Max Weber's Types of Rationality: Cornerstones for the Analysis of Rationalization Processes in History'. *The American Journal of Sociology* 85(5): 1145–1179.

Kamali, Masoud (1998) *Revolutionary Iran: Civil Society and State in the Modernization Process*. London: Ashgate Publishing.

Kassab, Suzanne (2012) 'A Post-Colonial Tragedy of Enlightenment?: Some Caribbean and Arab Thoughts'. Oral presentation at a workshop on the *Intellectual History of the Arab Left*, American University of Beirut, 7 July.

Kaufman, Asher (2001) 'Phoenicianism: The Formation of an Identity in Lebanon in 1920'. *Middle Eastern Studies* 37(1): 173–194.

Kazemi, Farhad (1996) 'Civil Society and Iranian Politics', in Augustus Richard Norton (ed.), *Civil Society in the Middle East*. New York: E.J. Brill, 119–152.

Keddie, Nikki R (2003) *Modern Iran*. New Haven, CT: Yale University Press.

Keinon, Herb (2012) 'We Could Destroy Parts of Lebanon to Stop Rockets'. *The Jerusalem Post*, 13 August.

Khalidi, Walid (1989) 'Lebanon: Yesterday and Tomorrow'. *Middle East Journal* 43(3): 375–387.

Khomeini, Ruhallah (2002) *Islam and Revolution*. Berkeley, CA: Mizan Press.

Kifner, John (2006) 'Hezbollah Leads Work to Rebuild, Gaining Stature'. *New York Times*, 16 August.

Koch, Andrew M. (1993) 'Rationality, Romanticism and the Individual: Max Weber's "Modernism" and the Confrontation with "Modernity"'. *Canadian Journal of Political Science* 26(1): 123–144.

Kochuyt, Thierry (2009) 'God, Gifts and Poor People: On Charity in Islam'. *Social Compass* 56(1): 98–116.

Koshul, Basit Bilal (2005) *The Postmodern Significance of Max Weber's Legacy: Disenchanting Disenchantment*. New York: Palgrave Macmillan.

Kroet, Cynthia (2016) 'UN: 30,000 Foreign Fighters in Syria and Iraq'. *Politico*, 5 July.

Kuran, Timur (1997) 'The Genesis of Islamic Economics: A Chapter in the Politics of Muslim Identity'. *Social Research* 64(2): 301–338.

Kuran, Timur (2001) 'The Provision of Public Goods Under Islamic Law: Origins, Impact and Limitations of the Waqf System'. *Law and Society Review* 35(4): 841–898.

Lancaster, Roger N. (1988) *Thanks to God and Revolution: Popular Religion and Class Consciousness in the New Nicaragua*. New York: Columbia University Press.

Layish, Aharon (1995) 'The Muslim Waqf in Jerusalem after 1967: Beneficiaries and Management', in Randi Deguilhem (ed.), *Le Waqf dans l'Espace Ismalmique Outil de Pouvoir Socio-Politique*. Damascus: Institut Français d'Études Arabes de Damas, 145–168.

Leopold, Todd (2015) 'Boy Scouts Change Policy on Gay Leaders'. *CNN*, 28 July.

Levine, Daniel H (1988) 'Assessing the Impacts of Liberation Theology in Latin America'. *The Review of Politics* 50(2): 241–263.

Lewis, Thomas A. (2005) 'Actions as the Ties That Bind: Love, Praxis and Community in the Thought of Gustavo Gutiérrez'. *The Journal of Religious Ethics* 33(3): 539–567.

Lister, Charles (2015) 'Yes, There are 70,000 Moderate Opposition Fighters in Syria. Here's What We Know About Them'. *The Telegraph,* 27 November.

Lister, Charles (2017) 'Al Qaeda is Starting to Swallow the Syrian Opposition'. *Foreign Policy,* 15 March.

London, Yaron (2008) 'The Dahiya Strategy'. *The Jerusalem Post,* 10 June.

Löwy, Michael (1988) 'Marxism and Liberation Theology'. *Notebooks for Study and Research* 10: 3–39.

Lupton, Robert D. (2011) *Toxic Charity: How the Church Hurts Those They Help and How to Reverse It.* San Francisco, CA: HarperOne.

Lynch, Sarah (2011) 'In Lebanon, Scouts Learn Loyalty – to a Political Movement'. *The Christian Science Monitor,* 2 February.

Lyotard, Jean-François (1984) *The Postmodern Condition: A Report on Knowledge.* Minneapolis, MN: University of Minnesota Press.

McCall, Leslie (2005) 'The Complexity of Intersectionality'. *Signs: Journal of Women in Culture and Society* 30(3): 1771–1880.

Macdonald, Geoffrey and Waggoner, Luke (2017) 'Why are so Many Tunisians Joining the Islamic State?'. *Washington Post,* 27 January.

McGovern, Arthur F. (1989) *Liberation Theology and its Critics: Toward an Assessment.* Maryknoll, NY: Orbis Books.

MacIntyre, Alasdair (2007) *After Virtue: A Study in Moral Theory.* Notre Dame, IN: University of Notre Dame Press.

Mahdawi, Dalila (2011) 'Israel's Cluster Bombs Continue to Kill and Maim in Lebanon'. *The Electronic Intifada,* 14 September.

Mahmood, Saba (2005) *Politics of Piety: The Islamic Revival and the Feminist Subject.* Princeton, NJ: Princeton University Press.

Makdisi, Ussama (1996) 'Reconstructing the Nation-State: The Modernity of Sectarianism in Lebanon'. *Middle East Report* 200: 23–26.

Malcolm X with Alex Haley (2007) *The Autobiography of Malcolm X.* London: Penguin Books.

Maldonado-Torres, Nelson (2007) 'On the Coloniality of Being: Contributions to the Development of a Concept'. *Cultural Studies* 21(2–3): 240–270.

Maldonado-Torres, Nelson (2008) *Against War: Views from the Underside of Modernity.* Durham, NC: Duke University Press.

Mallat, Chibli (2005) *The Renewal of Islamic Law: Muhammad Baqer as-Sadr. The Shi'i International.* Cambridge: Cambridge University Press.

Marable, Manning (2011) *Malcom X: A Life of Reinvention.* New York: Penguin Books.

Marei, Fouad Gehad (2016) 'Preaching Development: Shi'i Piety and Neoliberalism in Beirut', in Sabine Drehe and Peter J. Smith (eds), *Religious Activism in the Global Economy.* London: Rowman & Littlefield, 167–188.

Marino, Nick (2017) 'How to Party in Beirut Like it's Your Last Night on Earth'. *GQ Magazine,* 8 May.

Marotta, Vince (2002) 'Zygmunt Bauman: Order, Strangerhood and Freedom'. *Thesis Eleven* 70: 36–54.

Marusek, Sarah (2017a) 'Inventing Terrorists: The Nexus of Intelligence and Islamophobia'. *Critical Studies on Terrorism*, 20 July. www.tandfonline.com/doi/abs/10.1080/17539153.2017.1351597. Accessed 14 December 2017.

Marusek, Sarah (2017b) 'Islamophobia: Racism, the State and Social Movements', in Narzanin Massoumi, Tom Mills and David Miller (eds), *What Is Islamophobia? Racism, Social Movements and the State*. London: Pluto Press, 186–214.

Marusek, Sarah (2018) 'Beyond Secular Liberalism: Islamic Activism in Lebanon'. *The American Journal of Islamic Social Sciences* 35(1): 1–30.

Marx, Karl (1844) 'On the Jewish Question'. www.marxists.org/archive/marx/works/1844/jewish-question/. Accessed 11 July 2017.

Marx, Karl (1867) 'Das Kapital'. www.marxists.org/archive/marx/works/1867–c1/ch01.htm. Accessed 11 July 2017.

Marx, Karl and Engels, Frederick (1970) *The German Ideology*. New York: International Publishers.

Masri, Ridzuan (2013) 'The Idea of Love in al-Ghazali's Literature'. *Infrastructure University Kuala Lumpur Research Journal* 1(1): 67–74.

Matthiesen, Toby (2012) 'Saudi Arabia's Shiite Escalation'. *Foreign Policy*, 10 July.

Memmi, Albert (1992) *The Coloniser and the Colonised*. Boston, MA: Beacon Press.

Merhi, Zeinab (2012) 'Hezbollah's Unorthodox Fans'. *al-Akhbar English*, 19 May.

Mignolo, Walter D. (2011) *The Darker Side of Western Modernity: Global Futures, Decolonial Options*. Durham, NC: Duke University Press.

Miller, David and Mills, Tom (2009) 'The Terror Experts and the Mainstream Media: The Expert Nexus and its Dominance in the News Media'. *Critical Studies on Terrorism* 2(3): 414–437.

Mobarez, H. (1972) 'Iran: Documents of Repression'. *Middle East Report* 8: 20–22.

Moin, Baqir (2005) 'Khomeini's Search for Perfection: Theory and Reality', in Ali Rahnema (ed.), *Pioneers of Islamic Revival*. London: Zed Books, 64–97.

Morrow, John Andrew (2012) 'Malcolm X and Mohammad Mehdi: The Shi'a Connection?'. *Journal of Shi'a Islamic Studies* 5(1): 5–24.

Morton, Adam David (2007) *Unravelling Gramsci: Hegemony and Passive Revolution in the Global Political Economy*. London: Pluto Press.

Moussawi, Ibrahim (2011) *Shi'ism and the Democratisation Process in Iran*. London: Saqi Books.

Mulholland, Kenneth B. (1987) 'Book Review: Liberation Theology by Emilio A. Nuñez'. *Evangelical Missions Quarterly* 23(3) July.

Mullings, Beverley (1999) 'Insider or Outsider, Both or Neither: Some Dilemmas of Interviewing in a Cross-Cultural Setting'. *Geoforum* 30: 337–350.

Nandy, Ashis (2009) *The Intimate Enemy: Loss and Recovery of Self Under Colonialism*. Delhi: Oxford University Press.

Nash, Jennifer C. (2008) 'Re-Thinking Intersectionality'. *Feminist Review* 89: 1–15.

Nash, Jennifer C. (2011) 'Practicing Love: Black Feminism, Love–Politics And Post-Intersectionality'. *Meridians* 11(2): 1–24

Nasr, Seyyed Vali Reza (1996) *Mawdudi and the Making of Islamic Revivalism.* New York: Oxford University Press.

Nasrallah, Sayyed Hassan (2009) 'Hizbullah's New Political Manifesto – We Want Lebanon Strong and United'. *Al-Ahed News,* 30 November.

Ndlovu-Gatsheni, Sabelo J. (2013) 'Why Decoloniality in the 21st Century?'. *The Thinker* (48): 10–15.

The New Arab (2016) 'North Lebanon Local Elections Dethrone Traditional Sunni Leaders'. *The New Arab,* 30 May.

News24 (2012) 'A United Afrikanerdom'. *News24,* 7 May.

Nickoloff, James B. (1996) 'Introduction', in James B. Nickoloff (ed.), *Gustavo Gutiérrez: Essential Writings.* New York: Orbis Books, 1–22.

Noe, Nicholas (ed.) (2007) *Voice of Hezbollah: The Statements of Sayyed Hassan Nasrallah.* New York: Verso.

Norton, Augustus Richard (1987) *Amal and the Shi'a: Struggles for the Soul of Lebanon.* Austin, TX: University of Texas Press.

Norton, Augustus Richard (2000) 'Hizballah and the Israeli Withdrawal from Southern Lebanon'. *Journal of Palestine Studies* 30(1): 22–35.

Norton, Augustus Richard (2005) 'Musa al-Sadr', in Ali Rahnema (ed.), *Pioneers of Islamic Revival.* London: Zed Books, 184–207.

Norton, Augustus Richard (2007) *Hezbollah.* Princeton, NJ: Princeton University Press.

OCHA (2016) 'Lebanon: North and Akkar Governorates Profile'. United Nations, 4 August. http://reliefweb.int/report/lebanon/lebanon–north–and–akkar–governorates–profile–august–2016. Accessed 28 May 2017.

Offe, Claus (1984) *Contradictions of the Welfare State.* Cambridge, MA: The MIT Press.

Ostrower, Francie (1995) *Why the Wealthy Give: The Culture of Elite Philanthropy.* Princeton, NJ: Princeton University Press.

Packer, Martin J. and Addison, Richard B. (eds) (1989) *Entering the Circle: Hermeneutic Investigation in Psychology.* Albany, NY: State University of New York Press.

Patterson, Alexander and Raustol, Lauritz V. (2011) 'Tough Times Don't Dampen Charity Giving'. *The Daily Star,* 27 August.

Perry, Grayson (2014) 'The Rise and Fall of Default Man'. *New Statesman,* 8 October.

Piedra, Alberto M. (1985) 'Some Observations on Liberation Theology'. *World Affairs* 148(3): 151–158.

Pierret, Thomas (2013) *Religion and State in Syria: The Sunni Ulama from Coup to Revolution.* Cambridge: Cambridge University Press.

Plantinga, Alvin (1983) 'Reason and Belief in God', in Alvin Plantinga and Nicholas Wolterstorff (eds), *Faith and Rationality: Reason and Belief in God.* London: Notre Dame University Press, 16–93.

Press Association (2010) 'Amnesty Links British Jets to Saudi Attacks in Yemen'. *Press Association,* 24 August.

Press TV (2007) 'Shari'ati Busts Unveiled in Tehran'. *Press TV*, 22 June.

Qassem, Naim (2005) *Hizbullah: The Story from Within*. London: Saqi Books.

Quijano, Anibal (2000) 'Coloniality of Power, Eurocentrism, and Latin America'. *Nepantla: Views from South* 1(3): 533–580.

Rahnema, Ali (2005) 'Introduction', in Ali Rahnema (ed.), *Pioneers of Islamic Revival*. London: Zed Books, 1–10.

Ramadan, Tariq (2013) 'The Transformation of Malcolm X'. Lecture at the Shabazz Center in New York City, 21 February.

Ramesh, Randeep (2014) 'Quarter of Charity Commission Inquiries Target Muslim Groups'. *The Guardian*, 16 November.

Renick, Timothy M. (1991) 'From Apartheid to Liberation: Calvinism and the Shaping of Ethical Belief in South Africa'. *Sociological Focus* 24(2): 129–143.

ReOrient (2015) 'Introduction'. *ReOrient: A Forum for Critical Muslim Studies* 1(1): 5–10.

Rettig Gur, Haviv (2007) 'It's All in the Plans'. *The Jerusalem Post*, 11 June.

Reuters (2008) 'Israel Warns Hizbullah War would Invite Destruction'. *Reuters*, 10 March.

Reuters (2014a) 'Four Die during Saudi Police Raid to Arrest Wanted People'. *Reuters*, 20 February.

Reuters (2014b) 'IAF Chief: Israel will Destroy Hezbollah bases in Lebanon, Even Ones in Residential Areas'. *Reuters*, 29 January.

Reuters (2014c) 'Lebanese Army Advances in Border Battle with Islamists'. *Reuters*, 5 August.

Reuters (2016) 'Sunni Hawk Wins Lebanon Vote, Risking New Tensions'. *Reuters*, 30 May.

Roelofs, Joan (2007) 'Foundations and Collaboration'. *Critical Sociology* 33(3): 479–504.

Rose, Gillian (1997) 'Situating Knowledges: Positionality, Reflexivities and Other Tactics'. *Progress in Human Geography* 21(3): 305–320.

Rosen, Nir (2010) *Aftermath: Following the Bloodshed of America's Wars in the Muslim World*. New York: Nation Books.

RT (2012) 'Christian School in Louisiana: Loch Ness Monster Exists, Disproving Theory of Evolution'. *RT*, 26 June, www.rt.com/usa/loch-ness-monster-louisi-ana-creationism-evolution-790/

Saad-Ghorayeb, Amal (2002) *Hizbu'llah: Politics and Religion*. London: Pluto Press.

Sadeghi-Boroujerdi, Eskandar (2011) 'Ali Shariati and the Ideologisation of Religion'. *Tehran Bureau*, 30 October.

Said, Edward (1979) *Orientalism*. New York: Random House.

Said, Edward (1994) *Culture and Imperialism*. New York: Vintage Books.

Said, Edward (1997) *Covering Islam: How the Media and the Experts Determine How we see the Rest of the World*. New York: Vintage Books.

Salehi-Isfahan, Djavad (2006) 'Revolution and Redistribution in Iran: How the Poor have Fared 25 Years Later'. Paper presented to the *Third Annual World Bank Conference on Poverty*, Washington, DC, 5–6 June.

Salloukh, Bassel F., Barakat, Rabie, Al-Habbal, Jinan S., Khattab, Lara W. and Mikaelian, Shoghig (2015) *The Politics of Sectarianism in Postwar Lebanon*. London: Pluto Press.

Sandoval, Chela (2000) *Methodology of the Oppressed*. Minneapolis, MN: University of Minnesota Press)

Sankari, Jamal (2005) *Fadlallah: The Making of a Radical Shi'ite Leader*. San Francisco, CA: Saqi Books.

Santos, Boaventura De Sousa (2007) 'Beyond Abyssal Thinking: From Global Lines to Ecologies of Knowledges'. *Review* 30(1). www.eurozine.com/beyond-abyssal-thinking/. Accessed 5 September 2017.

Sartre, Jean-Paul (1955) 'An Explication of The Stranger', in *Literary And Philosophical Essays of Jean-Paul Sartre*, trans. Annette Michelson. New York: Criterion Books, 108–121.

Sayyid, Salman (2003) *A Fundamental Fear: Eurocentrism and the Emergence of Islamism*. New York: Palgrave.

Sayyid, Salman (2014a) *Recalling the Caliphate: Decolonisation and World Order*. London: Hurst.

Sayyid, Salman (2014b) 'Politics of Islamism', in Frank Peter and Rafael Ortega (eds), *Islamic Movements of Europe*. London: I.B. Tauris, 73–79.

Schütz, Alfred (1944) 'The Stranger: An Essay in Social Psychology'. *American Journal of Sociology* 49(6): 499–507.

Schwartz, Leonard (2009) 'A Conversation with Michael Hardt on the Politics of Love'. *Interval(le)s*, II.2–III.1, Fall/Winter: 810–821.

Schwartz, Michael (2007) 'CIA Terror Bombings, Bob Gates, and the Rise of Hezbollah'. *The Huffington Post*, 28 June.

Scott, James C. (2016) 'Resistance That Dares Not Speak its Name: Ancient and Modern'. Keynote presentation at the 'Resistance(s)-Between Theories and the Field'. Université libre de Bruxelles, Brussels, 14 December.

Sentilles, Sarah (2017) 'We're Going to Need More Than Empathy'. *Literary Hub*, 6 July.

Shaery-Eisenlohr, Roschanack (2008) *Shi'ite Lebanon: Transnational Religion and the Making of National Identities*. New York: Columbia University Press.

Shari'ati, Ali (1980) *Marxism and Other Western Fallacies*. Berkeley, CA: Mizan Press.

Shatzmiller, Maya (2001) 'Islamic Institutions and Property Rights: The Case of the "Public Good" Waqf'. *Journal of the Economic and Social History of the Orient* 44(1): 44–74.

Sick, Gary (1985) *All Fall Down: America's Tragic Encounter with Iran*. New York: Random House.

Simmel, Georg (1950) *The Sociology of Georg Simmel*, trans. Kurt Wolff. New York: Free Press. www.cardiff.ac.uk/socsi/undergraduate/introsoc/simmel13.html. Accessed 2 July 2017.

Singh, Simran (2016) '"Personal-is-Political": Decolonial Praxis and the Future (or How I Learnt to Stop Worrying and Tried to Love Neoliberalism)'. *Ethnomusicality Review*, 10 November.

Smith, Adam (2003) *The Wealth of Nations*. New York: Bantam Classic.

Smyth, Marie Breen, Gunning, Jeroen, Jackson, Richard, Kassimeris, George and Robinson, Piers (2008) 'Critical Terrorism Studies: An Introduction'. *Critical Studies on Terrorism* 1(1): 1–4.

Speetjens, Peter (2016) 'Saad Hariri's Saudi Problem: Desperate Needs, Desperate Deeds'. *Middle East Eye*, 6 December.

Stampnitzky, Lisa (2011) 'Disciplining an Unruly Field: Terrorism Experts and Theories of Scientific/Intellectual Production'. *Qualitative Sociology* 34(1): 1–19.

Steele, Jonathan, McCarthy, Rory and Tisdall, Simon (2006) 'Israel to Suspend Air Attacks for 48 Hours After Qana Deaths'. *The Guardian*, 31 July.

Steinberg, Guido (2016) 'Ahrar al-Sham: The "Syrian Taliban"'. *SWP Comments* (27): 1–7.

Stewart, Dona J. (1996) 'Economic Recovery and Reconstruction in Postwar Beirut'. *Geographical Review* 86(4): 487–504.

Strickland, Patrick (2015) 'Tripoli: A Microcosm of Syria's War in Lebanon'. *Deutsche Welle*, 4 October.

Szanto, Edith (2013) 'Beyond the Karbala Paradigm: Rethinking Revolution and Redemption in Twelver Shi'a Mourning Rituals'. *Journal of Shi'a Islamic Studies* 6(1): 75–91.

Taleqani, Seyyed Mahmood (2003 [1985]) *Islam and Ownership*. Lexington, KY: Mazda Publishers.

Tamez, Elsa (1995) 'Women's Rereading of the Bible', in R.S. Sugirtharajah (ed.), *Voices from the Margin: Interpreting the Bible in the Third World*. London: Orbis.

Tareen, Sherali (2013) 'Narratives of Emancipation in Modern Islam: Temporality, Hermeneutics and Sovereignty'. *Islamic Studies* 52(1): 5–28.

Tavernise, Sabrina (2006) 'Charity Wins Deep Loyalty for Hezbollah'. *New York Times*, 6 August.

Taylor, Adam (2016) 'The "Obama is a Muslim" Conspiracy Theory is Still Reverberating in the Middle East'. *Washington Post*, 21 January.

Taylor, Charles (1994) 'The Politics of Recognition', in Amy Gutmann (ed.), *Multiculturalism: Examining the Politics of Recognition*. Princeton, NJ: Princeton University Press, 25–74.

Taylor, Charles (2005) *The Qur'an*. New York: Tahrike Tarsile Qur'an Inc.

Totten, Michael J. (2011a) 'Hanging with Hezbollah, Part I'. *World Affairs*, 8 May. www.worldaffairsjournal.org/blog/michael-j-totten/hanging-hezbollah-part-i. Accessed 11 July 2017.

Totten, Michael J. (2011b) 'Hanging with Hezbollah, Part II'. *World Affairs*, 9 May. www.worldaffairsjournal.org/blog/michael-j-totten/hanging-hezbollah-part-ii. Accessed 11 July 2017.

Toolis, Kevin (2004) 'Rise of the Terrorist Professors'. *New Statesman*, 14 June.

Traboulsi, Fawwaz (2007) *A History of Modern Lebanon*. London: Pluto Press.

Turley, Jonathan (2014) 'Big Money Behind War: The Military–Industrial Complex'. *Al Jazeera*, 11 January.

United Nations (2016) 'Syria Regional Refugee Response'. Inter-Agency Information Sharing Portal, 31 December. http://data.unhcr.org/syrianrefugees/country.php?id=122. Accessed 19 June 2017.

UNHCR (2007) 'Twin Treasury Actions Take Aim at Hizballah's Support Network'. US Department of the Treasury, 24 July. www.treasury.gov/press-center/press-releases/Pages/hp503.aspx. Accessed 11 July 2017.

UNHCR (2016) 'The Situation of Palestinian Refugees in Lebanon'. United Nations Relief and Works Agency for Palestine Refugees in the Near East, February. www.refworld.org/pdfid/56cc95484.pdf. Accessed 6 December 2017.

Wallerstein, Immanuel (1974) *The Modern World System*. New York: Academic Press.

Walshe, Peter (1987) 'The Evolution of Liberation Theology in South Africa'. *Journal of Law and Religion* 5(2): 299–311.

Walshe, Peter (1991) South Africa: Prophetic Christianity and the Liberation Movement'. *The Journal of Modern African Studies* 29(1): 27–60.

Ward, Trina (2012) 'Negotiating Contradictory Information in Chinese Medicine Practice', in Joy Hendry and Laara Fitznor (eds), *Anthropologists, Indigenous Scholars and the Research Endeavour: Seeking Bridges Towards Mutual Respect*. New York: Routledge, 128–137.

Weber, Max (2003) *The Protestant Work Ethic and the Spirit of Capitalism*. New York: Dover Publications.

Wedeman, Ben (2017) 'How Saad Hariri's Resignation Could Backfire on Saudi Arabia'. *CNN*, 18 November.

Wehbe, Mouhamad (2011) 'Living Sectarianism: Lebanon's Demographic Cold War'. *Al Akhbar English*, 5 September.

Weich, Ben (2017) 'Sadiq Khan to Urge Home Secretary to Impose Full Ban on Hezbollah'. *Jewish Chronicle*, 6 July.

Weiss, Max (2010) *In the Shadow of Sectarianism: Law, Shi'ism, and the Making of Modern Lebanon*. Cambridge, MA: Harvard University Press.

Westphal, Merold (1992) 'Preface', in James L. Marsh, John D. Caputo and Merold Westphal (eds), *Modernity and its Discontents*. Fordham, NY: Fordham University Press, ix–xiv.

Whimster, Sam and Lash, Scott (eds) (2006) *Max Weber, Rationality and Modernity*. Abingdon: Routledge.

Wiley, Joyce (2001) 'Alima Bint al–Huda, Women's Advocate', in Linda S. Walbridge (ed.), *The Most Learned of the Shi'a: The Institution of marja' taqlid*. New York: Oxford University Press, 149–160.

Williams, Patricia (1987) 'Spirit-Murdering the Messenger: The Discourse of Fingerpointing as the Law's Response to Racism'. *University of Miami Law Review* 9(1): 127–157.

Williams, Raymond (1985) *Keywords: A Vocabulary of Culture and Society*. New York: Oxford University Press.

Williams, Rowan (2001) 'What Does Love Know?'. *The Aquinas Lecture*, Oxford, 24 January, 260–272.

Wilson, Rodney (1988) 'The Contribution of Muhammad Baqir al-Sadr to Contemporary Islamic Economic Thought'. *Journal of Islamic Studies* 9(1): 46–59.

Wing, Adrien Katherine (1990) 'Brief Reflections Toward a Multiplicative Theory and Praxis of Being'. *Berkeley Journal of Gender, Law & Justice* 6(1): 181–201.

Wintour, Patrick (2017) 'Qatar Diplomatic Crisis – What You Need to Know'. *The Guardian*, 5 June.

Wolterstorff, Nicholas (1983) 'Introduction', in Alvin Plantinga and Nicholas Wolterstorff (eds), *Faith and Rationality: Reason and Belief in God*. London: Notre Dame University Press, 1–15.

Wood, Josh (2011) 'In Lebanon, a More Patient Protest'. *New York Times*, 13 April.

Worth, Robert (2009) 'Billion–Dollar Pyramid Scheme Rivets Lebanon'. *New York Times*, 15 September.

Wright, Robin (1990) *In the Name of God: The Khomeini Decade*. New York: Simon and Schuster.

Yassine, Dalal (2010) 'Unwelcome Guests: Palestinian Refugees in Lebanon'. *al-Shabaka Policy Brief*, July.

Yassin-Kassab, Robin and al-Shami, Leila (2016) *Burning Country: Syrians in Revolution and War*. London: Pluto Books.

Ybema, Sierk, Yanow, Dvora, Wels, Harr and Kamsteeg, Frans (eds) (2009) *Organizational Ethnography: Studying the Complexities of Everyday Life*. London: Sage Publications.

Zabad, Ibrahim (2017) *Middle Eastern Minorities: The Impact of the Arab Spring*. London: Palgrave Macmillan.

Žižek, Slavoj (2008) *Violence: Six Sideways Reflections*. New York: Picador.

Zurayk, Rami (2010) *War Diary: Lebanon 2006*. Charlottesville, VA: Just World Books.

Index

Abdel-Samad, Mounah 101, 106, 107, 118–19, 120, 162
Abduh, Muhammad 20
Abisaab, Rula Jurdi 107–8
Abrahamian, Ervand 30, 31, 33–4
Abu-Lughod, Lila 166
African-Americans 157–8, 183–5, 183–6
African National Congress (ANC) 63
Ahrar al-Sham 169–70
Ajami, Fouad 49
al-Akhbar English newspaper 164
Al-e Ahmad, Jalal 31, 53, 54
al-Hadi Institute 110
Al-Intiqad newspaper 91
al-Khiam attacks 112
al-Mabarrat Association charity network
  activities 53–4, 108–13, 130, 197n32
  economic policy and 174–5, 186
  Israeli strikes on 74
  values 113, 118–21
  Western opposition to 66, 112
  Western researchers and 87
al-Manar television channel 65, 87, 91, 98, 117, 189n4
al-Nabi Ibrahim Orphanage attack 112
al-Nour Broadcasting 65, 91, 189n4
al-Qaeda 169
Alagha, Joseph Elie 69
Alawites 151, 155, 169
Algeria 190n7
Ali, Imam (Prophet's cousin) 41, 88, 151
Alleik, Hajj Kassem 102–4, 117, 177
Amal militia
  Arab spring marches and 165

division within 89–90, 195n2
evolution of 193n26
founding of 49, 68
hijackings by 124
Hizbullah and 126
in Parliament 85, 126
piousness and 138
al-Amin, Sayyid Ibrahim 90
apartheid, South African struggle against *xii*, 1, 59–62, 63, 185
Arab Spring 164–5, 166
Araki, Mohsen 39–41
Arquilla, John 64
Asad, Talal 7–9, 10, 11, 83, 190n6, 190n7
Ashura 28, 98–9, 101fig
Aslan, Reza 16
al-Assad, Bashir 92, 165–6, 170
Assaha Traditional Village 111, 174, 177, 197n33
awqaf 17, 30
Ayatollah, meaning of title 19

Baathist regime 38, 42, 89, 151
Bahman Hospital 110–11, 119, 197n28
Bahrain 191n1
Barthes, Roland 23
Bassam, Mohammad 129–31, 142
Battle of Algiers, The (film) 190n7
Bauman, Zygmunt *xii*, 78, 187
Bazargan, Fereshteh 37–8
Behdad, Sohrab 29
Beirut Souks 194n9
Bender, Courtney 14
Benjamin, Walter 77
Berger, J.M. 167
Berri, Nabih 49, 195n2
Biko, Steve 185